CW01513088

THE LIFE
AND TRIALS OF

CLIFF RICHARD

Also by

Somebody to Love: The Life, Death and
Legacy of Freddie Mercury

83 Minutes: The Doctor, the Damage and the
Shocking Death of Michael Jackson

The Hidden Army: MI9's Secret Force and the
Untold Story of D-Day

THE LIFE AND TRIALS OF
CLIFF RICHARD

MATT RICHARDS & MARK LANGTHORNE

First published in the UK in 2025 by Blink Publishing
An imprint of Bonnier Books UK
5th Floor, HYLO, 105 Bunhill Row,
London, EC1Y 8LZ

A CIP catalogue record for this book is available from the British Library.

Hardback ISBN:9781911600435
eBook ISBN 9781788709743

Also available as an ebook and an audiobook

1 3 5 7 9 10 8 6 4 2

Design and Typeset by Envy Design Ltd
Printed and bound by CPI (UK) Ltd, Croydon CR0 4YY

The authorised representative in the EEA is
Bonnier Books UK (Ireland) Limited.
Registered office address: Block B, The Crescent Building
Northwood, Santry
Dublin 9, D09 C6X8, Ireland
compliance@bonnierbooks.ie

www.bonnierbooks.co.uk

For Lucy, for everything.
Matt

*For my sister Sara, and to Marc and Lucian for
their encouragement.*
Mark

*And for Cliff Richard who has endured so much
and his fans who never doubted.*
Matt & Mark

People say there's no smoke without fire. I'm afraid that does not work anymore. People will absolutely fabricate a complete story where there is no smoke or fire. They create it themselves.

CLIFF RICHARD, Parkinson, BBC TV, 2004

CONTENTS

FOREWORD

WHY THEY PRESSED HIM TO THEIR HEARTS

People of gargantuan fame suddenly become inscrutable. This is because people who are unique *are* inscrutable. Each man is forever driven by whatever he missed as a child, and fame can be the perfect contracting party. In a way, many who seek fame are unable to manage existence by themselves. But perhaps they don't want to – because there are *other* destinies, and there are awaiting fantasies and vanities in every corner of the world. Cliff Richard is as famous as England itself, and it takes a long strider in a discrediting world to peak in the 1950s, the 1960s, the 1970s, the 1980s, the 1990s, and the savage beyond. His success lends strength to others because most of us are standardized lumps when the seas get choppy and there's no sign of land. Cliff has shown no battle fatigue, and is thus the crowned authority on pop life because he has always been there for as long as I can remember time itself. At the start, cracked-tooth giggle-girls from Croydon screamed and steamed their love-goggles simply because Cliff had very slightly moved his body this way or that

– to which the girls felt certain that Cliff might possibly chew the buttons off their blouses in an era when butter coupons were still in peoples' memories. His music made the girls understand something about their bodies that they did not previously know. He was, *then*, an intruding question, magically developed at an exciting time in a country that no longer exists. Yet he is still with us, and still connecting with everything. There is not enough time to list all of his achievements – it would be chaotic to try to. He has lived, and there is proof. If you need him, his voice will always be there for you – in his as yet unspent capacity for song. Suddenly even the songs step aside, and then the life itself becomes the work of triumph.

He has coped very well with success, and that's what makes him *him*. He has mirrored the times in many decades, and only the golden chosen ones have achieved this – because very few had the commitment necessary to even give it a go. He is never spotted with his wildly over-praised counterparts, and therefore his reputation strikes mystery because he moves so carefully around the spotlight. Righteous oblivion is not for him.

When the mills of fame grind long and hard, it takes Chinese patience to immune yourself from enemy fire, and Cliff (for *there is only one* Cliff) has shown great moral courage when those who object for a living suddenly positioned him in their sights. The truth of Cliff Richard is enough. The level of determination exerted by the press in order to destroy him was a reflection of his power and his appeal: but the Grub Street gremlins overlooked how much he is loved – *and how much they* are scrounging, passionless, money-sick crones who mistakenly believe that they have a morality that we all need.

Tomorrow is always another day to be lived – even if it is true that most humans generally do not know very much about themselves. Cliff is an identification, a cherished flesh and the utmost authority on superstardom; he who never once chose the wrong future for his career. He made feature films full of friendships and high spirits, his role always a model of healthy humanity. His prize was a smile charged with devotion, and he nationally became someone for whom it is easy to have a protective feeling towards. Some songs were soft, some songs were tough, and he rose as a star whom it gave people pleasure to know existed. His early hits were felt throughout the rest of his life, even when the teen screams ceased and the peach-lipped sophisticates of Portugal and Spain felt intoxicated just by saying his name. Look at the video for *The Day I Met Marie* from the Steve Allen Show: Cliff is at his best, his impeccable suit is a masculine moral code, and he is a desirable object so generous to the camera at any angle; the voice from nature is love inspired. But what has he done and how did he do it? Like many, he started with scant advantages and blurred distinctions everywhere, therefore his task was to produce something. One of the most radical things we can do is sing. In a way, it is effrontery. He made this the altar of his duty for a lifetime, and he succeeded because his career set its own terms even if his smile belonged to the world. He knew how to announce the lover within the song. It is not an easy thing to do. He might even approach the stage as others approach lovers, and how quickly he became a question in every household throughout Europe. But there was never a belief that his success would be fleeting. In the 1980s, when we all wondered if any meaning could be found anywhere, Cliff was there – suggesting *take it as it is and enjoy it*. He represented order and meaning into the 90s – having given nothing of his private self away, whilst producing new hits in America and still building his life's work when, let's be frank, it would generally take your average pop success just three years to discover their own irrelevance. Without money it is not possible to participate in the world, and Cliff had by now earned enviable freedom whilst still being Cliff. Into the sexless 2000s, audiences still held their breath because he was due on stage in fifteen minutes. Given such a life, it is impossible to imagine how or why death might strike. Perhaps the screaming girls of Wood Lane of 1958 – of dirty hair and gawky specs – were still here, too, *his journey theirs.*

Even Jesus took a day off. But not Cliff Richard. That's the funny and that's the lonely side of it. For decades he stayed the same age, a fragrant skin untouched by constant air travel and inhospitable schedules. However, there is no way back from this choice, because to not sing is to retreat into darkness, and once the world has rushed to touch your hand ... nothing else will do.

Singers should command your attention. This is the entire reason why anyone should sing. Cliff has never once mourned a lost career, even if his life must, of course, become a walled paradise – for these are the rules, and that's what you get when you give your all to the microphone – as if somehow it keeps the secrets of a sacred confidant. Finally – and ultimately, his singing tone comes through in all circumstances as the voice of a friend, and it will be heard – *somewhere, everywhere* – long after our graves are obscured by fallen leaves.

MORRISSEY.
Rome, 2025.

PROLOGUE

The date is 18 July 2018.

The events of the last four years have taken their toll on Cliff Richard mentally and physically. Last night he slept intermittently. He woke earlier than usual, ate a light breakfast and prepared himself for the day ahead, which, after 1,434 torturous days, would be *his* day in court. This would be a defining moment in his life, one that would finally offer him some form of vindication.

As Christopher Hitchens said, 'What is your idea of earthly happiness? To be vindicated in your own lifetime.'[1]

Feelings of anxiety flood his every thought. He struggles to decide what to wear. Black felt too sombre. Pale blue too establishment. He eventually settles on a charcoal two-piece suit with blue satin lapel trim and matching blue knitted tie, with a chalk blue shirt that is unbuttoned at the collar, creating his casual signature look. 'In life we don't usually get to choose the time of our defining moment,' wrote Darren Shan. 'We just have to stand and face them when they come, no matter what sort of state we are in.'[2]

Before his car arrives, Cliff arranges his thinning hair and applies a small amount of base foundation.

This was theatre after all.

And he was the star of this show. Regardless of how it would end.

Arriving at London's High Court with his close friend Gloria Hunniford, he stands momentarily outside before the throng of photographers, closes his eyes, and joins his hands in the familiar praying position.

Then he turns. And goes in.

CHAPTER 1

The human reality of what happens to millions is only
for God to grasp; but what happens to individuals is another
matter and within the range of mortal understanding.
MARION STARKEY, *The Devil in Massachusetts*, 1949

Everything has a beginning.

Ours is the Indian city of Lucknow, the capital of Uttar Pradesh. Here the Gomati River, a tributary of the Ganges, meanders lazily through the city and the sweet, long-lasting fragrance of the Saptaparni or Devil Tree hangs in the air.

It's a city of enchanting mornings with a bright melodic soundtrack of native birds, where bicycles form the main mode of transport and children play marbles, satoliya, or cricket in the shade of the rising sun.

It is 14 October 1940. And at King George's Hospital on Victoria Street in Lucknow, at that time part of British India, Dorothy Marie Webb (née Dazely) gives birth to her first son. With her husband Rodger Oscar Webb, they have travelled 500 miles to Lucknow from their modest home in Dehradun, at the foothills of the Himalayas. There was no British hospital in Dehradun, so Dorothy and Rodger had wanted to make sure the birth of their first child went smoothly in a reputable and clean hospital. They named their son Harry Rodger Webb and returned to Dehradun, where Rodger held down steady employment managing the restaurant at the local railway station.

In June 1942, a younger brother for Harry was born. Named Frederick, after Harry's paternal grandfather, the child only lived for a few months owing to a blood disorder and was likely buried in the British Cemetery in Dehradun.

In 1943, Rodger gained promotion and the family uprooted and moved 1,000 miles south-east to Howrah, an important industrial and transportation hub located on the western bank of the Hooghly River, directly opposite Calcutta.

The smells of Howrah were different to the scents of Dehradun but, nevertheless, they hold the key to so many memories for an impressionable four-year-old growing up: the aroma of dry summer shimmering above asphalt, dusty earth, and the blond grass of the foothills. The scent of tropical rain, of night-blooming jasmine, and a touch of ashram. The soft smoke blanket of incense pierced by a fretwork of spice – mace, nutmeg, and clove.

It feels like memories of a film that I saw a long time ago. I remember the heat, and potholed streets, and playing in dirty water up to my waist with my best friend, Lal, in the monsoon season.[3]

The sweet fragrance of freshly cut hay, the Siri cows somewhere nearby. The odour of muddied water dried on the skin, of childhood sweat, and of the Ganges water that flows from the spring high in the mountain. The perfumes of his young life.

I remember eating curry with my fingers and fighting kite battles.[4]

Childhood for Harry Webb was carefree, full of mystery and privilege; the family had servants at their beck and call in their first-floor, river-view apartment, which was provided by Rodger's employers, Kellners, and was situated right above a chocolate factory.

I adored the delicious smells that used to waft up from downstairs.[5]

In 1945, the young Harry Webb started attending St Thomas Church of England School, which catered mostly for expats. There he learned Hindi and a smattering of Bengali. Being too far to return home for lunch, every day one of his family's servants, Habib, would deliver him lunch served with a napkin. Outside of school he would visit tea rooms or the botanical gardens with his Aunt Olive or go to the cinema to watch cowboy films and cartoons. Sometimes he would go fishing with his father and their home-made rods. At week-ends he would go to Sunday school at St Thomas Church, where he would sing in the church choir, the boys being expected to provide the treble section.

I don't think I was a very good one [choirboy] as it was difficult for me – or anyone else, come to that – to distinguish one note from another. However, in red cassock and white ruff I looked the part and, without being too cynical, I think that's what mattered.[6]

The world seemed perfect for young Harry and his family, untouched as they were by the Second World War and cocooned in their comfortable existence of secure employment, happy schooldays, and family devotion.

But unbeknown to young Harry, the family was hiding a scandalous secret, one that was finally revealed to the world during an interview on BBC's *Woman's Hour* in 2011. Although born in India, Harry Webb was primarily of English heritage. His paternal grandfather, Frederick William Webb, was born in Woolwich, south London, and travelled to India in 1884 aged just twelve to join his own father, Thomas Benjamin Webb, and work on the railways. Some years later he moved to Burma (now Myanmar), and Frederick was employed in bridge construction. While in Burma, Frederick met and eventually married Donella Eugenie who, it was said, had Burmese royal blood in her family. Their marriage produced eleven children of which Harry's father, Rodger, was one, born in 1904.

However, it's the maternal side of Harry's family that sparked a scandal in the shape of his grandfather, William Edward Dazely. Born in 1896 in Bombay, he enlisted in the army in India and married Dorothy Bridgewater in Madras in 1919. The marriage produced two daughters: Harry's mother Dorothy and her younger sister, Olive. In 1924 tragedy struck when William disappeared while serving in the army, presumably killed fighting Afghan tribesmen. But all was not what it seemed, as Harry – now Sir Cliff Richard – disclosed out of the blue on the BBC in 2011.

His wife, my mother's mother, thought he was killed in the war. It turns out that he left her... and set up a new home in Coventry.[7]

4

In fact, not only had he set up a new home in the UK, but William had also remarried and moved to Birmingham, where he worked for the car giant Rover, and had five sons with his second bride, Maizie.

William was a bigamist.

Sir Cliff mentioned having never known this other family and teased that it was all revealed in his 2008 book, *My Life, My Way*. However, careful examination of the 308 pages fails to find any mention of a bigamist grandfather or the secret family he created. Instead, the book focuses on his successful career and charitable endeavours, with little insight into his personal or family life and certainly no references to any bigamous relatives. And in his 2020 autobiography, *The Dreamer*, the whole episode gets a brief, cursory paragraph.

CHAPTER 2

In August 1947, the Webbs were living a contented and privileged life in Howrah. By now, the seven-year-old Harry had two siblings, Donna born in 1942 and new arrival Jacqui, but while everything seemed perfect for the family, outside on the streets of India violence was erupting. After directly ruling India since 1858, the British had finally agreed to leave and the subcontinent was partitioned into two independent nation states: Hindu-majority India and Muslim-majority Pakistan.

Almost immediately one of the greatest migrations in history began as millions of Muslims headed to West and East Pakistan (later known as Bangladesh) while millions of Hindus and Sikhs headed in the opposite direction back to India. But it was a bloody and murderous journey, as communities that had co-existed for generations attacked each other with brutal levels of sectarian violence.

By 1948 the violence was getting close to Howrah as civil unrest spread across India. But the young Harry Webb had other innocent pleasures on his mind.

I was more concerned with flying kites and nicking chocolate from the shelf with Lal, but at nights we would sometimes hear gunshots.[8]

As riots and fighting continued to encroach on their doorstep, it was becoming obvious to the Webbs that it was too dangerous to remain in the country.

There was a big park not far from where we lived. We'd gone there for an outing and as we came back there was the terrible sound of gunfire. We had to rush into a friend's house to escape.[9]

The Webbs discussed fleeing to Australia, the land of plenty, but instead decided to head for England, a country ruined, rationed, and rebuilding after the horrors of the Second World War. None of them had ever been to Blighty, as they called it, but given their ancestral heritage, they felt they were going home. On 24 August 1948, having sold all their belongings to cover the cost, they began their epic journey, and at six in the morning on 13 September 1948 the ship that carried them back, the *SS Ranchi*, berthed at Tilbury Docks in Essex.

We arrived with five pounds sterling, which I looked up, I think it's about two hundred pounds now. If you can imagine how you have a wife and four children and survive on two hundred pounds and no work.[10]

Initially the family stayed in Carshalton in the London suburbs with Harry's maternal grandmother, Dorothy, and her seven children, at their three-bedroomed house in Windborough Road. Living conditions were close to impossible with so many crammed in. Later they rented the spare box room in the next-door neighbours' house, but their existence was a far cry from the life they had in India, made worse by the fact that Rodger was struggling to find employment. Eventually he found work as a porter at a local hospital. Harry, meanwhile, had been enrolled in Stanley Park Primary School, but the eight-year-old was immediately treated as an outsider.

I got bullied at school, because I talked differently to the other kids and my skin was darker from years in India – they hit me and called me 'Indi-bum'. But I fought back. I'm a lot tougher as a person than people assume.[11]

After a year in Carshalton, the family moved to Waltham Cross in Hertfordshire, where they lived with Rodger's sister, her husband and two sons, occupying a small room in the house which was now even more crowded following the arrival of Rodger and Dorothy's third daughter, Joan, in 1950. Due to the cramped conditions, the family were quickly offered council housing; a small red-brick council house at 12 Hargreaves Close on the new-build Bury Green Estate in Cheshunt, thirteen miles north of Central London. The family moved there in April 1951. The move coincided with an upturn in the family's fortunes. Rodger found a new job with Atlas Lamps, part of Thorn Electrical Industries in Enfield, and Dorothy took some part-time work to boost the family coffers.

A change in location also meant another change in school for Harry. He left King's Road School in Waltham Cross, where the bullying had simply continued where it left off in Carshalton, and enrolled at Cheshunt Secondary Modern, where he settled in well and enjoyed going to school for the first time in England.

The school also encouraged students to have pen pals in faraway places and Harry chose to strike up correspondence with a girl in Australia.

His introductory letter read:

Dear Catherine,
My name is Harry Rodger Webb. I go to Cheshunt Secondary Modern School in Cheshunt, Hertfordshire. I am twelve and a half years old. My ambition is to be a famous singer. [12]

While he showed little inclination towards music at school, Harry threw himself into acting in the school productions. It was in one of these, *Toad of Toad Hall*, that Harry's character was expected to sing a song. He protested vehemently that he didn't want to sing, but was threatened with losing the part by his teacher if he did not. So, he sang 'Ducks' Ditty' for three nights and found that he enjoyed singing and the attention it brought and, also, that he was quite good at it. By the age of fifteen, music was really beginning to grab him and in May 1956 one piece of music changed his life forever.

Harry would still visit Waltham Cross on Saturdays to hang out with friends and on one of these visits, as he was walking down a road with some of them, a car pulled up at a nearby newsagents, the driver leapt out and rushed into the shop, leaving the engine running and the car radio on. It was playing a song unlike anything Harry and his mates had heard before: 'Heartbreak Hotel' by Elvis Presley.

It felt like something from outer space. I'm convinced now that that's the reason I followed my dreams.[13]

Harry quickly became obsessed with rock 'n' roll, particularly with Elvis. He started brushing back his hair, shaping it meticulously with Brylcreem, and began mimicking his moves before a mirror in the privacy of his bedroom. He saved his money and bought Elvis's records as well as tuning in religiously to the radio to hear Jerry Lee Lewis, Little Richard, Buddy Holly and Ricky Nelson. But it was Elvis who fascinated him most. He obsessed over him, and it was Elvis he wanted to be.

By the age of sixteen, Harry had formed his own small vocal group, the Quintones, and had been given a guitar for his birthday by his father who, being an enthusiastic banjo player, began teaching Harry the rudiments.

He taught me my first three chords – G, C and D – and how to play the first song I ever learned on a guitar: 'The Prisoner's Song', later sung by Fats Domino.[14]

The guitar made Harry feel like a true rock 'n' roller and after watching Bill Haley & His Comets play live at the Regal in Edmonton in March 1957, Harry knew where his destiny lay – he was going to make good his ambition laid down in the letter he had sent to his Australian pen-pal and become 'a famous singer'.

But that was easier said than done in Cheshunt and having failed all his O-levels bar English Language, he left school to an uncertain future. His father pulled some strings and secured him a job at Atlas Lamps. It involved mundane form-filling, which Harry, his mind elsewhere, rarely undertook with due diligence, but it did lead to an encounter that would change his life forever. Unable to cycle to work as his bicycle had a flat tyre, Harry took the bus and bumped into an old friend from school.

She told me that her boyfriend, Terry Smart, who I also knew from school, was playing drums in a local skiffle group led by a guy called Dick Teague. Their singer had just been called up to do his National Service and so they were looking for a replacement.[15]

The skiffle craze had been sweeping across the country since Lonnie Donegan released his version of 'Rock Island Line' in 1955, which reached the Top 10 in the UK *and* the USA. It was essentially American Deep South music, but infused in the UK with trad jazz and blues and, for the first time, the guitar was placed at the centre of the music with accompaniment from an unusual array of instruments such as washboard and washtub bass.

Appearing just before rock 'n' roll, skiffle was also the first opportunity for the youth of Britain to reject the culture of their parents, to break away from swing bands and schmaltzy crooners. 'Skiffle was grassroots, it came from below, it surprised everyone,' says British singer-songwriter Billy Bragg. 'Every generation needs something like that. For me it was punk.'[16]

By 1957 there were an estimated 50,000 skiffle bands in the UK, including early incarnations of the Beatles and the Rolling Stones, but for Harry skiffle was simply a means to an end. It gave him the chance to sing with a group. but pretty quickly both Harry and band-mate Terry Smart realised their passion was for the edgier, more exciting rock 'n' roll sound, so together they decided to break away and form their own rock 'n' roll band.

They recruited another old schoolfriend, Norman Mitham, to play guitar (although he had never played guitar in his life) and, calling themselves The Drifters, they began rehearsing at Harry's house with the support of his parents. By 1958 they were playing local gigs and at one of these, the Five Horseshoes pub in Hoddesdon, the group were approached after the gig by Johnny Foster.

Despite having no management experience (he was a lorry driver at a local sewage works), Foster offered to manage the group and suggested he could fix it that they perform at the 2i's coffee bar, a renowned live music venue run by two wrestling promoters in the heart of Soho in London. Two years earlier, Tommy Hicks had been spotted performing there and was duly signed up by Decca, whereupon he changed his name to Tommy Steele and released his first single 'Rock The Caveman', which reached Number 13 on the charts, leading to him being dubbed 'Britain's Elvis'.

Even though not being masters of their craft by a long way, a date at the 2i's and potential discovery by a record executive was simply too good to turn down for The Drifters. After an audition at the venue, they secured a week-long residency, but much to their disappointment no record executives turned up to see them, the only silver lining being the £25 they received for their work.

There were, however, two people in the crowd that week who would prove to be pivotal; one was Ian Samwell. He was a songwriter and guitarist and offered his services as a lead guitarist to the band. Following a hasty audition, which impressed the three Drifters, he was in. The second person was concert promoter Harry Greatorex. He had seen them at the 2i's and offered them a booking at his Regal Ballroom in Ripley, Derbyshire, for another £25 but on one condition – they had to change their name. He wanted them to be billed as Harry Webb & The Drifters to follow in the fashion of American rock 'n' roll bands of the time such as Buddy Holly & The Crickets and Bill Haley & His Comets.

Nobody in the band wanted their stage name to be Harry Webb & The Drifters, so they headed for the Swiss Tavern pub in Soho to brainstorm. 'Someone said Russ because of Russ Hamilton,' recalls guitarist Norman Mitham. 'Then someone said Clifford. So, Russ Clifford was tossed around. Then it was Cliff Russard. He liked the ring of that. It was getting close to what he wanted.'[17]

Harry was drawn to idea of Cliff as a name. It denoted a cliff face made of rock, which, to him, connected with rock 'n' roll. Richardson was mulled over as a surname, that was shortened to Richards and it was seemingly settled: Cliff Richards & The Drifters. Then Ian Samwell suggested losing the 's'. 'It sounds a bit like Little Richard,' Samwell said, 'which is cool.'[18] So, on Saturday 3 May 1958, Cliff Richard made his stage debut at the Regal Ballroom, Ripley, under the billing: 'Direct from Soho's famous 2i's Coffee Bar, Cliff Richard and The Drifters.'

They played for an hour, going through their repertoire of Ricky Nelson, Jerry Lee Lewis and Elvis songs and suddenly they felt confident things might be happening for them. More shows followed, the audiences started getting bigger, girls began rushing to the front row, crowds started screaming. And Cliff was the focus. He had only recently started going out with his first serious girlfriend, Janice Berry, but he was already conscious of how he had to cultivate his image, particularly in respect of how female fans viewed him.

Being a male singer, my fans like to see themselves as perhaps having a chance of dating me. Or they look on me as being the boy they'd like to have next door. I have to stay this way as long as I can.[19]

Soon they were headlining a monthly talent show at the Shepherd's Bush Gaumont and it was here for the first time that Cliff experienced the trappings of being a rock 'n' roll star, albeit still a fledgeling one.

> *After the show some three hundred fans hung around outside the theatre chanting my name: 'We want Cliff! We want Cliff!' When I left, they chased me down the street and I had to take refuge in a men's toilet on Shepherd's Bush Green. The police helped get me out of there. Some of them were on horseback.*[20]

Everything Cliff had wanted, everything he dreamed of, was finally beginning to happen. He had witnessed kids screaming at Bill Haley, he had seen fans chasing Elvis. Now it was happening to him. But there was a casualty. Following the show, Cliff ended his relationship with Janice. He says in his autobiography that they were 'going steady' and that he 'really liked her'. But, in truth, Cliff only had one love – rock 'n' roll. And Janice had to pay the price. 'The actual end was upsetting for me in the same way that it is when any relationship finishes,' reflected Janice years later, 'but it may not have been upsetting for him. I don't know how he felt about it.'[21]

By this point, Cliff and his band had already cut a demo at the HMV store in Oxford Street. It had cost them five pounds to get an acetate of their rendition of 'Lawdy, Miss Clawdy' and Jerry Lee Lewis' 'Breathless' and it proved money well spent after it landed on the desk of Norrie Paramor, head of A&R at Columbia Records, a label run by EMI. Suitably impressed, Norrie invited the band to do a test recording at EMI Recording Studios in Abbey Road, London, and after going on holiday and keeping Cliff and his bandmates on tenterhooks, Norrie finally called them to say he was going to offer them a contract. He wanted them to find a bass player and record 'Schoolboy Crush', previously a hit in the USA for country star Bobby Helms.

At 7 p.m. on 28 July 1958, barely ten weeks after he appeared on stage as Cliff Richard for the first time, the singer and his two bandmates arrived in Studio 2 at Abbey Road to record 'Schoolboy Crush'. With backing vocals provided by the Mike Sammes Singers, who got £4 each for their time, and with two session musicians in Ernie Shear on lead guitar and Frank Clarke on bass supplying the professional musical touch, it took just under two hours to record.

In fact, the recording session went so well that the veteran engineer scheduled for the recording, Peter Brown, decided he would depart early to go to the opera and leave the session in the hands of Stuart Eltham and young engineer Malcolm Addey, who was barely older than Cliff himself and a new boy at Abbey Road. 'I did it the way that felt natural to do and everybody loved the sound,' recalls Addey. 'Cliff had a great recording voice, he always did. You put any microphone in front of Cliff and you'd get a good sound, there's no question of that.'[22]

The intention was that 'Schoolboy Crush' be Cliff Richard & The Drifters, first single release, but Ian Samwell had been working on another track, his own composition, on his daily rides on the 715 Green Line bus from London Colney to Cheshunt. Titled 'Move It', he had written it in response to an article in *Melody Maker* suggesting that the days of rock 'n' roll were numbered. 'So rock 'n' roll is dead, is it? My funeral oration consists of just two words: "good riddance",' wrote Steve Race. 'Perhaps now we shall see some sense of proportion returning to the pop music business.'[23]

With the backing singers having done their work on 'Schoolboy

Crush' and left the session, talk turned to the prospective B-side for the single and 'Move It' seemed the ideal throwaway track. Consisting of just three chords, Ian Samwell demonstrated the song to the others and scribbled down the lyrics for Cliff. In the final forty minutes of the session they recorded 'Move It' with Ernie Shear providing the iconic guitar introduction.

'Ernie played an absolutely wonderful introduction,' confirms Malcolm Addey. 'He was one of those guys who would play whatever was required without getting uptight, and so he just turned up his EQ and let it rip. It came out really great, and that's what got everybody's attention. For his part, Cliff liked to play while he was singing, so Norrie allowed him to hold onto his guitar, and after a false start we completed the song in a couple of takes. There were no edits whatsoever.'[24]

Music publisher Franklyn Boyd hawked 'Schoolboy Crush' around, looking for airplay. He managed to get a meeting with TV producer Jack Good, the man helming ITV's early-evening pop-music show, *Oh Boy!*. Hearing the A-side, Good wasn't particularly excited. But that changed when he heard 'Move It', saying, 'This disc could sell 50,000 on its first eight bars alone!'[25] Good offered them a slot on the ITV show on the basis they performed 'Move It'.

'When I first saw him,' recalled Good, 'he did have these long sideboards and this ruffled hair and this rather scraggy white shirt and he carried this tinny guitar and he quivered his legs with monotonous regularity and the first thing I did was to take off his guitar and say, "Now, you've got to sing without it," and he found this quite impossible because he didn't know what to do with his hands. In fact, his right hand was continually strumming these imaginary strings.'

Good continued, 'Then we asked him to shave off his

sideboards and this was going too far. Not even a debut on television was worth that! What would the kids think, you know. In the end we persuaded him it was very necessary in order that he shouldn't look like Elvis and he didn't want to look like Elvis, did he? A-ha, but he did! So, we got the sideboards off and the first rehearsal was called and he was so shy that you couldn't get him to rehearse in front of his backing group so we had to take him away into a little room and let him mime to his record and work through it slowly.'[26]

It's wonderful to be going on TV for the first time, but I feel so nervous that I don't know what to do. I mean, I only turned professional five weeks ago, and before that I was working as a clerk and only playing at local dances and things in my spare time. I wore sideburns then, but I shaved them off last night – Jack thought it would make me look more original. I think he's right.[27]

By this point, recording contract signed, Cliff had left his job at Atlas Lamps. He now had a record, was on ITV's flagship pop-music show and was about to hit the big time. 'Move It' became the A-side and swiftly rose up the charts to peak at Number 2, becoming acknowledged as the first home-grown rock 'n' roll song out of the UK. 'This is Sir Cliff's "It's Alright Mama", states presenter and producer Dominic King. 'It's a taut, edgy debut that augured well for a career, which like the King's, only too frequently ended up mired in slush. Sure, the lead guitar sound was dangerously thin and echoey, "ballet and calypso" seemed lyrically middle-aged, and the production on this repetitive twelve-bar tune rang hollow, but that drawling vocal and driving rhythm guitar made it a coffee bar smash.'[28]

Cliff had exploded onto the scene, had become Britain's very own Elvis, and was about to embark on a career that, at the time of writing, has extended into its eighth decade.

Nobody at that moment could have predicted that, and nobody – least of all Cliff – could have foreseen the triumphs that lay ahead, and amongst them, the catalyst for the trial to which that stardom ultimately led.

CHAPTER 3

SHEFFIELD 28 JUNE 1985

I am the way and the truth and the life.

John 14:6

Sheffield, South Yorkshire, England. 28 June 1985. Twenty seven years since Cliff had burst onto the pop scene with 'Move It'.

Much had happened in the intervening years: Number 1 singles, movies, falling in and out of fashion and, of course, Cliff's proclamation of faith which, in many ways, had come to define him. One of the singer's guiding lights in his devotion to Christianity was the American evangelist and preacher Billy Graham.

In 1985, Graham had returned to the UK for a twelve-week campaign of preaching and between 22 and 29 June he addressed almost 330,000 people at Bramall Lane Stadium, home to Sheffield United Football Club since 1889.

On 28 June, Cliff was invited to join Billy onstage in front of 47,200 of Graham's evangelical followers.

But outside the stadium trouble was brewing, as members of Sheffield's anti-apartheid movement gathered to protest at Cliff's decision to participate in charity gospel concerts in apartheid-era South Africa, in direct opposition to a United Nations ban on cultural and sporting links with the country.

I go wherever Christians invite me to speak about Jesus. It's a platform I've been given by God.[29]

The consequences of his charity performances in South Africa meant that Cliff was perceived as supporting the apartheid regime at a time of international boycott. As a result, he had been placed on a register – or blacklist – of performers that ranged from Frank Sinatra and Liberace to the Vienna Boys Choir.

In an attempt to assuage the protestors at Sheffield, Cliff met with the Bishop of Sheffield prior to the rally to discuss the row over his refusal to boycott anti-apartheid South Africa and his appearance eventually went ahead that day without any trouble. One of the policemen guarding him remembered what a 'nice bloke' Cliff was and how 'he had tea and biscuits sent to the police room for the duty officers with a note thanking us for looking after him.'[30]

Appearing on the final day of the event, Cliff looked relaxed and confident. Dressed in all-white jacket and trousers with a pale blue shirt open at the collar, wearing aviator glasses and strumming an acoustic guitar, Cliff serenaded the crowd with a series of Christian and gospel songs following Billy Graham's sermon, which focused on sex and peer pressure and sinful pleasures: 'We are sinners by choice, we are sinners by practice. We are heading towards some sort of Armageddon before the end of the century, things are getting worse and worse.'

One of those in the crowd that day was 36-year-old Pauline Wraith. She arrived a devoted fan of Cliff and left the rally a committed Christian. 'He [Cliff] was just singing on his own from a platform on the pitch and talking. It was a very full stadium. At the time Cliff was a big star, but his Christianity came before everything else.'[31]

During the rally, Billy Graham invited members of the crowd to step forward as a public commitment to Jesus. Pauline found herself doing just that. 'I went forward and gave my life to Jesus. Somebody came to speak to me and gave me a card. I was put in touch with a Methodist church and I've been going ever since.'[32]

A number of photographs appeared in the national press showing Cliff clutching his acoustic guitar as he spoke to the audience and then backstage smiling and clasping his hands as he stood beside Billy Graham. It is these images that confirm Cliff was present at the rally that day.

Also present among the tens of thousands of Cliff fans and pilgrims of Billy Graham were numerous youngsters from various Christian organisations across the country who had travelled to Bramall Lane to experience the evangelical charisma of Graham – not necessarily drawn by the 'star appearance' of Cliff Richard, who was likely deeply unfashionable and uncool for many of the youngsters. However, whatever their thoughts of Cliff and his musical talents, he was undeniably a star, a celebrity, an icon – a national treasure if you will, regardless of how old you were.

Among those youngsters there was one young man who would claim, much later on, that he and his friend were sexually assaulted by the singer backstage after the main festivities had finished. When the allegation finally emerged in 2014 – almost thirty years after the alleged assault – the details involved a boy under the age of sixteen and a friend (now deceased), who had come forward to claim that they had been sexually assaulted by Cliff in a storeroom after the Billy Graham rally at Bramall Lane football ground in the mid-1980s.

However, the allegation appeared riddled with uncertainty and inconsistencies: the complainant was unclear as to what night of the week it was when the assault actually took place. Billy Graham had appeared at Bramall Lane for six consecutive nights, but Cliff was only present for the one night on 28 June. The complainant wasn't sure who had accompanied them (the two boys) to the rally or why they even went. There were uncertainties about who had secured them tickets to the event, or how they had managed to get backstage, or how they gained access to Cliff's dressing room, or how they ended up in the storeroom (where the assault allegedly happened), or how long they were alone in there with him. Seemingly, for the police, none of these uncertainties mattered, regardless of the fact that they never established the accusers were even there.

By the time the allegations were made, at the height of Operation Yewtree but over three decades after the alleged assault, the police were prepared to take it seriously.

Friends rallied round the singer, unable to believe the allegations. Cilla Black said, 'I, like everyone else, was shocked to hear of these allegations and I am absolutely positive that they are without foundation,'[33] while broadcaster Michael Parkinson commented, 'I think the Cliff Richard case only highlights the feeling there is some kind of witch-hunt going on.'

Appearing on the *Studio 10* TV show in Australia, Bonnie Lythgoe, a dancer and friend of Cliff's, jumped to his defence, though it was never clear how she got the details. 'Cliff was with two security people and he was evidently, supposedly, seeing this young boy who was in the bathroom and evidently, he exposed himself or something happened and it is totally untrue. I know Cliff so well.'[34]

Cliff, however, was not about to settle. In fact, he was up for a fight to prove his innocence. It was reported that in his police interview he told them that 'he was never alone with the boys' who claim he sexually abused them at the rally.[35] This appears an odd thing to say, as it suggests he remembers the boys and recalls not being alone with them. He would later refute even remembering any boys.

As is the case in allegations of sexual abuse, the people who allege they are victims – though legally only complainants until proven – receive lifelong anonymity, so Cliff had no idea who was alleging the assault and never will do so. 'Cliff has never seen this person, he doesn't know who this person is,' stated Bonnie Lythgoe, 'and the sadness of all of this is that Cliff will never know who this person is.'[36]

To prove his innocence, Cliff would have to fight a faceless adversary, an accuser able to hide behind anonymity, while Cliff saw his name and image plastered across the national and international news.

Already he was presumed guilty in the eyes of many who form their opinions solely on lurid headlines, misleading soundbites, and the desperate appetite of rolling twenty-four hours news channels, which put audience figures, advertising revenue and sensational clickbait above the lives of those embroiled in such cases and who, by the very definition of British justice, are innocent before proven guilty.

CHAPTER 4

Cliff's second single, 'High Class Baby', was another Top 10 hit in 1958 and he embarked on a major nationwide tour supporting the Kalin Twins for £200 a week. It soon became clear that Cliff Richard & The Drifters were upstaging the headline act.

By now, The Drifters had a changed line-up. While Terry Smart and Ian Samwell were still in place on drums and guitar respectively, Norman Mitham had left the band as had Ken Pavey, and there were two newcomers. Geordies Hank Marvin and Bruce Welch had ventured south from the north of England to seek fame and fortune in London and had become best friends in the process. Both guitarists, Hank had been performing at the 2i's in Soho when Johnny Foster, still Cliff's manager, spotted him and asked if he wanted to join the band for the tour.

'Of course, I said I'd do it, I wanted to eat!' Hank said. 'I asked if they needed a rhythm guitarist and I recommended Bruce, so we did that tour and Cliff loved what we were doing and asked us to stay on.'[37] At the end of the tour, Ian Samwell was replaced by Jet Harris on bass and the following tour saw Terry Smart give up his seat behind the drums for Tony Meehan. Owing to a legal dispute over naming rights, The Drifters became The Shadows in time for the release of Cliff's sixth single 'Travellin' Light'. This became his second Number 1 hit after 'Living Doll', which had become the year's biggest selling single and Cliff's first song to crack the US Billboard charts, peaking at Number 30.

Success in the charts encouraged Cliff to make his first foray into movies – after all, Elvis was doing them – with a small role where he either sulked or crooned in the film *Serious Charge* directed by Terence Young, who would later go on to find fame as the director of the Bond films *Dr No, From Russia With Love* and *Thunderball*.

In *Serious Charge*, Anthony Quayle's vicar faces a barrage of abuse after being falsely accused of molesting a teenage boy, the accusations maliciously backed up by a local woman after the vicar had rejected her advances. Relatively ground-breaking for its day, the film has an undercurrent of repressed homosexuality, with the vicar appearing to avoid women like the plague throughout the film and the implication he is gay. At one point in the film, the actor Percy Herbert says of the vicar in a less than subtle moment of implication: 'We haven't got one of them in the parish, have we?'

The 'wrongfully accused' theme of the film would be a portent of what was to come in Cliff's life.

On a rock 'n' roll stage, by now I at least had some idea what I was doing. On a film set, surrounded by proper experienced actors, I felt completely out of my depth. Luckily, Terence Young, Anthony Quayle and everybody else were kind. I think they found me a bit of a novelty: their own tame, teenage rock 'n' roll star.[38]

The strain of combining a hectic music career with acting – Cliff had been playing shows at the Finsbury Park Empire while filming during the day – was beginning to take a toll on the singer's health and his father was becoming worried. By now Franklyn Boyd was Cliff's manager, having supplanted Johnny Foster following the success of 'Move It', Foster having taken Cliff as far as he could. Boyd had previously had a fledgling career as a teenage crooner, winning the All-British Crooning Championship aged just fifteen, before abandoning his singing career and going into publishing. Here he had met Norrie Paramor, the man who had offered Cliff his first contract, and by the autumn of 1958 Boyd was managing Cliff. But he was pushing his protégé too hard, causing Cliff to collapse with exhaustion.

Unbeknown to him, wheels had already been set in motion to get rid of Boyd.

At a party in October 1958, Cliff had met Ray Mackender, an underwriter for Lloyds during the day, a DJ by night and a budding talent scout and manager. 'Ray Mackender was gay,' revealed poet Royston Ellis, 'but I don't think anyone knew what that was all about.'[39] Ray was introduced later to Cliff's father, who expressed his concern for Cliff and suggested Ray help him manage Cliff's career.

'When Cliff's dad met me, I seemed like a godsend,' recalled Mackender. 'Everything was happening too quickly for them and he confided in me that he was looking to get rid of Franklyn Boyd. His sole interest was in preserving Cliff's health, but he also imagined that he would be quite good himself at managing Cliff's career and he asked me to help him do so.'[40]

Mackender went on to inform Rodger Webb it would be a huge task and they should bring in someone on a full-time basis. The singer's father took matters into his own hands and sacked

Boyd. 'I started to get problems from his father saying I was working him too hard,' remembered Boyd. 'And eventually I got a letter from him saying that he no longer wanted me to manage him. I never had any quarrel with Cliff or his mother. It was his father who was a pain in the neck.'[41]

Franklyn is a music publisher and he's also an entertainer in his own right. In a way, I was just another job to him and what he couldn't have realised at the time he undertook to manage me was the speed with which things were going to happen.[42]

With Boyd gone, Tito Burns, one-time bandleader and now talent manager, was appointed but despite Rodger's concerns and the appointment of a new manager, Cliff's workload didn't let up. He took on a major role in the film *Expresso Bongo*, a gritty and cynical satire of the pop music business. Tommy Steele and Marty Wilde had been considered for the role, but Cliff landed the £2,000 contract. The movie provided Cliff with his first Top 10 single of the sixties, 'A Voice in the Wilderness'. Two more Top 10 hits followed in 1960 along with two chart-toppers: 'Please Don't Tease' and 'I Love You'. He also recorded and released a Top 10 album, *Me & My Shadows*.

In 1960 Cliff and The Shadows also undertook their first tour of the USA and Canada. Part of a huge travelling roadshow that included acts such as Frankie Avalon, Bobby Rydell and Clyde McPhatter amongst others, it ran for six weeks beginning in the Kitchener Memorial Auditorium in Ontario, Canada and ending at the Orpheum Theatre in Wichita, Kansas. Throughout, their set-list remained constant: 'Thirty Days to Come Back Home', a Chuck Berry cover; 'My Babe', a Willie Dixon cover; his UK hits 'A Voice in the Wilderness' and 'Living Doll', which the

American audiences knew, and finishing with 'Whole Lotta Shakin' Goin' On', the Big Maybelle cover.

Despite audience approval, the tour did nothing to further Cliff's career in the USA. He needed, and expected, his record company to commit time and investment to make him a major attraction across the Atlantic.

In America, more than anywhere else in the world, there has to be a co-ordinating promotion machine... That didn't happen. So, we missed out.[43]

It would be another sixteen years before he cracked the Billboard Top 10.

While on tour in North America, Cliff was receiving the same adoration from girls screaming at him on stage or chasing him down the street as he encountered back in Britain. It continued once he returned to the UK, too, but he was aware of remaining true to himself, of sacrificing any female relationships so he could retain his fanbase. That was what was most important to him. He was adamant he wouldn't be seen to be in a relationship, he didn't want it damaging his career, which is what he lived for. His new manager, Tito Burns, couldn't help but notice. 'From the moment I first knew Cliff, women were of no interest to him. I'm not saying that he was gay. I just don't think sex meant anything to him.'[44]

But while he might not have had a visible relationship, unbeknown to anyone, Cliff was having an affair and, in doing so, finding himself part of an intricate love triangle.

Carol Costa was just seventeen years old when she was spotted by The Shadows' bass player Jet Harris at the Finsbury Park Astoria in 1959 and a relationship between them developed quickly. So quickly, in fact, that they were married within two months. In April 1959, Cliff met her for the first time at the Chiswick Empire. Her looks blew him away.

I always had a thing for Brigitte Bardot and Carol had just that look.[45]

Another strange quote from Cliff: Carol Costa had dark hair, Brigiette Bardot was famously blonde.

There was a noticeable chemistry between Cliff and Carol, but the problem was that she was married to Jet, Cliff's bandmate. When Carol discovered Jet had been unfaithful, she used Cliff as a shoulder to cry on, him becoming her emotional bedrock. shoulder to cry on, him becoming her emotional bedrock.

'Cliff was always in my corner. He was cautious about talking to other women. I think he's always been scared of girls and what they might be after,' Carol recalled many years later.46 Their discreet relationship grew stronger and, eventually, turned sexual. Carol, becoming distanced from Jet owing to his spiral into drink, began to believe that she might marry Cliff and start a family together but, after sleeping with her twice, Cliff ended the relationship. And he got bandmate, drummer Tony Meehan, to do his dirty work.

'I remember the moment the phone went,' she remembered. 'It was Tony Meehan. Tony was the only one of The Shadows who knew then what was going on. He said Cliff had asked him to tell me he wasn't coming back that night, that Cliff loved me and wouldn't marry anyone else. He said it was over. Tony said Cliff had been crying about it and couldn't bring himself to phone. He should have had the decency to tell me himself. I was shattered, completely heartbroken.'[46]

Carol suspects that it was Cliff's parents who doomed the

relationship after they discovered one of the many intimate letters the young lovers had written to each other.

'Cliff's mother found it under his pillow. It described the fact that we'd had sex at last, everything. Cliff's dad was very ill at that time and Mrs Webb said it would kill his father if he went ahead with the relationship. I don't think it was a money thing with Mrs Webb, and maybe not entirely a moral thing, but I think they felt it would ruin his career.'[47]

Cliff finally had his own say on the termination of the relationship decades later.

What my father was angry about was the fact that I was having this relationship – any relationship – behind his back... Had he known the full truth he would not have been pleased. If my affair with Carol had become public knowledge, or if she and Jet had divorced and I had rushed off and married her, it would almost certainly have wrecked my career.[48]

There it is again: 'career'. Cliff's sole *raison d'être*, even at the beginning of his journey, even in the face of the temptations of the flesh. He was focused, determined, nothing nor anyone was going to get in his way.

'I pretty much knew something was going on between him and my wife,' said Jet Harris many years after, 'but I went on stage every night and stood there behind the man, looking at the back of his head, backing him up. I never once rocked the boat, asked questions, made things difficult. I just kept schtum. Got up there. Did the job.'[49]

But Jet's drinking got to the point where he could no longer do the job. One night, in Liverpool's famous Cavern Club in January 1961, he fell off stage. The band offered to stop work for three months so he could sort out his issues with drink, but Harris was convinced he didn't have a problem so refused the suggestion. In April 1962, however, when Harris had spent the day of the NME Poll Winner's Party at Wembley taking full advantage of the free bar, Cliff and the other Shadows sacked him backstage, moments before they went on to collect the NME Best Instrumentalist Award. Jet took to the stage, played his three final songs with the band, put his bass down and walked out. He would never return, his place taken in the line-up by Brian Locking.

Forty-nine years later Jet Harris died of cancer and his manager, Peter Stockton, took the opportunity to launch a stinging attack on Cliff Richard, accusing him of neglecting his former bandmate during his struggle with the illness by refusing to offer him financial support.

'This man is meant to be a born-again Christian and humanitarian, but he's just a bloody hypocrite. Cliff was contacted eighteen months ago by a friend of Jet named Audrey, about Jet's cancer. She explained that Jet didn't have the necessary funds to get specialist treatment and wondered if Cliff might be able to be of assistance in some way or other. Audrey just got a letter back saying something like "I'm sorry to hear about Jet. I suggest he contact the Macmillan cancer people for help." It wasn't even signed by Cliff, but instead by someone in his office, which is absolutely disgusting,' Stockton said.[50]

If that wasn't all, in 2013, the spectre of Cliff's relationship with Carol reared its head again when 53-year-old Ricky Harris claimed he was the secret lovechild of Cliff and Carol. Raised as the son of Carol and Jet, Ricky had little contact with his father growing up. He said: 'I started to wonder who my father was in my teens when I thought, I need a father in my life. The doubts in my mind were fuelled by the Chinese whispers in and around my grandparents – not necessarily that Cliff was my dad, but that people weren't sure that Jet was.'[51]

Harris planned to launch legal proceedings to secure a DNA test, but almost as quickly as the story surfaced it disappeared again and neither Cliff, nor his representatives, ever commented on the matter.

CHAPTER 5

It was a bittersweet year in 1961 for Cliff. Professionally it was incredibly successful: he had his first Number 1 album with *21 Today*, he had four Top 10 singles and he toured South Africa. He also filmed his starring role in *The Young Ones*, which was to become the third most successful film at the British box-office in 1962, beaten only by *The Guns of Navarone* and *Dr No*. He was also dating a dancer, Delia Wicks, whom he had met while filming *The Young Ones*. They dated for over eighteen months, but it was a sexless relationship. They would spend time at the movies, going for drives or simply chatting.

Despite never having sex, Delia believed in the intensity of their relationship and that 'it would have happened eventually'.[52] But like Janice Berry before her, Delia was to find out that Cliff's only real love was rock 'n' roll. He dumped her via a letter, writing that 'showbiz is in my blood now and I would be lost without it'[53] and 'being a pop singer I have to give up one priceless thing – the right to any lasting relationship with any special girl.'[54]

Delia wasn't the only relationship Cliff lost in 1961.

Despite a brave fight against illness, his father, Rodger, died from complications with thrombosis. At the age of just twenty, Cliff now had to support his mother, who had become a widow at forty, and his three sisters, both emotionally and financially.

My stiff-upper-lip upbringing has often made me loath to show public emotion, but I sobbed like a baby at Dad's funeral and I didn't care who saw me.[55]

It signalled the beginning of a period of profound change for Cliff. He wanted to hire a medium to try to communicate with his dad, but The Shadows' new bass player, Brian Locking, a devout Jehovah's Witness, warned him against it as such an action would offend God. Cliff questioned why it would offend God, so Brian duly picked up a copy of his Bible and read Deuteronomy 18:10 which forbade consulting the dead and other forms of the occult arts. So started a period of Cliff exploring faith and religion more deeply with Brian Locking. 'We used to gather around hotel rooms and have some very nice and interesting discussions about religion,' recalled Brian.[56]

Meanwhile Cliff and The Shadows went from strength-to-strength. In 1962 'The Young Ones' and the double-A side 'The Next Time/Bachelor Boy' both got to Number 1 ('Bachelor Boy' being the first song Cliff had written or co-written that was released as a single). Two other singles peaked at Number 2 while his album reached Number 3 in the UK and topped the album charts in Canada.

In 1963, 'Summer Holiday' was not only a chart-topping single, but the film of the same name it came from was the second-biggest film at the UK box office after *From Russia With Love,* and Cliff was voted the most popular star at the British box-office.

Brian Locking then left The Shadows in October 1963 to pursue his activities with the Jehovah's Witnesses, and his place in the band was taken by John Rostill.

A string of eight consecutive Top 10 hits culminated in 'The Minute You're Gone' topping the charts in April 1965. This had been an unabashed attempt to crack the USA market recorded, as it was, in Nashville with US session musicians. Cliff had broken into the Billboard Top 30 in 1963 with 'It's All In the Game', but success there continued to elude him with other releases and 'The Minute You're Gone' failed to even chart. Tom Jones appeared to have stolen his thunder in the US with his energetic and provocative performances and, of course, the Beatles heralded the British Invasion in 1964, enabling groups such as the Dave Clark Five, Herman's Hermits, the Rolling Stones and the Searchers, to name but a few, to storm their shores.

Having missed the boat, Cliff slipped into being a comfortable middle-of-the-road act in the mid-60s, appearing in anodyne films that were box-office misfires, releasing singles that generally had lukewarm sales – only two of his twenty singles in the rest of the decade broke into the Top 5, although 'Congratulations' did reach Number 1. He even represented the United Kingdom in the 1968 Eurovision Song Contest, coming second with 'Congratulations' to Spain's 'La La La'.

The sixties were a revolution in sound and society, fashion and music. An artist like Cliff, once the performer heralding the arrival of British rock 'n' roll, was suddenly on the outside. The music he was making wasn't keeping up with the groundbreaking experimentation and rule-breaking of the Beatles or the Beach Boys, it couldn't compete with the poetry of Bob Dylan, and it fell way short of the rawness of the Rolling Stones and the Who. Cliff remained hungry for hits, but became unable to record great records as the sixties became the seventies, and the more he chased hits the more his slow decline into a family-friendly pop entertainer began.

Rock 'n' roll had had its day, new sounds and musical genres had ushered in. Perhaps Cliff had had his day, too.

While it's true the musical revolutions of the sixties hastened Cliff's decline, another possible reason was religion.

Cliff had considered becoming a Jehovah's Witness after his talks with Brian Locking following the death of his father, and even attended some meetings alongside Brian and Hank Marvin. But Cliff couldn't quite accept the philosophies of Jehovah's Witnesses. He needed something else. In July 1965 he was introduced to Bill Latham at a birthday party for his old English teacher, Jay Norris. Jay was fervently anti-Jehovah's Witness and had become concerned at Cliff putting out religious feelers with them. Bill Latham was head of religious education at the school and was 'recruited' by Jay to help Cliff forge his path.

Later, at a Sunday afternoon Crusaders class,[57] Cliff experienced a relaxed atmosphere where youngsters were taught about Christian life. He went back regularly and as the months passed, he found the evangelical Christian teachings of the Crusaders getting under his skin. While filming *Finders Keepers* at Pinewood Studios in 1966, and having had a year of discussions with Bill Latham, Cliff became a Christian.

> *I lay on the bed and mouthed a very hesitant prayer. It was something like: 'All right, Jesus, I'm aware that you're knocking – you'd better come in and take over'.*[58]

Later in June 1966, Cliff went public. The American evangelist Billy Graham was coming to Britain. One of his rallies was going to be at Earl's Court and a message had been sent to Cliff's office asking if he would speak about his faith in front of 25,000 people.

I jumped at the chance, because it's every Christian's wish to say that he's a Christian to as many people as he can.[59]

Cliff addressed the crowd, pronounced his faith and sang the southern gospel song 'It's No Secret What God Can Do'. As a committed Christian, Cliff was now out. He soon found his circle of friends changing; they were vicars, schoolteachers or youth workers. He spent more time hanging out with Bill Latham and the rock 'n' roll world seemed a different planet. Cliff's career was taking a back seat, whether intentionally or not, and as God and religion became his guiding light, the press ridiculed him and the public began to desert him.

'To declare it [his Christian faith] was just the most unfashionable, the most daring, courageous and brave act you could imagine,' says Manfred Mann singer Paul Jones. 'You could have said the world was flat and people would have had more time for you.'[60] Becoming a Christian or, at least, displaying it so publicly, was the last thing a rock 'n' roll performer should do. 'The rock star is a rebellious creature,' states Queen guitarist Brian May. 'And he's scornful of the morals of the time, and for Cliff to cast himself in the role and still maintain his open faith is a hard thing to pull off.'[61]

Some saw it as a gimmick, a clever piece of image-building, concocted by the PR men to broaden my appeal. And there were those who viewed it as professional suicide.[62]

Cliff's first album following the Billy Graham rally was *Good News*, a collection of Christian songs. It spent one week on the album charts, reaching Number 37. In 1968 he starred alongside Dora Bryan in the film *Two A Penny*, made by Billy Graham's World Wide Pictures production company. It tells the story of a girl becoming a drug dealer to earn money before being converted to Christianity (by Billy Graham, no less) and seeing the error of her ways. It was called 'a naive piece of propaganda which makes its intentions clear from the start' by the *Monthly Film Bulletin*, while the *Radio Times* commented: 'The obstacle is Cliff himself, who was already a popular family entertainer, but is awkwardly miscast as a hoodlum.'

> *To my mind it's the best film I've done and it was a shame it never got a general release. The critics didn't exactly go overboard: secular press thought it was too Christian, and Christian press thought it was too secular. But what's important is that, through its story and its message, people have encountered Christ.*[63]

Whether he liked it or not, Cliff had become the poster boy for Christianity, but while the Beatles met with the Maharishi at the height of their creative peak and continued to push boundaries and Elvis recorded his gospel album *How Great Thou Art*, which sold over three million copies and earned him a Grammy, Cliff's career stuttered and stalled following the Billy Graham rally.

The singer was just twenty-six years old, but he was no longer cool. He briefly contemplated becoming a teacher, but friends talked him out of it.

> *Ever since I had emerged and been called an English Elvis, I had got used to being feted, admired, and screamed at. Everyone*

loves to be loved and it was tough suddenly to be viewed as a figure of fun, a wimpy Bible-bashing Goody Two-Shoes.[64]

As he threw himself into his Christian endeavours, attempting – and failing – to marry pop and religion with any critical or commercial success, Cliff kept his relationship with Billy Graham firmly intact. It was a friendship built on faith, on spirituality and, to a certain extent on Cliff's part, hero worship.

In 1984, Billy Graham returned to the UK to preach in arenas and stadiums to tens of thousands. At Villa Park in Birmingham, Cliff joined him, proclaiming, 'For me being a Christian has become the most important part of my life.'[65]

A year later, in 1985, Cliff again joined Billy Graham on stage, this time at a rally at Bramall Lane in Sheffield. As Cliff sang to the crowd, he couldn't possibly imagine how this event would come back to haunt him thirty-nine years later, threaten to destroy him, and throw into the public eye the role of broadcasters and the police, striking at the very heart of British justice.

CHAPTER 6

Perhaps there was a grim inevitability – particularly in the swirling maelstrom of Operation Yewtree – that the name of Cliff Richard would be trawled up in connection with allegations of sexual abuse or misconduct.

The public image of Cliff was one of an extremely private man wedded to his career, committed to his Christianity and content to spend his spare time playing tennis (he once memorably said he preferred tennis to sex). Coupled with his ever-attainable yet untouchable Bachelor Boy-persona, this image of never-wedded fantasy-lover popstar who has never settled down with a woman (and who has barely had any heterosexual relationships) has long given way to speculation that he must be a repressed homosexual.

For much of the latter part of his career he had been sniggered at, leered at, and derided by those not in his fanbase, seen as a middle-of-the-road Man At C&A-type entertainer. While Elvis, the performer he aspired towards, was powerful and potent, Cliff was a sweet, soft, unthreatening version. Being a pop idol – as the writer Philip Norman once said – should represent sin in its most enviable forms. Cliff was almost the exact opposite: no drugs, no swearing, no guitar-smashing or room-wrecking, no hedonistic indulgence, and no sex. Even the sex he sold on stage to his legion of middle-aged and increasingly elderly female fans is a peculiarly antiseptic choreographed form of sex: more arthritic than anarchic. He isn't sexy because he doesn't know how to be, and maybe that is simply because he hasn't had sex.

Cliff's lifestyle feeds into constant speculation about his sexuality and that, in turn, fed rightly or wrongly into the narrative that he would inevitably be caught up in the tangled web of Operation Yewtree.

Yewtree, by default, stems from our national obsession with paedophilia, and irresponsible politicians linking it to homosexuality. It leads therefore into the suspicion that bachelors, especially older bachelors, must have – or have had – a sexual interest in underage boys.

And Cliff is the ultimate bachelor.

But simply being a bachelor is not reason enough for police forces to believe allegations of sexual abuse. Certainly not an excuse to leak suspects' names to the press prior to being arrested or charged, celebrity or not.

From the beginning of 1970 to the end of 1975, only two of Cliff's eighteen single releases made the British Top 10 and one of these, 'Power To All Our Friends', was the British entry into the 1973 Eurovision Song Contest, decided by BBC viewers via a postal ballot after Cliff had performed six songs on Cilla Black's BBC1 Saturday evening show *Cilla*. Although it reached Number 4 in the UK charts, Cliff once again failed to conquer Eurovision. Having come second in 1968 with

'Congratulations', this time he finished third behind runner-up Spain and winner Luxembourg.

During this fallow period, Cliff was also without his Shadows. The band had disbanded in December 1968 when relationships within the group became strained. 'It amazes me that people expect four guys to work together, play together and virtually live in each other's pockets – and still be best of pals all the time, and behave like brothers,' recalled guitarist Bruce Welch. 'We had been working together now almost non-stop for nearly ten years, touring the world without let-up. We were on a treadmill of tours, recording sessions, live engagements, TV work … and so it went on, year after year. Although we were established as an international act, the domestic hits slowly came to an end.'[66]

Tensions within the band came to a head before a performance at the Talk of the North nightclub in Eccles, when Hank Marvin's apparent lack of punctuality, arriving five minutes before the band were due on stage, almost caused a fight within the band that resulted in Welch storming out and bassist John Rostill exploding with anger.

'I just broke down,' said Marvin. 'Bruce was about to run out on us, John had got it in for me and my fuse just went. I ran out of the building and gulped in a mouthful of cold Lancashire air. I went back in ten minutes later having regained my composure a bit, to find Olivia [Newton-John, Welch's girlfriend at the time] had persuaded Bruce not to go home, as we'd got a job to do and a contract to fulfil. As far as I was concerned it was all over that night.'[67]

An uneasy truce enabled the band to agree to complete their run at the London Palladium with Cliff before they disbanded, their final performance being on 14 December 1968.

With The Shadows no more, Hank continued collaborating

with Cliff, writing 'Throw Down a Line' for him, backed by the Mike Vickers Orchestra, which they recorded in 1969 and it became Cliff's last Top 10 hit of the decade. Marvin also appeared regularly on Cliff's BBC1 Saturday show, *It's Cliff Richard*, which ran between January 1970 and September 1974, attracting audiences of up to fifteen million at its peak.

It was basically a family variety show that aired on BBC1 on Saturday teatimes at 6.15. Hank and Una [Stubbs] were on it every week with me, and we would do songs and sketches and have special guests.[68]

Cliff had known Una Stubbs since 1963 when she made her film debut alongside Cliff in *Summer Holiday*. They appeared together again the following year in *Wonderful Life* when, off-screen, romance briefly flickered between them. Years later Stubbs would say, 'We loved each other madly, we had a romantic attachment, but it wasn't a sordid affair.'[69] In 2020, Cliff said, 'Una Stubbs and I hit it off from the start,' before continuing, 'There was no question of any romance between us, although I loved her and still do to this day.'[70]

The probing into Cliff's private life lengthened in the early seventies when he bought a house just outside Weybridge in Surrey. Still a bachelor, Cliff wasn't alone in moving in. He was joined by Bill Latham, the man who had helped turn him on to Christianity after they had met in 1965. Remaining close friends ever since (he would ultimately go on to become part of Cliff's management team), from 1973 Cliff and Bill lived together. Both appeared single – Cliff definitely so – and it wasn't long before newspaper gossip began.

The papers looked at the fact of two single guys, in their thirties, sharing a house, and put two and two together to make five.[71]

In fact, Cliff and Bill weren't alone; also sharing the house was Bill's mum Mamie and, later, Bill's girlfriend Pia Hoffman. The whole fascination with the fact Cliff was living with Bill bemused Latham. 'I can never understand society's assumption that if someone is single after a certain age then they must be homosexual,' commented Latham. 'I suppose the assumption is that if two men share a home, they have to be having a sexual relationship.'[72]

When Bill and I lived together, there were always stories about what people believed our real relationship was, but what nobody realised was that Bill's girlfriend was living with us, too. Nobody asked about that, not that it was anyone else's business.[73]

Their living arrangements were one of convenience – nothing more – despite the prying eyes and sordid headlines of the tabloids. Cliff hated loneliness; he loved having people around him, he was sociable and he needed – maybe craved – company. Perhaps he suffers from autophobia, an intense fear of being alone. It likely stems from a complex mix of factors, including past experiences, a lack of self-esteem, social conditioning (father, shame, fear of failure), and even potential mental health conditions. Abandonment fears and feeling inadequate or sexually shameful can also contribute to this fear. Additionally, some individuals may simply not be used to having time to themselves, or may have learned to associate being alone with negative emotions.

Despite being on-stage, the life of a singer can be intensely lonely, leading to autophobia. Performing is an intense communion between artist and audience, a singer in front of thousands of adoring fans sharing the moment. But once the show is over and the tour moves on, a nomadic, lonely lifestyle of dark, empty motorways begins. Hotel rooms that blend one into another, constantly moving and never settling, the rush of the stage and the comedown after, let alone carrying your life in a suitcase, all create an emotional and chemical rollercoaster that a performer's body and mind goes through every day.

Yes, there are bandmates, crew, managers, promoters close by, but travelling, working, eating and staying with the same people can be socially exhausting, which can make being alone seem extraordinarily isolating. In a 2009 study of American celebrities, psychologist Donna Rockwell found that celebrity status results in a kind of death – an 'irreversible existential alteration' that includes loss of privacy and freedom to go about life with anonymity. The famous, she found, are alone on the 'island of recognition', where they find 'a loneliness that happens because you are separate'.[74]

In her Netflix documentary,[75] Lady Gaga is heard saying she is 'married to her loneliness' and during a phone call with her designer, she reveals: 'I'm lonely, Brandon. Every night. And all these people will leave. They'll leave and then I'll be alone. And I'll go from being touched and talked to all day long to total silence.'[76] 'The big pop stars are all lonely, even with thousands of people screaming at them,' said singer Lulu. 'I married Maurice Gibb, and looking back I can see we were drawn to each other because we were both lonely.'[77]

Cliff wasn't looking for any kind of romance with Bill, he was simply looking for companionship, friendship, and an antidote to the loneliness of the performer and artist.

Bill's friendship is not only special but consistent. Although I don't feel lonely because of Christianity, I can feel alone, so Bill and my friends are very important to me. I enjoy loving my friends and being loved by them in a platonic way.[78]

He was also looking for a return to pop recognition. Like an addict, fame and adulation had become his addiction and with that comes the problems of adulation stopping, no longer being in the limelight. He was in danger of becoming a 'has been', because a bright light can't shine forever.

As his hits dried up, the early-70s saw him turn to television to keep him in the public eye. Alongside Cliff's teatime family BBC show, appearances on children's TV shows such as *The Sooty Show* and entertainment shows like *Morecambe & Wise* seemed to reinforce his position as a middle-of-the-road, wholesome, safe family entertainer, far removed from the wild world of rock 'n' roll.

By the mid-70s, Cliff had recorded only one album so far in the decade, *Tracks 'n Grooves*, released in 1970.[79] It barely troubled the Top 40.

If somebody had told me at that time that I had lost my way in my music career, I'm sure I would have been offended and denied it indignantly, but the truth is that I think I had. My band had split, and I was preoccupied with my faith and doing TV.[80]

Cliff's final major film role to date was *Take Me High* in 1973, an instantly forgotten dud best summed up by a *Radio Times* review that said: 'The "comedy" plods along with all the zip of Spaghetti Junction at rush hour. Indigestible.' While working on the movie, Cliff met the Australian music producer David Mackay, who was responsible for the film's soundtrack. Mackay had an idea to get Cliff's pop career back on track, feeling the singer had slumped into a routine and was no long feeling the song. 'He would turn up at the studio, he'd be handed some lyric sheets and then he'd go in and sing the songs through perfectly,' Mackay recalled. 'Then it would be goodnight. He'd put the lyric sheets in his bag and leave. It had just become a mind-set for him. When you've had that much success over that long a period, you don't feel the need to change. But then you start to see that it's becoming less and less successful. You also see that other people are coming around you who are doing great things, and what you're doing is rather pedestrian in contrast. It was a long hard slog to turn him around.'[81]

Mackay's idea was that Cliff work with a band in the studio again and he introduced him to some Australian musicians working in London. 'This was happening just as he emerged from those years of terrible variety shows on TV, which were just so mindless and horrible,' said Mackay.[82] With Cliff writing a number of songs and playing guitar, these sessions resulted in Cliff's 1974 album, *The 31st of February Street*.

I thought it was a sweet, sensitive album, and after getting immersed in writing and recording it, I felt closer to it than I had to any album in years.[83]

His fans didn't feel the same way, though, and the album failed to chart. What it did do, however, was reignite Cliff's interest in music.

It really felt like a rebirth.[84]

Plans were hatched to record a new album later in 1975. But first they needed a producer. Cliff's then manager, Peter Gormley, put the word out and one of Cliff's old acquaintances, Bruce Welch, who had become a successful producer since leaving The Shadows, particularly with Olivia Newton-John, answered the call. 'Cliff had come through a time where he was making crap movies, putting out crap singles, and hadn't had a hit single in a year,' remembered Welch. 'When someone said that there was a chance of producing Cliff if I could find the songs, I went out and found the songs.'[85]

One of the songs was 'Miss You Nights', which Welch had discovered on an unreleased album by Dave Townsend.

Bruce had come round, cos my manager, the late Peter Gormley, had asked him if he would like to produce an album. And he started collecting songs. He came up and played me 'Miss You Nights', and we sat on the balcony of my house and I said, 'I've got goosebumps.' He said, 'Look at my arm! It's got to be on the album.'[86]

Cliff had also been presented with a song by Terry Britten, who had been playing guitar in his band for a couple of years. The song was 'Devil Woman'.

I had loved it instantly, and I'd had it for weeks while not being particularly sure that it was right for me. But Bruce thought it was fantastic the second that he heard it.[87]

It has been suggested Cliff appeared resistant to recording it, because he didn't like some of the lyrics and the fortune-telling theme of the song. But Bruce Welch persuaded Cliff to sing it –

with some minor lyric changes to align with Cliff's beliefs – and, upon hearing it Tony Clark, the engineer, predicted it would be a hit in America.

However, it was 'Miss You Nights' that became the lead single for the forthcoming album, *I'm Nearly Famous*, and it reached Number 15 in the UK charts, perhaps not as high as it should have done given the quality of the songwriting and the performance by Cliff.

'"Miss You Nights" is for sure in the top 100 of best British singles of all time,' suggests Tris Penna, who worked at EMI from 1987–97 as a producer, A&R and manager. 'A heartbreaking performance by Cliff of a Dave Townsend song.'[88]

But it was the success of 'Devil Woman' that truly heralded the beginning of Cliff's pop comeback and helped turn *I'm Nearly Famous*, released in May 1976, into Cliff's most successful album since 1962. The album also became Cliff's first to chart in the USA, thanks, in part, to Elton John.

He heard I'm Nearly Famous *– somebody played it to him but didn't tell him who it was. He heard the first track [*'I Can't Ask For Anymore Than You'*], which was one of the first times I used falsetto, and said, 'Who's that? Cliff Richard? It can't be.' Then he heard 'Devil Woman' and went, 'Oh my God, this is great stuff, let's see if we can get it for Rocket.' And I wasn't signed in the US with EMI at that moment, so I said, 'Yes, please, anything you can do.'*[89]

The album peaked at Number 5 in the UK album charts and as well as being a commercial success, it was also a critical one. Writing in *Melody Maker*, Geoff Brown said, 'Cliff Richard has at last made the sort of album he could, and should, have been making for years. It is with some incredulity that I have to say that for the past ten days I've been playing two albums constantly. One is Marvin Gaye's *I Want You*. The other is *I'm Nearly Famous*. The renaissance of Richard, for that is what I believe this album heralds, is long overdue... it is the best album of new songs ever and, if there are enough unprejudiced ears around, could well mark the start of a fresh Cliff Richard buying public.'

The second single from the album, 'Devil Woman', reached Number 9 in the UK charts and Number 6 in the US Billboard charts, Cliff's first ever Top 10 hit in the USA.

When I went to America with 'Devil Woman', it sold 1.4 million copies. When I came back people said to me, 'You've cracked America!' The only thing I could think of was that 249 million people did not buy it.[90]

A third single, 'I Can't Ask For Anymore Than You', also broke in the UK Top 20 giving Cliff a hat-trick of hits from the album and he was back in the game. From his UK resurgence and cracking America, Cliff then went behind the Iron Curtain, embarking on a brief tour of the Soviet Union, playing dates in Moscow and St Petersburg before being rushed back by EMI to record his next album at Abbey Road, keen to ride his current wave of popularity.

Every Face Tells A Story was released in March 1977, but the musical landscape in the UK had changed significantly since Cliff's previous album release a year earlier.

The previous year had seen the arrival of punk, born out of the fiery rebellious spirit of a discontented youth faced with lack of opportunities and boredom. 'In 1976 Britain was a cultural wasteland with stuff like Genesis and the dregs of glam rock,'[91] says Damned guitarist Brian James, while John Lydon of the Sex Pistols describes the Britain of the time as 'a very depressing place. It was completely run-down, there was trash on the streets, total unemployment – just about everybody was on strike.'[92]

Disillusioned and desperate with an air of delinquency, they turned to music, with punk embracing a DIY mentality. 'Everybody was brought up with an education system that told you point blank that if you came from the wrong side of the tracks … then you had no hope in hell and no career prospects at all,' says Lydon. 'Out of all that came pretentious *moi*, and the Sex Pistols, and then a whole bunch of copycat wankers after us.'[93] In fact, it was the Damned who released punk's first single, 'New Rose'. 'We thought we were a fast rock 'n' roll band,' says Brian James, 'but the journalist Caroline Coon coined the term "punk rock", so suddenly "New Rose" was "the first British punk single".'[94]

In the USA, disco had emerged from nightclubs like Studio 54 and Paradise Garage to become more mainstream and was to firmly establish itself in 1977 with the *Saturday Night Fever* soundtrack following in the formative footsteps of Van McCoy, Donna Summer and the Trammps. Faced with the shift in musical tastes alongside a society racked with disorder, unrest and unemployment, Cliff's new album flopped in comparison to his previous release, only reaching Number 8 on the UK album charts and failing to chart at all in the USA. Of the three singles released from it, two failed to break into the Top 30 and only 'My Kinda Life' penetrated the Top 20, peaking at 15.

I went into the album feeling really confident . . . but it didn't quite scale the heights of its predecessor. It's hard to say exactly why. Maybe we had rushed into it a little too quickly, and our song choices weren't as good.[95]

Cliff's reaction in 1978 was to follow-up with an album of contemporary Christian music titled *Small Corners*. Bruce Welch declined the offer to produce it. 'I thought the timing was wrong,'[96] Welch recalled, but Cliff was undeterred and pressed ahead producing the album himself and recording songs such as Larry Norman's 'Why Should the Devil Have All the Good Music', Kris Kristofferson's 'Why Me', and ending with the eighteenth-century hymn, 'When I Survey the Wondrous Cross'. The album scraped into the Top 40 and neither of the singles released charted.

His next studio album, *Green Light*, released later in 1978, didn't do much better. Full of commercial expectations, it only reached Number 25 on the album charts and the title track was the only single to register a chart position, peaking at a lowly Number 57. It was the first year since his debut single in 1958 that Cliff had failed to have a Top 20 hit.

I began to worry: was my comeback starting to stall?[97]

Nobody, least of all Cliff, was prepared for what would come next.

CHAPTER 7

Operation Yewtree was set up in 2012 by the Metropolitan Police with the aim of investigating allegations of child sexual abuse by the TV and radio presenter Jimmy Savile and others. Also launched in 2012 was Operation Fairbank, an investigation into allegations of sexual abuse by politicians. Two years later, Operation Midland was formed to investigate a paedophile ring allegedly operating from a property in Dolphin Square, London, in the 1970s and 1980s.

By 2014, Operation Yewtree had found damning evidence against Savile that proved him to be Britain's worst sex offender. A predatory paedophile who, over six decades and with access granted through his charity work, which masked his crimes, abused hundreds of victims, young, old and dying, and even participated in necrophilia. Savile died in 2011, escaping punishment, but others were snared in subsequent investigations.

Entertainer Rolf Harris, broadcaster Stuart Hall, weatherman Fred Talbot, disc-jockey Chris Denning, publicist Max Clifford and pop star Gary Glitter were all given custodial sentences following investigation by Yewtree or other police authorities. The public appeared fully behind the Yewtree investigations, their thirst for the next celebrity arrest insatiable. 'The public's support for pursuing non-recent cases is reassuring for victims of sexual abuse,' Peter Watt, Yewtree lead for the NSPCC said. 'Despite long investigations and often shocking revelations, the public remain supportive of Operation Yewtree. And they strongly support pursuing offenders in other cases even after a number of years have passed.'[98]

But for every household name arrested, there were other celebrities who became collateral damage. Radio presenter Paul Gambaccini was arrested at 4.38 a.m. in October 2013 accused of sexually assaulting a minor. The claim was made by a drug addict with a history of making false allegations. It took Gambaccini eleven months to clear his name, during which time he was publicly hung out to dry, lost around £100,000 in earnings, was forced to sell belongings to meet his legal costs and suffered panic attacks. *Pop Idol* judge Neil Fox was another publicly accused, yet no charges were ever brought.[99]

Comedian Jim Davidson was arrested twice and feared his career was over. 'Suddenly I was arrested at Heathrow. I had a load of accusations. And me and my lawyers went and got all the evidence and gave it to the police. And they basically said, "Jim, there's not going to be any more action, so no further action."'[100]

Jimmy Tarbuck was another arrested by Yewtree following allegations of historic sexual abuse, but was released without charge. 'You get a knock on the door. I was in my dressing gown making a cup of tea and fourteen policemen came in my house, fourteen! I thought it's [the ITV show] *Surprise Surprise*,' the veteran comedian said, before continuing, 'And the real thing that annoys me about it all is these people can remain anonymous.'[101]

Freddie Starr was arrested four times and spent eighteen months on bail as a result of Operation Yewtree before prosecutors announced there was insufficient evidence to prosecute him over sexual offence allegations. Starr's lawyer accused the police of a 'flagrant breach' of Starr's human rights over their handling of the case, continuing, 'You can see the toll it has taken on him. He is a man of good character and remains a man of good character and I would ask the public to now stand by this man. There can be no doubt about it – his innocence has been proven.'[102]

In October 2012, the man overseeing Operation Yewtree, Commander Peter Spindler, announced, 'This is a watershed moment for child abuse investigations and Yewtree will be a landmark investigation.'[103] But in 2015, after dramatically quitting the Yewtree investigation two years previously, Spindler admitted that the police had got some things wrong during the investigations. 'One of the things we didn't get right was we completely underestimated what was going to happen. We didn't have sufficient resources in place. We didn't have the knowledge and the skills amongst our more general detectives,' he commented, during a talk at the NSPCC's HQ in London to address whether the investigations had turned into a 'media witch-hunt'.[104]

Whether it was a media witch-hunt or not, Cliff Richard was about to have his collar felt by the full force of the law.

In March 2014, South Yorkshire Police (SYP) received an allegation from Operation Yewtree, which centred around a complainant who alleged that he was molested by Cliff Richard during a Billy Graham event at Bramall Lane in the 1980s.

Five months later, at 10.20 a.m. on 14 August 2014, officers from South Yorkshire Police entered Cliff's Berkshire apartment in the full glare of the media, specifically – and crucially – the BBC.

Cliff was not at home, he was at his villa in Portugal and was able, like millions of others, to watch the raid in horrifying detail on television due to the BBC reporters, camera crews and helicopter – hired exclusively by the BBC – obtaining footage as the officers searched Cliff's property. And all this on the basis of a single allegation of historic sexual abuse.

More than a decade ago it used to be common practice for police to let reporters know they were about to raid a celebrity's house or make a high-profile arrest. It was part of the trade of information and favours between the police and hacks. Procedures began to change in 2008 when the High Court considered the lawfulness of such a search at the home of the football manager Harry Redknapp, who was being investigated for allegations of corruption in football. Officers from the City of London Police were accompanied by photographers from a national newspaper when they searched Redknapp's property.

Regarding Redknapp, the court described as 'understandable' his complaint that journalists from the *Sun* newspaper had been present. A Home Affairs Committee Report in 2009 said that leaks, while not illegal, were 'wrong' and damaged the reputation of the police and that the person being investigated could turn out to be innocent and the resulting press coverage could 'unjustifiably taint individuals' reputations'. The Leveson Inquiry subsequently concluded that police operations involving the media should be 'controlled more tightly' to avoid the 'risk of violating the private rights of individuals'.

Guidelines following these various committee reports and inquiries led to police tip-offs to hacks greatly reducing – although not disappearing completely – in the years that followed. In the College of Policing's 2013 publication, *Guidance on Relationships with the Media*, it states that the decision to disclose the name of a suspect on arrest or disclose such information to the press should be 'on a case-by-case basis but, save in clearly identified circumstances, or where legal restrictions apply, the names or identifying details of those who are arrested or suspected of a crime should not be released by police forces to the press or the public. Such circumstances include a threat to life, the prevention or detection of crime or a matter of public interest and confidence.'

This all begs the question: how was the BBC outside Cliff's Berkshire apartment as the police went in?

Between March and June 2014, following presentation of the allegations to the South Yorkshire Police by the Metropolitan Police Yewtree team, various discussions had taken place between the two Forces before an agreement was reached on 2 July 2014 that an investigation into Sir Cliff Richard by South Yorkshire Police was ready to proceed.[105] Detective Superintendent Matt Fenwick, a man with twenty-seven years' experience, was appointed Senior Investigating Officer under the command of Jo Byrne, a strategic firearms commander who, in July 2013, had become the first woman to be appointed to a chief officer position with South Yorkshire Police.

Aware of the allegations circling Sir Cliff was the Chief Constable of South Yorkshire Police at the time, David Crompton. 'I cannot remember who told me about this at first,' he said, 'but I do recall that I had a number of conversations with Matt Fenwick. Although I did not have any direct involvement in investigations, I was kept informed of any high profile or important investigations within SYP. I recall from these briefings that Matt did not consider that the evidence against Sir Cliff Richard was particularly strong and he was unsure whether the investigation would lead to charges.'[106]

CHAPTER 8

On 9 June 2014, another character entered the story: BBC crime correspondent Dan Johnson. Graduating from Leeds University, where he had been one of six Student Feature Writers of the Year at the 2006 *Guardian* Student Media Awards, he had joined BBC Radio Sheffield in 2008 and then moved into television as a reporter within the newsroom at BBC *Look North* in 2011.

A year later, while working on the regional programme *Inside Out*, Johnson investigated the acquittal of 95 miners charged with rioting at Orgreave during the miners' strike. During his investigation he uncovered new evidence about the alleged manipulation of statements made by South Yorkshire Police detectives to describe 'scenes they'd simply never seen'[107] and using language that Sheffield barrister, Mark George QC, said pointed to 'widespread collusion'.[108]

This award-winning programme was broadcast a month after the Hillsborough Independent Panel, which looked into the fatal crowd crush at the 1989 FA Cup semi-final at Hillsborough Stadium in Sheffield that resulted in the deaths of 97 Liverpool football supporters. It revealed that 164 South Yorkshire Police statements had been altered after the disaster.[109]

Chief Constable David Crompton, who was also Chief Constable during the Cliff Richard investigation, was suspended in 2016 by Alan Billings, the South Yorkshire Police and Crime Commissioner, following a statement Crompton gave that was interpreted as blaming Liverpool fans for the disaster. After being forced to resign, Crompton successfully took his case to court and the High Court ruled that Billings had acted unlawfully in removing him.[110]

In light of what was to come, it's interesting at this point to note Mr Justice Mann's 2018 observations of Dan Johnson as a witness in the Approved Judgement of Sir Cliff Richard versus the BBC and South Yorkshire Police. Mann comments:

> Mr Johnson was the reporter whose investigations started the whole ball rolling in this case, so his evidence was central to the BBC's case. He was, at the time, a relatively junior member of the news gathering team, covering the north of England, though he was not without experience. He was, like any responsible reporter, anxious to get knowledge of, and become involved in, big stories, and in my view was anxious to make a bit of a name for himself by getting this story and bringing it home. I do not believe that he is a fundamentally dishonest man, but he was capable of letting his enthusiasm get the better of him in pursuit of what he thought was a good story so that he could twist matters in a way that could be described as dishonest in order to pursue his story.[111]

It was on 9 June 2014 when Dan Johnson spoke to a confidential source and received a tip-off about the police investigation into Sir Cliff Richard. This source was never identified, Johnson's case being that the source was associated with, but was not part of, Operation Yewtree. At this point in June, South Yorkshire Police had been working with the Metropolitan Police officers involved in Operation Yewtree for three months while they put the case against Cliff together, although it must be reiterated that the investigation was not connected to the Metropolitan Police's Operation Yewtree.

It is possible that Dan's source came from within South Yorkshire Police, it could even have come from within Thames Valley Police, who were involved in the raid as part of their jurisdiction was Berkshire and may have had advance warning, but it is more likely – although not certain – that it came from within the Metropolitan Police. In fact, it is interesting to note, following the raid on Cliff's Berkshire apartment on 14 August, that Thames Valley Police vigorously denied any leak to the press from them: 'Thames Valley police did not speak to any media outlets prior to the warrant being executed in Sunningdale, Berkshire, yesterday. This is a South Yorkshire police investigation and local officers from Thames Valley police assisted South Yorkshire officers in their search of the property.'[112]

In Andrew Trotter's independent review, commissioned by the Police and Crime Commissioner for South Yorkshire into the Disclosure of Information to the BBC, it is stated quite clearly that 'The BBC acknowledged publicly on 15 August 2014 that the source of the information provided to the BBC journalist (who had made contact with South Yorkshire Police on 14 July 2014 and following this date), was not South Yorkshire Police.'[113]

That appears to leave the Metropolitan Police (Operation Yewtree) as the source of the leak.[114] But in 2017 they were adamant in denying any such leak: 'To date, the Metropolitan Police Service has found no evidence to substantiate the damaging and, we believe, unfounded, allegation that Operation Yewtree was the source of leaked information to the BBC regarding South Yorkshire Police's investigation.'[115] Given that this was a case of the Met investigating themselves, their findings need to be cautionary.

Whoever was the leak, Dan Johnson received the tip-off that Cliff Richard was being investigated on 9 June 2014.

On 2 July, an agreement was reached that the investigation into Cliff by South Yorkshire Police was ready to proceed and they formally took control of the investigation on 3 July.[116] Chief Constable David Crompton recalls, 'It was not until the summer that I became aware that South Yorkshire Police would be conducting the investigation. When the investigation came to South Yorkshire Police it was at a very early stage and not all of the details were known to the South Yorkshire Police. From the outset, my overriding concern was to ensure that, whatever the outcome of the investigation, it was dealt with properly and thoroughly.'[117]

A few days later, on 9 July 2014, Dan Johnson called South Yorkshire Police, specifically Carrie Goodwin, the Head of Corporate Communications.[118] A large part of her job was to liaise with the media over police issues. Johnson said he wanted to discuss a number of matters with Goodwin, one of which was the investigation into Cliff Richard.

The recollections of this phone conversation between Johnson and Goodwin differ. Johnson, in his witness statement, said he had come across the story in June 2014 when he was discussing high-profile cases involving celebrities with a 'confidential source', who told Johnson there was 'just one more major figure' the police were looking at. Johnson said, 'I guess[ed] this to be Sir Cliff Richard because of previous rumours I'd heard about him. The contact confirmed I had guessed the right name.' When Johnson asked Carrie Goodwin if Cliff was on their 'radar' during the phone call, she had responded with an 'audible gasp'.[119] According to Johnson, Goodwin said that she was not sure how much she could say, that she would check and would get back to him.[120]

Carrie Goodwin, who had known since April of the possibility of the Cliff Richard investigation moving to South Yorkshire Police, because Matt Fenwick had informed her, was surprised and caught off-guard by Johnson's information, but she later revealed, in a letter to the Chair of the Committee on 17 September 2014, that her recollections were that Johnson made clear that his source was Operation Yewtree.

'When Dan Johnson first contacted me, he detailed a conversation he said he had with Operation Yewtree. He said that he had told the source that he probably wouldn't have many dealings with them [Op Yewtree] in future. He asked Operation Yewtree if there were any more [other suspects] to come. Operation Yewtree said, "Just one more, Cliff Richard." Dan Johnson said it [Cliff Richard] probably wouldn't be his and the reply from Yewtree was, "You cover Sheffield, don't you?" Dan Johnson went on to detail the allegation accurately and the location the allegation related to. Specifically, he spoke about a boy aged between eleven and fourteen alleging that he had been taken to a room at Bramall Lane, where he was made to carry out a sexual act. There was some question over the date, but Dan Johnson indicated it was in the 1980s.'[121]

A few sentences later in the letter she reiterated: 'Dan Johnson told me explicitly that it was Operation Yewtree that had provided the information regarding Cliff Richard to him. He said this in the initial phone call I had with him.'[122]

Carrie Goodwin was significantly concerned at what she had heard from Johnson on the 9 July call that she was 'left with the impression that Johnson was ready to publish the story and seeking a comment.'[123] The prospect of him proceeding with the story before a search of Sir Cliff's UK residence could result in evidence being lost. She decided to speak with Matt Fenwick and they discussed the possibility of giving Johnson a pre-recorded interview and she made a note that said: 'Pre-rec may keep him quiet.'[124]

She then went to raise the matter with Chief Constable David Crompton. 'Carrie explained to me she had been approached by a BBC journalist, Dan Johnson, who was aware of the South Yorkshire Police investigation into Cliff Richard. Carrie explained that he knew all the details of the allegation, that he had obtained this information from Operation Yewtree, which is obviously a very credible source, and was effectively ready to publish a story.'[125]

Crompton was shocked there was a journalist who appeared to know as much about the allegations as he did. 'This information was deeply concerning to me, because I thought that a media report on a high-profile case, which was in its infancy, could fatally compromise South Yorkshire Police's ability to carry out a thorough investigation which, as I have said, was my priority.'[126]

Chief Constable Crompton and Carrie Goodwin spent some time discussing their options, even considering bringing forward the date of the search so it could be completed before the BBC published their story. They talked about the integrity of the investigation and Sir Cliff Richard's privacy and they worked through the College of Policing Guidance. It was decided to provide the BBC with the date of the search, but that this would not be an invitation for the BBC to accompany them.

'It seemed to me now,' Crompton said, 'that the media were alive to the investigation [and] the story was bound to come out at some point. As the BBC already had all the information about the allegation from a credible source, it appeared to me that they were likely to report it imminently. Therefore, to provide information about the search was a small concession and we would not be naming Sir Cliff Richard.'[127]

At 2.37 p.m. on 14 July, a month before the raid would happen, Carrie Goodwin emailed Dan Johnson asking him if he wanted her to 'set something up with the officer in the celebrity case?' She pointed out that the officer [DS Fenwick] was shortly going on holiday 'if you want to get a pre rec' (i.e., a pre-recorded statement). Johnson replied two minutes later saying, 'Oh that would be fab if you could, need to give the boss a few details to get a cameraman, haven't said anything yet. How much can I say?'[128]

As Justice Mann observed, this reply from Johnson is significant in that it is false in saying that he [Johnson] had not said anything yet. In fact, he *had* spoken with his superior, Declan Wilson – then the manager running the BBC's North of England Bureau – at some point between Johnson's conversation with the source and 15 July.[129]

Following Johnson's email, Carrie Goodwin responded at 2.46 p.m.: 'No one else has picked up on it yet, so while ever it stays that way the story is all yours. If you can get away with saying the bare minimum, I'd be grateful but accept you may have to give the name if pushed.'[130] After nine minutes, Johnson replied: 'Can you give me a quick call and we'll agree what I can pass on?' [Number supplied.]

A meeting was arranged for the following day, 15 July at 1 p.m. Prior to the meeting, DS Matt Fenwick had told Carrie Goodwin that he did not wish to do a piece-to-camera and instead he would brief Dan Johnson. He asked for, and was given, a precis of the investigation in order to remind himself of the state-of-play. This precis summarised the statement of the complainant and the complaint and that the incident took place at the ground of Sheffield Wednesday, because he [the complainant] remembered a lot of blue and white and he described going into a sports-equipment-type room.

It seems odd that, at this point, nobody was questioning the validity of the complaint based on this very statement. Throughout, the complainant stated the alleged assault took place at Bramall Lane, where Billy Graham was preaching and where photos of the event very clearly place Cliff Richard. Bramall Lane is the home of Sheffield United Football Club, who have played in red and white stripes for most of their history, beginning in the 1890–91 season. Blue and white is the colours of their nearest rival, Sheffield Wednesday Football Club, who have played in those colours since 1867.

It seems inconceivable that Sheffield United would countenance the use of blue and white, the colours of their fiercest rivals, in their stadium. All the main investigators involved, and Dan Johnson, had spent enough time in Yorkshire to know the rivalry of the two teams yet, at no point, does anyone feel the need to question the validity of the complainant's statement when such a basic error in fact is obvious.

At the meeting on 15 July – a meeting Matt Fenwick was apprehensive about, but felt he had to undertake in order to hear what Johnson had to say given his apparent knowledge of the investigation – it was confirmed that Sir Cliff Richard was the celebrity in question, that an allegation against him involved a boy under sixteen and a friend (now deceased). He had come forward to say they had been sexually assaulted by Sir Cliff in a dressing room (note that earlier this had been described as a 'sports-equipment-type room'. Would a room such as this really be a dressing room for a 'star performer'?) in the early 1980s. Again, the event was in 1985, surely this would be classed as mid-1980s.

During the meeting Fenwick again reiterated his view that he was not convinced that the complainant's evidence was strong enough to go to court, which Dan Johnson says he wrote down as 'unlikely charge'.[131] Johnson asked what would be likely to happen next and was told that South Yorkshire Police were planning to search Sir Cliff's Sunningdale property[132] on 7 August.[133] Johnson recalls being told that if Sir Cliff was at the house then he would be arrested and a joke had been made about considering arresting Sir Cliff when he had attended Wimbledon a few weeks before.[134] Fenwick added that he would give a pre-recorded interview for the BBC either late in that week or when he returned from leave on 6 August.

The important fact about all this information, noted by Johnson, was that it was volunteered to him by South Yorkshire Police for no apparent reason. Johnson's starting point had simply been that he knew and said only that Sir Cliff was on their (South Yorkshire Police's) radar.

For their part, South Yorkshire Police's case is that the starting point was different, in that Johnson had given more detail when he first rang and a belief that he knew those matters were South Yorkshire Police's starting point. Carrie Goodwin was keen to work with Johnson to make sure that the story did not emerge too early for the South Yorkshire Police's purposes, hence the meeting on 15 July. Fenwick recalled that Johnson told them he had got his information from Operation Yewtree (a fact Johnson denied)[135] and stated that the South Yorkshire Police would be prepared to give Johnson the date and location of the search if he agreed not to publish the information he had got from his source. According to Fenwick's notes, Johnson agreed.[136]

CHAPTER 9

Following the meeting, Johnson updated his superior at the BBC, Declan Wilson, about the story. Later that day, following Johnson's update, Wilson wrote to Gary Smith, the UK news editor for BBC News. A man with an extensive background of senior leadership experience throughout broadcasting, Smith had worked on many of the major news stories of the 1980s and 1990s, including the fall of Margaret Thatcher, the end of the Berlin Wall, the Dunblane shootings and the assassination of Rajiv Gandhi. 'I've a passion and commitment for providing accurate, clear, informative, honest journalism with integrity and impartiality,' he commented.[137]

Under the subject line 'SIT DOWN WHEN YOU READ THIS', Wilson wrote, 'Dan had a meeting with South Yorks Police today. On August 7th this year South Yorkshire Police plan to go to the house of Cliff Richard the singer in Surrey and arrest him there in connection with historical sex offences against a boy in Yorkshire. Dan [Johnson] will get an interview ahead of the operation on Aug 6. This is all I have for now.'[138]

Smith replied with a message: 'Congratulations. And jubilations. I want the world to know I'm happy as can be.' These are, unmistakably, the opening lyrics to Cliff's famous 1968 chart-topper and Eurovision runner-up, 'Congratulations'. The frivolous tone of communication continued between the two men with Wilson writing, 'Soon to play "Jailhouse Rock", or was that Elvis?' Both Smith and Wilson would later tell the court that it had been a private communication that was not meant for publication[139] and was 'just a bit of a joke between colleagues who knew each other very well', saying that in no way did it 'set a tone for our coverage of the story.'[140]

Commenting on their performances as witnesses, Justice Mann summed up Declan Wilson with the words: 'I found various aspects of his evidence unsatisfactory,' and, 'the totality of his evidence needs to be approached with caution.'[141] While, of Smith, he stated: 'He was, in my view, one of the employees of the BBC who became very concerned (I am tempted to use the word "obsessed") with the merits of scooping their news rivals and that probably affected some of his judgement at the time.'[142] Dan Johnson himself wasn't immune to adopting the banterish-tone at the BBC, telling one colleague that 'it wasn't just the hand of God doing the touching', a reference to evangelist Billy Graham speaking at the Bramall Lane rally central to the allegations against Sir Cliff.[143]

Later in the day Wilson reported some of the details of the alleged crime to Smith and said that: 'The police considered gripping CR at Wimbledon this year – imagine that!? Dan's source is the SIO, who will go on camera the day before under embargo and name CR. I suppose there could still be a defamation risk, however we are in an amazing position knowing who the target is direct from the police. Off record, they want the publicity as they believe there are others. Sallie is IC on Aug 6 and Suzanne Aug 7 (raid day). I'd really like Dan in Surrey to reward his work on this, it's bloody cracking.'

As a select band of people at the BBC began researching and putting together some Cliff Richard-related material on a 'need-to-know' basis, Dan Johnson made an approach on 18 July via email to see if arrangements could be made to enable him to speak with the victim of the alleged crime. His audacious request was, naturally, turned down and, as Justice Mann observed, 'his email demonstrated a concern that other media should not be alerted, and asked when he would be allowed to break the story. He obviously anticipated (and made clear his anticipation) that the BBC would attend at the search site.'

Later on 18 July, Carrie Goodwin replied to Johnson and said they needed to 'put the brakes' on their plans, because the address that South Yorkshire Police thought was Sir Cliff's address turned out not to be correct and on 24 July, Goodwin texted Johnson to say the matter was on hold while South Yorkshire Police concentrated on a murder manhunt.

While South Yorkshire Police attempted to locate and confirm Sir Cliff's actual address, at the BBC research continued into Sir Cliff to create a package that could be broadcast once the story became public. Strangely, a reporter at the BBC had already identified Sir Cliff's address. David Sillito, another University of Leeds alumnus and, in 2014, Media and Arts Correspondent at the BBC, had sent an internal email identifying Sir Cliff's Berkshire residence as a 'gated development' and stating, 'It's impossible to get within 100 yards of the flat.'[144] It would take South Yorkshire Police another two weeks to confirm what the BBC already knew.

On 6 August, Chief Constable David Crompton went on

holiday with his family to Wales. 'As I went on holiday my understanding was that the investigation team were trying to establish Sir Cliff Richard's current UK address in order to apply for a search warrant.'[145]

No sooner had he left than the UK address of Sir Cliff was confirmed as an apartment at a private residential complex in Sunningdale, Berkshire and on 7 August – the date originally proposed for the search to take place – a search warrant was obtained under the Police and Criminal Evidence Act 1984 from Sheffield Magistrates' Court. The warrant authorised officers of South Yorkshire Police, Thames Valley Police (the force local to the residence in Berkshire) and the Metropolitan Police to search the property. Those authorised to accompany them also included police civilian media staff.

Here the question has to be asked: why was the search warrant even granted? The 1984 Police and Criminal Evidence Act requires police to satisfy a Justice of the Peace that, not only are there reasonable grounds for believing an offence has been committed, but that the premises to be searched hold material that is both relevant and of substantial value. If the police believed there was reasonable grounds that an offence had been committed, why had they not already arrested Sir Cliff? And could there really be the prospect of the premises holding material that was relevant and of substantial value in the case of an alleged sexual assault almost thirty years previously?

Additionally, and perhaps more pertinently, a warrant should only be issued if it is 'not practicable to communicate' with the owner of the premises. Admittedly, the police were finding it hard work to establish the actual location of Sir Cliff's apartment, but surely even the most inept police force could find a way of contacting him.

Nevertheless, the warrant was granted and a decision was taken to conduct the search on Thursday, 14 August 2014. A plan was made by South Yorkshire Police's media team for DS Matt Fenwick to read a statement to the media in due course in connection with the search when it took place and the statement prepared for him would NOT BE naming Sir Cliff.

It wasn't until 13 August, the day before the raid, that Dan Johnson at the BBC was informed. He was working in the north of England and didn't get notification from South Yorkshire Police until an email was sent to him at 4.32 p.m. on the 13th by one of Carrie Goodwin's staff members. This meant Johnson would have to hotfoot it overnight to get to Berkshire in time for the search.

Johnson wasn't sent an address of the property, but was forwarded an aerial view of the location with the message: 'From what I have been told by the officers who are down there now, there won't be much to see from the street.' As it happened, Johnson had already worked out the address and internal BBC emails had been sent saying the story would need to be 'red flagged'[157] – a system for alerting higher levels of management within the organisation to things that may require their attention in due course.

With the date of the search confirmed, arrangements were made by the BBC for the level of coverage required. Journalists – such as Dan Johnson – were already on their way. Additional reporters David Sillito and Jane Peel were ready to go and supporting technicians and equipment were sourced. Nothing was being left to chance. But there was the issue of visibility for the cameras. As Sillito had already pointed out, it seemed impossible to get within 100 yards of the flat. Any footage would be distant and unremarkable, far removed from the door-smashing and cop-rushing raids so familiar on TV.

An idea was mooted within the BBC to use a helicopter to secure aerial footage of the inside of the estate. The BBC had permanent contractual arrangements for the use of a helicopter and it planned to have the helicopter fly over the property during the search. Contractually, the use of the helicopter was shared with ITN and there was an agreement in place with ITN that for a stated fee, the BBC would share all footage on 'breaking news' with ITN and also inform ITN of any launch to cover a breaking story as soon as possible.

However, despite knowing of this agreement, BBC officials decided not to tell ITN. Gary Smith, BBC UK News Editor at the time, later sought to justify the decision in court on the basis that it was not a 'breaking news story' within the meaning of the agreement until the BBC started to broadcast it, and therefore the BBC was not under any obligation to inform ITN until that point in time. Until that moment the BBC might not have broadcast anything, in which case it would not have been a breaking story.[146] However, in an email on 13 August, Smith described the BBC's conduct in not informing ITN as 'slightly breaking the terms of our deal'.[147]

In addition to the helicopter and reporters outside Sir Cliff's Berkshire residence, the BBC had also learned that the singer would most likely be at his property in Portugal.

Sir Cliff had been a frequent visitor to Portugal for decades and had owned houses there before, but in 1993, while visiting a local restaurant, learned of a 350-year-old former farmhouse for sale with thirty acres of land just to the south of the town of Guia, a five-minute drive from the Algarve coast.

*I had to have it. I bought it for less than a million pounds, but
I had to spend nearly as much again to repair it and make it
habitable.*[148]

By 2014, Sir Cliff had transformed the property into a mini
estate. A long, cobbled drive flanked with olive trees passed the
old windmill to lead to the main farmhouse with its six ensuite
bedrooms, an outdoor swimming pool, sun terrace, hot tub and
tennis court. Another three-bedroom cottage and two-bedroom
apartment stand within the manicured grounds and alongside the
seven hectares of vines, which produced Sir Cliff's own wine, the
Adega do Canto (Winery of the Singer). Knowing Sir Cliff was
most likely in Portugal, the BBC arranged for a reporting team
to travel there so that some form of coverage could take place.[149]

As Dan Johnson raced south on 13 August, Carrie Goodwin
at South Yorkshire Police briefed Lesley Card, a media relations
officer within the force. 'I would be the bronze media relations
officer on the search warrant. This meant that I was responsible
for performing actions on the ground. Carrie Goodwin was the
gold media relations officer who set the overall strategy and Joanne
Wright was the silver media relations officer who was responsible
for implementing the strategy,'[150] said Card. Goodwin gave her
Dan Johnson's number, saying, 'Once you know what time the
warrant will start, let him know so he doesn't get there before
you. He's pretty good at working with us.'[151]

Lesley Card had travelled down to Berkshire on 13 August
and stayed in a hotel overnight. 'I was aware that the operation
was highly confidential and I remember telling my family that I
was going to a conference and had to stay overnight.'[152]

At 6.53 p.m. on 13 August, Gary Smith alerted Jonathan
Munro, then the Head of Newsgathering at the BBC and his

deputy, Sara Beck, with an email that said, 'Just so you know …
we think South Yorkshire Police are going to raid Cliff
Richard's house in Berkshire tomorrow morning to arrest
him for questioning about an alleged sexual offence in the
80s against a 13-year-old boy. (At a Billy Graham rally!)'[153]
A brief correspondence continued between Smith and Munro,
with Smith writing at 10.24 p.m.: 'The money shots will be
police going in and out of his flat and loading bags of hard
drives or whatever into their vans. We can only get this from
the helicopter.'[154] As Justice Mann observed, 'The reference to
"money shots" shows the importance attributed by Mr Smith
to the helicopter's participation and the emphasis the story was
likely to be given.'[155]

On the morning of 14 August, a briefing was held at a Thames
Valley Police Station prior to the search. Following this Lesley
Card called Dan Johnson to inform him the search team was on
its way to the location and would be entering via the main front
gates.[156] Johnson, however, was already at the property, having
arrived earlier, expecting the police to be there at 9.30 a.m.

At 8.57, Johnson was sent an email from a senior media and
public relations officer for South Yorkshire Police with the text of
a statement that the police intended to release if there was no one
at the property. The significant part of this is that it confirmed
that the police did not intend to name Sir Cliff Richard. Johnson
forwarded the email to Matthew Shaw, the UK Deployment
Editor of the BBC, and he replied: 'Fran [Unsworth] will sanction
the naming of Cliff.'[157]

At 9.35 police entered the gates to the estate. At 10.20 they
gained access to Sir Cliff's apartment.

Lesley Card texted BBC's Dan Johnson: 'Going in now Dan.'[158]

CHAPTER 10

With the relative failure of his albums since 1976's *I'm Nearly Famous*, Cliff decided a change of approach was required. He turned to Terry Britten, who had written 'Devil Woman', persuading him to co-produce the new album, to be called *Rock 'n' Roll Juvenile*, alongside Cliff. Furthermore, the album wouldn't be recorded in the UK, but in Paris.

Britten had become a prolific songwriter – of the twelve tracks on the new album he wrote or co-wrote ten of them – but wasn't convinced he should produce. 'I'm more interested in writing than producing,' he said. 'I've seen it happen with a lot of people. They start producing and go from one project to the next and the writing stops. I'm always worried that might happen to me.'[159] Nevertheless, with ten of his own tracks to produce, Britten accepted the offer.

Many of the backing tracks of the album had already been recorded by Terry Britten and Cliff in the UK in 1978 and so, in early 1979, Cliff went to Paris to record his vocals at the Pathé Marconi EMI Studios. Recording in the studio next door to Cliff were the Irish rockers Thin Lizzy.

'We were in doing the *Black Rose* album,' recalls Thin Lizzy guitarist Scott Gorham, 'and Cliff Richard, of all people, was in the next studio and the album was getting to the point where it was getting towards the end of the album and Phil [Lynott] goes, "You know, Cliff is just next door, why don't we get him over here and see what he thinks." And I forgot all about there was two drug dealers literally chopping out lines of coke, racking them up, right. Cliff walked in and you know that he saw what was going on, you just know this right, but he did not look in that direction, sat down, faced forward, played him a couple of songs and he never looked behind him no matter what was said. I mean he could hear the scraping of the razor blades for God's sake, but he never looked around and I gotta give it to him, and at the end of the two tracks he goes, "Wow, yeah, that was really great, thank you so much for letting me come over and listen," got up, left and still never looked at these two guys behind him. It was just this weird, surreal situation that you found yourself in with Cliff Richard.'[160]

Eleven songs had been recorded for *Rock 'n' Roll Juvenile*, ten of which had been written by Terry Britten, and the other song, the title track of the album, had been composed by Cliff himself. But with the album virtually complete, they were presented with another song by Alan Tarney, who had been Cliff's bass guitarist since being introduced to him by David Mackay for *The 31st Of February Street* album in 1974. He had already written three minor hits for Cliff earlier in the decade.[161]

Alan had been working alongside Bruce Welch producing tracks for the English singer Charlie Dore, including the soon-to-be US hit 'Pilot of the Airwaves'. During a break in the recording sessions, Tarney played Welch a demo of a song he had written called 'We Don't Talk Anymore'. 'I said, "This is a terrific song,"' recalled Welch[162] and took a tape of it straight to Cliff's then-manager Peter Gormley, who agreed Cliff should record it. But Cliff wasn't so sure.

I didn't think it suited the feel and mood of what Terry and I were doing on Rock 'n' Roll Juvenile.[163]

However, Bruce Welch was adamant that Cliff should record it, as were his record label EMI. So, in May 1979, Cliff went to RG Jones Recording Studios in Wimbledon to record the track. 'When he eventually did record it, he started by just going through the motions. It was only on the third chorus that he really started to get into it,' said Tarney.[164]

Anyway. I put my voice on it. It was one tone too high – I hit a falsetto that I could barely do then! I couldn't honestly look you in the eye and say I knew it was going to be number one, but you do get a goosebump and you think, "Oh my God, this could be a hit." I'm always terrified to think it might be number one, so I don't. Nobody knows; no one can say that.[165]

For years, there have been rumours that Bryan Ferry of Roxy Music provided backing vocals to the song, but in 2015 Cliff appeared to put these rumours to rest.

No, I don't think it is [true that Bryan Ferry sang backing vocals on 'We Don't Talk Anymore']. *I'd love the idea. If he'd offered at the time, I'd of course said 'yes'.*[166]

The song was released as a single in July 1979 and on 19 August it replaced the Boomtown Rats' 'I Don't Like Mondays' at the top of the UK charts, so becoming Cliff's first Number 1 single since 'Congratulations' in 1968. It sold over half a million copies in the UK alone, topped the charts in ten other countries and reached Number 7 in the US Billboard charts, on its way to selling two million copies worldwide, Cliff's biggest-ever-selling single.

I think I was lucky to get probably one of the best pop rock songs ever written and that was 'We Don't Talk Anymore'. It sold so much around the world and so I would say that that was probably the best one I've done.[167]

It was only natural that EMI add it to the forthcoming album and, in doing so, helped propel *Rock 'n' Roll Juvenile* into the Top 3 in the UK, his most commercially successful album since 1962. Another single off the album, 'Carrie', was a Top 10 hit in the UK and broke the Top 40 in the USA and it appeared the unexpected resurgence of Cliff Richard was complete.

'He was dead for six or seven years. He was like yesterday's papers,' said Tony Meehan, drummer and founder member of The Shadows. 'The fact that he bounced back in the 1970s shows how strong willed he is. I think it shows the nature of his motivation in that he never got silly or lazy. He stuck with it. He never gave in. I think that he is much more intense than comes across and I think he has staked his life completely on his career.'[168]

The next four years saw Cliff's career continue to flourish. More hit singles followed: 'Dreamin'', 'Wired For Sound', 'Daddy's Home', 'The Only Way Is Out', 'She Means Nothing To Me' and 'True Love Ways' all reaching the UK's Top 10, while 'Dreamin'', 'Suddenly' and 'A Little Love' all broke into the US Billboard Top 20.

The next four albums he released after *Rock 'n' Roll Juvenile* all went Gold or Platinum in the UK, but by the time of the Billy Graham rally in Sheffield in 1985, Cliff had experienced two lean years. His 1984 album *The Rock Connection* had flopped, selling only 60,000 copies in the UK and failing to break into the Top 40, and his chart presence in the USA had all but vanished.

Of the four singles he released in 1984 only one, 'Baby, You're Dynamite', scraped into the UK Top 30 at Number 27. It would be two more years before he was back at the top of the charts once again with his first Number 1 hit of the decade.

But despite his lack of hits in the mid-80s, Cliff remained a public figure and his private life continued to fascinate the public. A 'romance' with tennis player Sue Barker at the beginning of the decade had briefly filled the tabloids with rumours of marriage but when that fizzled out attention once again turned to the bachelor boy's sexuality and, in 1985, around the time of Cliff's appearance in Sheffield alongside Billy Graham, he gave an interview to Anne Diamond for TV-am on ITV where the subject was front and centre with the topic coming up just a minute into the interview that was broadcast:

ANNE DIAMOND: It's not surprising really if you've had about twenty-seven years at the top that people buying your records and they end up idolising you, obviously they do, they're going to want to know about your private life.

CLIFF RICHARD: I don't want them knowing. I mean, I'll talk about it now but it's the fact that it's never represented correctly. You know, why should there be innuendo about the fact that I'm single?

And later in the interview:

ANNE DIAMOND: What about the constant innuendo that you're gay?

CLIFF RICHARD: Well, I mean, which are they going to have? Either I'm going to get married with Sue (Barker) or I'm gay. Either I'm a sex-maniac or I'm homosexual.

ANNE DIAMOND: They want to know your sexuality, you see. Don't they? They want to know.

CLIFF RICHARD: Well, I'm not going to tell them everything about me. I've denied my homosexuality, I've denied that I am so what else am I going to say? What am I going to tell people? I mean, that's ridiculous, really.

CHAPTER 11

It was the morning of 14 August 2014 when 63-year-old Malcolm Smith received the phone call from South Yorkshire Police.

Smith had been a chartered accountant at Touche Ross until he left in 1987 to become managing director of the Cliff Richard Organisation, ostensibly becoming Cliff's business manager. He was regarded as the last of the old guard in Cliff's coterie. Bill Latham, the man Cliff described as having changed his life 'fully and completely'[169] and who had been his confidant, had retired in 2010 after thirty years taking care of Cliff's Christian and charity work as well as dealing with the press. 'He is in his seventies,' said Cliff's PR, Liza Davies, 'and not everyone wants to go on like Cliff.'[170]

David Bryce, Cliff's long-standing tour manager also departed and to her shock, Gill Snow, Cliff's Girl Friday and his PA from 1972, was sacked in 2011. 'Sir Cliff is a nice person,' commented Bryce, 'but Malcolm Smith is an accountant. You know what they are like: if they can save a penny, they will.'[171]

But as well as these departures, there had also been an addition.

By 2014 Cliff's charitable activities and property interests were being looked after by John McElynn, a tennis-loving Catholic priest whom Cliff had met in New York in 2000. Within a year, McElynn had given up the priesthood and, like Latham before him, had moved in with the singer.

> *This was great for me. When he moved over, John instantly gave me good company, companionship and the invaluable help I needed. It banished the loneliness that I felt living on my own and gave John the reboot and kickstart he thought his own life needed. It was good for the both of us – and long may it last.*[172]

On 14 August 2014, Cliff and McElynn were together in Portugal, initially unaware of the drama unfolding at the singer's Sunningdale residence. When his phone rang, Malcolm Smith was the first one within Cliff's 'family' to find out what was unfolding. Coincidentally, he was in Portugal himself at his own property.

Smith immediately called Gideon Benaim, a partner in Simkins LLP, solicitors who acted for Cliff's various affairs. Among others, Benaim had represented model Naomi Campbell in her libel action against the *Daily Telegraph* and Oscar-winning film director Roman Polanski in his successful bid to give evidence at his libel trial by video link from Paris. Smith told Benaim that the police were at Cliff's Sunningdale property with a search warrant and that there was a media presence outside.

Gideon Benaim was not a criminal specialist, so he contacted BCL Burton Copeland, a law firm founded by Ian Burton, one of Britain's most successful and experienced lawyers. Upon receiving Benaim's call, Paul Morris, a partner in BCL Burton Copeland, was immediately sent to attend the search with a colleague, Omar Khan. At this point none of the lawyers – or even Malcom Smith – knew exactly what the police were doing at Cliff's property and had no idea what suspected offences they were investigating.

Leaving their offices at 11 a.m. to travel to Sunningdale, Morris and Khan attempted to get any information during the journey about what was happening, but were unable to do so. According to his own notes used later in court, Morris recounted, 'I phoned Mr Benaim at 11.47 a.m. (whilst Mr Khan and I were still travelling) and told him that we still did not know why the police were at the Claimant's apartment and had been able to obtain no further information about what was going on.'

Just before Morris and Khan had left their offices, Malcolm Smith *had* managed to get a copy of the search warrant. He emailed it to the solicitors at 10.59. But, as we have seen, questions could be asked about the validity of this search warrant.

As Geoffrey Robertson QC stated, 'It is not known who issued this warrant (although the High Court has held that the identities of JPs should be made public). What qualifications did he or she have and what steps were taken to protect the occupier's privacy? What justification did the police give for this general search, with world-wide publicity? Was there any questioning of the police, so as to ensure that they could identify what they were looking for, and that it had "substantial value" for a prosecution? How was the Justice of the Peace satisfied that this whole exercise was not an improper means to publicise an uncorroborated allegation against the singer, in the hope of "shaking the tree" to attract further allegations which might give it some credibility?'[173]

Morris and his colleague arrived at the public entrance to the singer's property at about 12.15 p.m. on 14 August only to be denied access by the security team. Already a crowd of media had started to gather. In fact, the whole scene was one of chaos, with furious residents swearing at journalists and demanding that the helicopter stop hovering overhead. One of Cliff's neighbours apparently seemed more concerned that the journalists were investigating his own, unknown misdemeanours.[174]

Eventually, Morris and Khan were granted access to the property and were escorted to Cliff's apartment. It was while walking to the apartment that Morris became aware of a helicopter circling overhead at a seemingly low level. At the apartment Morris and Khan were shown the search warrant by DI Mayfield, one of the search team from South Yorkshire Police.

In his evidence to the court, Morris stated:

Immediately after that I phoned Mr Benaim to tell him what we knew. From my notes, I can see that this call took place at 12.51 p.m. and I was able to provide him with the following information at that time: 'We are getting information. An allegation. 1985. Said to have taken place in Sheffield. A boy, under sixteen at the time. This was an Operation Yewtree investigated matter but as there is only one complaint, it has been passed by Yewtree to South Yorks Police. There was another potential matter but "that has not been substantiated". I will keep you updated. Police want to interview CR in due course.'

I spoke to DI Mayfield at around 1 p.m. and she clarified that in fact there was only one complaint against the Claimant and that South Yorkshire Police had received no other complaints.

At this point.

CHAPTER 12

RECOLLECTIONS MAY VARY

The weather in Wales was particularly topsy-turvy on 14 August 2014. There was flash flooding in Cardiff while Anglesey enjoyed eleven hours of sunshine. The unpredictability of a British summer wasn't bad enough though to stop Chief Constable David Crompton of South Yorkshire Police taking a Welsh holiday with his family.

'On the morning of 14 August, I was on the beach with my family,' testified Crompton. 'I received a text message timed at 11.11 hours from my deputy, Andy Holt, which informed me about the media presence at the location of the search warrant. I responded, "It should be on Sky by 1 p.m. I will tune in!"'[175] Presumably he meant it would be on the BBC.

Somebody else enjoying a summer holiday was Philip Hall. He had flown further afield, to somewhere with guaranteed sunshine, Spain. Hall was Cliff's PR man who, following a career as editor of such titles as *News of the World* and *Hello!*, had founded the PHA Group in 2005, a London-based PR company with three simple aims in mind: 'I wanted to work with passionate people, I wanted to be known for delivering a strategy, not just talking a good game, and I wanted the industry to talk about us.'[176]

His first PR client was Heather Mills McCartney, then seemingly happily married to former Beatle Paul and at the time looking for opportunities to promote her charity. 'I thought "great". She had a nice peaceful life at that time,' Hall says. 'Within seven days I'd made her a very large sum from a magazine deal and I was off and running.'[177]

His PR relationship with Mills McCartney continued during her highly public divorce from Paul in 2006, during which Hall commented on the behaviour of the British press revelling in the acrimony of their break-up. 'I just think it's naivety. There are people who I've spoken to laughing down the phone. They think it's absolutely hilarious that she has been driven out of her home by a paparazzi photographer. They see it almost as a movie rather than real life, but there's a woman here with a daughter and no protection at all. It's an impossible situation.'

He went on describing reporters who deliberately made up stories. 'You learn very quickly that there's only so much you can do. There are four or five people in particular who just make it up and don't care about what they write. One of them . . . his stuff is unbelievable, so inaccurate it's just incredible. He's going to get found out one day.'[178]

For those cynics thinking such a statement a bold revelation for an ex-*News of the World* editor, Hall says, 'I didn't have a libel writ in my entire career, and everything I did was from a standpoint of being accurate and properly corroborated.'[179]

At some point mid-morning on 14 August, Hall became aware of the police searching Cliff's Berkshire apartment and the media interest around the property after it was brought to his attention by either Malcolm Smith or a lawyer from Simkins LLP. Naturally, it was the first he had heard of it and it appears that nobody on Cliff's side had yet been contacted by either South Yorkshire Police or the BBC – certainly not before 11 a.m. UK time – and the police had entered Cliff's apartment at 10.40 UK time.

But as far back as 23 July, an email was sent by BBC reporter David Sillito to Bernadette Kitterick, a BBC employee tasked with some background research before the search *and* with contacting Cliff's representatives for comments on the day of the search.

The email clearly identified Philip Hall as the singer's 'crisis PR' and also the details of his publicist as Lisa Davies. Telephone numbers for both of them were provided on the email,[180] so the question is why had no contact been made as soon as the search began and images of the search were being recorded by the BBC?

Of course, this is open to interpretation, but the most likely scenario is that the BBC were anxious to preserve their exclusivity. After all, they were working on the assumption that Cliff Richard – a national treasure – was about to be arrested on allegations of historic sexual abuse. It was undoubtedly a major story (if the allegations were true), one that, according to Gary Smith – the BBC's UK News Editor at the time – fell into the category of 'in principle' stories, which the BBC would report on as being in the public interest subject to editorial checks.[181] It was definitely a story that would be picked up quickly by the BBC's competitors, particularly in the age of the 24-hour rolling news cycle.

Dan Johnson, on the ground outside the singer's property, was not involved in the editorial discussions going on within the BBC but was, as Justice Mann observed, 'personally very anxious to preserve the "exclusive" for which he was responsible.'[182] He was eager to know the outcome of the deliberations going on back at the BBC. Gary Smith appeared keen to preserve the exclusivity of the story also and, to that end, he procured that the 'red flag' list (of forthcoming sensitive matters, prepared for the benefit of senior management at the BBC) should refer to the matter, but not in a way that would identify Cliff Richard, in order to keep the internal knowledge of it as confined as possible.[197]

Smith had been diligent in briefing Fran Unsworth on the matter in the run-up to 14 August. Unsworth, who had held previous senior posts at the BBC, was Deputy to the Director of News at the BBC, James Harding. Harding was on holiday at the time, so Smith briefed Unsworth to keep her up to date with developments. On 13 August, Smith informed her that the search of the singer's property would be going ahead the following day. Smith also had a conversation with an internal lawyer and emailed Jonathan Munro, Head of Newsgathering at the BBC, to let him know about the raid and that the police would arrest Cliff Richard if he was present.[183]

On 14 August, Gary Smith was at his desk in the BBC taking directions, to an extent, from Matthew Shaw, who was the UK Deployment Officer at the BBC, the person in charge of all the news coming in. As we have seen, Matthew Shaw had already been in email communication with Dan Johnson and told him that 'Fran will sanction the naming of Cliff', as he likely knew the police would not.

At 9.41, six minutes after South Yorkshire Police had entered the gates to Cliff's property, Shaw decreed that Philip Hall was not to be contacted until it was known whether the search team was in and whether the singer had been arrested or not.[184]

It was not until 10.40 that South Yorkshire Police gained

access to Cliff's apartment and three minutes later Dan Johnson was informed by Lesley Card, the Media Relations Officer at South Yorkshire Police, that they were in.

'I confirmed that the officers had gone in and gained access,' testified Card. 'He [Dan Johnson] continued to text me to ask me whether Sir Cliff Richard was at home, whether his property was the penthouse, and asking me to let him know when officers were going to bring out any items of the property so the BBC could get footage.'[185] Unable to answer Dan's queries, Card asked Carrie Goodwin what she should do. Goodwin told Card that '. . . it was up to Dan to do his own research.'[201] Card did not respond to him again.

At some point between 10.40 and 11.00, Bernadette Kitterick finally reached out to Philip Hall. Kitterick had been tasked (in advance) with being the liaison point between the BBC and Cliff's media representatives. This process was an established procedure, which BBC employees often referred to as a 'right of reply' procedure. It would allow the singer, or his spokespeople, an opportunity to respond *prior* to broadcast concerning information about the search of his property, and the allegation it was in connection with. Any such statement, or the thrust of it, could then be included in the BBC broadcast.

Kitterick called Philip Hall on his mobile but, being on holiday in Spain, he didn't answer. She left a message saying she was calling about Sir Cliff and asking him to call her back at the earliest possible opportunity. At no point did she mention the search of his property in her message.[186] Further attempting to get in touch with Hall, Kitterick called or emailed, amongst others, Lisa Davies, Cliff's publicist. Kitterick now, for the first time, revealed that the BBC had information that the singer's property was being searched by the police in connection with an allegation of a sexual nature. Davies recommended Kitterick continue trying Hall.[187]

At 10.57 at the BBC, Gary Smith emailed Matthew Shaw: 'How long do we give Phil Hall to get back to us?' Shaw replied, 'There's no rush to broadcast – so long as the police don't plan to release their statement to anyone else yet. And the longer we hold, the more difficult we make it for ITN.'[188] As Justice Mann concluded, 'This demonstrates the extent to which Mr Smith was keen to be the first to broadcast the story. The reference to ITN is probably a reference to its being difficult for ITN to broadcast the story in their 1.30 news if it broke close to that time.'[205]

At approximately 11.15, Philip Hall spoke with Bernadette Kitterick for the first time. 'Our conversation was relatively short,' recalled Hall. 'She said that the South Yorkshire Police were searching [Sir Cliff's] apartment and that the BBC were present onsite. She then informed me that the BBC was planning to run a story about the search later that day and they would like to have a statement about it from my client. She also said that the BBC were prepared to give me some time to do that. I replied by asking Ms Kitterick if the BBC intended to name [Sir Cliff] in their story. She replied that she did not know.'

He added, 'Under the circumstances, my response to Ms Kitterick was that I was not prepared to say anything on behalf of my client, not even "no comment". My reasoning, in essence, was in seeking to obtain a comment from the claimant, Ms Kitterick was not interested in anything he might have to say. What she was trying to do, in my view, was to "legitimise" the BBC's story, i.e. to obtain an "on-the-record" comment from the claimant, which enabled them to say that the claimant had confirmed that it was his apartment which had been searched.' He continued, 'Ms Kitterick said nothing which gave me any hint that the BBC was planning broadcasts of the nature that emerged at 1 p.m. UK time. Nothing was said about helicopters, or exclusives, or live or quasi-live rolling coverage, or any special deals with the police, or anything else of that nature. Nor was anything said at that stage about the BBC planning to go to air at 1 p.m.'[189]

Later in court, Kitterick and Hall contradicted each other when discussing what was said during this initial phone call. Kitterick said that she informed Hall that the search was in connection with an allegation of a sexual nature dating back to the 1980s and the BBC were in a position to broadcast that fact, while Hall said that no mention was made of such an allegation. For what it's worth, Justice Mann said, 'Although it probably does not matter, I think Miss Kitterick is probably right about that.'[190]

What seems evident though is that Kitterick gave no indication of *when* the BBC were planning to run the story and, by appearing to give him time to consider without a deadline, this led Hall, rightly or wrongly, to think the matter was not all that urgent. It also didn't occur to Hall that the police had briefed the BBC on the search. Why should it? Nothing was mentioned during the phone call in this respect and, in Hall's experience, it was very rare for the police to do such a thing. For his part, Hall spent the next hour waiting to find out more about what was going on.

An email from Matthew Shaw at the BBC, meanwhile, timed at 11.27, indicated that the organisation had decided to give Hall until 12.15 to make a decision regarding an on-the-record comment. However, it appears that this deadline was not communicated to Hall – although Kitterick did chase him for a response once or twice during that hour.[208] At 11.37, Detective

Superintendent Matt Fenwick read a pre-recorded statement on camera for the BBC, the only media outlet that received it because, thanks to South Yorkshire Police, they were the only media outlet that knew about the search.

The statement said: 'South Yorkshire Police has gained entry to a property in the Sunningdale area of Berkshire. Officers are currently searching the property. A search warrant was granted after police received an allegation of a sexual nature dating back to the 1980s involving a boy who was under the age of sixteen at the time. The owner of the property was not present.'[191]

There was no mention of Cliff Richard as the owner of the property searched, nor did it associate the singer with the search.

At 11.51 Smith, anxious to keep the story exclusive, emailed Jonathan Munro, Head of Newsgathering at the BBC: 'We're giving Phil Hall an hour to come back to us. Fran's coming down for another huddle at the desk at 12.15. Can you come too? We've heard from Danny Shaw who's at Scotland yard [sic] on a different story that Sky have heard rumours, although still no sign of them in Sunningdale.'[192]

Six minutes later, after Gary Smith had circulated Matt Fenwick's statement to camera within the BBC, Smith emailed Matthew Shaw and others, including Fran Unsworth saying, 'To be clear, this on camera statement is just to the BBC, so we're still holding off publishing till we've given Phil Hall time to respond on Cliff's behalf.'[193]

Bizarrely, the *Daily Telegraph* almost inadvertently stumbled upon the raid and scooped the entire story from under the noses of the BBC. A reporter from the newspaper had been sent to interview Martha Collison, a *Great British Bake Off* contestant, who was due to receive her A-level results at the private school opposite Cliff Richard's apartment. However, despite seeing the police vehicles, the reporter departed unaware of the potential scoop on their doorstep.[194]

Philip Hall, meanwhile, still unaware the BBC would be broadcasting at 1 p.m., was engaging help from those within his office back in the UK. One of them, Mark Gregory, emailed Hall at 11.51 saying, 'Wow . . . wow . . . wow . . . will be huge international story?!?' Hall responded to Gregory with, 'Sadly so. Based in [sic] very little from what we can gather.'[195] This suggests Hall had not been able to get much further useful information by that point.

But at 12.24, Bernadette Kitterick called Hall as well as sending him an email with the subject heading 'South Yorkshire Police', and the unreleased statement from DS Matt Fenwick. The email concluded: 'Phil we do need a response from you ASAP. I am on this email and number at all times. Talk soon.'[196]

During their concurrent phone conversation, Kitterick told him the apartment searched belonged to Cliff Richard, that there were a number of police cars at the property, that a statement was imminent and that the BBC would break the story within the hour.

This followed a high-level 'huddle' in the BBC newsroom involving, amongst others, Fran Unsworth. In the huddle the participants discussed whether to name Cliff Richard (which meant whether to go ahead with the story) and when to broadcast. In her testimony, Unsworth explained that, by this time, the legal risk was diminishing because they had got a lot of confirmation of the facts of the story – the flat was, indeed, Sir Cliff's, it was being searched by the police and the search was in respect of a historic sexual allegation. As Justice Mann observed: 'That indicated again that the principal concern of the BBC seems to have been factual accuracy and defamation, and not privacy-related concerns.'[197]

While crews waited at Sunningdale and the helicopter hovered overhead, in the huddle at the BBC it was decided that the story would be broadcast at 1 p.m. The final decision rested with Unsworth. Gary Smith said the discussion within the huddle centred around when they felt they could broadcast the story and how long they needed to wait for Philip Hall to get back to them. They also considered rumours that Sky might become aware of the story but, as Justice Mann again observed, 'missing from his [Smith's] summary of material at this point was any consideration of Sir Cliff's privacy (or other) rights.'[198]

The singer's privacy, at all times, appears to have been a secondary concern with the BBC. The BBC wanted the exclusive.

Unsworth was now satisfied that by the time of the broadcast they would have allowed a reasonable time for Cliff's representatives to come back with a response and took the view that the BBC had a responsibility in the public interest to report the investigation, whilst being sensitive to the position of the singer. She was satisfied that the BBC knew enough to be able to make the reporting accurate and was satisfied as to the source. She considered that it was 'strongly'[199] in the public interest that 'the public be informed of police activities being undertaken against individuals at their property'.[200]

Following the huddle, Unsworth approved the 'headline copy' and left it to the relevant editorial teams to decide how to report for their own respective outputs. She did, however, specify there was to be no live broadcast from the helicopter.[201]

The decision had been made: the story would break on BBC News at 1 p.m.

In his observations following the trial, Justice Mann wrote of Unsworth's cross examination in relation to some of her thinking that was underlying her decision to broadcast and her consideration of privacy rights: 'The thrust of her evidence, which I accept, was that she did not rationalise the privacy rights side of the matter, and focused more on the public interest in reporting, as to which she was satisfied. She acknowledged that she realised that the reporting would be capable of having a serious impact on Sir Cliff.'

Over in Spain, Philip Hall had received the news at 12.24 that the story would break within the hour. It gave scant time for the singer's representatives to release a statement. Perhaps that was the aim. In his observations, Justice Mann suggests as much: 'I think the decision to go ahead without giving more time for a statement was driven, as so much in this case, by the need to preserve the scoop and not risk letting another outlet go first with the story.'[202]

Hall had a conversation with Gideon Benaim at around 12.51, shortly after Benaim had been in touch with his colleagues Paul Morris and Omar Khan, who were on location in Sunningdale. Benaim had been informed by Morris that he had seen the search warrant by DI Mayfield and was able to relay some information about the allegation. Benaim's phone call with Hall was the first time Benaim knew that the BBC intended to break the story 'within the hour'. In his witness statement, Benaim expressed great surprise that the BBC did not give what he said would have been proper notice of Sir Cliff's privacy rights, allowing him an opportunity to protect them, if necessary, by seeking an injunction.[203]

Up to this point, Philip Hall was still pretty much in the dark. The singer's representatives had been in touch with South Yorkshire Police, but at no point did South Yorkshire Police tell them that they had collaborated with the BBC.[204] Similarly, the BBC had not indicated they were using a helicopter to obtain footage of the search. Hall later said that if he knew about the helicopter in the air, he would have taken immediate action, adding, 'I would have been straight to the lawyers about it and talking about an intrusive situation.'[205]

Also missing during the BBC's communication with Philip Hall was the fact that the police were not naming Cliff Richard in their statements. Hall noticed the absence of a naming reference in the email and made the point in his own email to Bernadette Kitterick at 12.45, writing, 'You don't say they mentioned the name of the property owner.'

Two minutes later, Kitterick responded with, 'Hi Phil, thanks for emailing me back. The police have not told us officially that the property is owned by Sir Cliff Richard, but BBC News knows the property is owned by Sir Cliff Richard. My apologies for the calls and emails, but could we have a statement please.'[206]

At 12.58, Hall responded: 'Hi Bernadette, We can't give you a statement until the police tell us what they are saying. We are waiting on that. I will get back to you asap when we have it [sic].'[207]

Two minutes later, just as the story broke on BBC News, Hall received an email from Kitterick: 'South Yorkshire Police have spoken on camera giving a statement if that is any help.'[208]

It was of no help at all at the time; with the broadcast on BBC News and the story spinning out across the world, the period of right of reply had vanished. In fact, the period for right of reply had barely existed in the first place, given the ludicrously short amount of time the BBC had imposed on Philip Hall and the rest of Cliff Richard's team to come up with a response, made even more difficult owing to the fact they didn't have all the information at hand and weren't fully aware of the BBC's intentions.

'Had I been forewarned by Ms Kitterick of what the BBC in fact had in mind, I and the rest of the Claimant's team may have reacted very differently, not least by seeking an urgent injunction from the court if that is what the lawyers advised,' explained Philip Hall in his court testimony.

'I have been involved in many cases over the years, both when I was at the *News of the World* and since I have "crossed the fence", where undertakings not to publish have been requested, and when refused, injunctions have been applied for and obtained in very short order. This would plainly have been one of the options that we would have been considering had Ms Kitterick been a bit clearer with me. As it happened on the basis of what she told me, I wasn't given to believe that there was any major issue in terms of what the BBC planned to do.'

In court the judge reflected, 'The question arises as to whether the dealings between Miss Kitterick on the one hand and Sir Cliff's representatives on the other, prior to publication at 1 p.m., was in fact sufficient to give a fair opportunity for a statement or discussion before the broadcast or not.' He added, 'Bearing in mind the professed objectives of the right of reply opportunity, I do not think that it was.'

But by then, it was too late. The news was out.

CHAPTER 13

NAMING HIM

At 1 p.m. on 14 August 2014, the police search and investigation at Sunningdale was presented as the 'top story this lunchtime' on BBC News, illustrated with a brief aerial shot of the apartment complex and grounds taken from the helicopter. After the headlines, the story was presented over just under two-and-a-half minutes. It was said that a search warrant had been granted to the South Yorkshire Police to search the claimant's home in Sunningdale, Berkshire, in connection with an allegation of a sexual nature dating back to the 1980s involving a boy who was under sixteen at the time.

The news then cut to a pre-recorded report by David Sillito, one of the BBC reporters on the scene. The narrative of this report was accompanied by aerial footage of the estate on which the apartment was located, the apartment building itself, and members of the plain clothes police officer team walking towards the penthouse apartment. This footage was then followed by the statement from DS Matt Fenwick, which had been pre-recorded

THE LIFE AND TRIALS OF CLIFF RICHARD

earlier that day for sole use (at that time) by the BBC. After the statement, the voiceover narrating the news story said that the claimant was believed to be in Portugal as he was interviewed by a Portuguese radio station earlier in the week. Over this narration a photo of Cliff Richard and another person was shown followed by footage of the singer meeting Her Majesty the Queen, with the narrator identifying the claimant as 'one of Britain's most successful performers'. It was said that Sir Cliff had so far made no comment on the allegation.

Then the broadcast cut live to Dan Johnson, the BBC reporter who had been integral in sourcing this story, who summarised that the search was continuing before saying on-air, '... despite our efforts this morning, we have not been able to get any response from Cliff Richard or his representatives.'

As had been decided by the BBC in their earlier 'huddle', the identity of the claimant was made public. Not by South Yorkshire Police, who simply released the statement with no reference to the identity of the claimant, but by the BBC, who named Cliff Richard and showed an image of him during the report which was watched by an audience of 3.2 million viewers.[209] In the world of no smoke without fire, Cliff and his team were now firmly on the back foot and with the media maelstrom of Savile, Glitter, Hall and Harris ringing so loudly and so recently in the minds of the watching public, the mantra of innocent until proven guilty no longer carried weight in a trial by media.

One of those viewing the unfolding news, but in no doubt that Cliff was innocent, was his close friend, Gloria Hunniford. The broadcaster, watching from her home in Sevenoaks, Kent, later gave a witness statement in which she said, 'That the police were searching my friend's apartment was of course a shock in itself, but to witness the search being carried out on television apparently in real time, with a helicopter filming overhead with details of the appalling criminal allegations that the police were said to be investigating, seemed beyond belief.'[210]

Another source close to Cliff who was watching events unfold, but who preferred to stay anonymous, accused the police of organising a 'fishing expedition' and told the *Daily Telegraph*: 'This is appalling, because what they are doing, they are just going in there making as much noise about it as they can and seeing if anyone comes out of the woodwork to back it up. And if they don't, they will still have wrecked someone's life.'[211]

By 2 p.m. a press release was issued on Cliff's behalf. 'By that time,' recalled Philip Hall, 'the BBC had identified [Sir Cliff] as the person whose property was being searched by the police in Sunningdale, and the story had gone all around the world.'[212]

Fifteen hundred miles away at his Portuguese home, Cliff Richard had spent the early morning packing his overnight bags. Along with his sister Joan, her partner Martyn and Cliff's live-in friend and advisor John McElynn, he was planning a trip to Alentejo.

Ninety-five miles north of his Guia home, Alentejo is an arid, unpretentious landscape, but irrigation systems installed in Moorish and Roman times mean the region is a major producer of wheat, wine and cork. Cliff and his travel companions were heading there for lunch with his wine consultant, David Baverstock, followed by a couple of nights in Alentejo's historic capital, Évora.

While he was packing, Cliff's phone rang. On the other end was the manager of his apartment block back in Sunningdale, advising the singer to go somewhere private and call him straight back. Cliff went to another part of the house and dialled his mobile.

The words he said next were the biggest shock I could imagine – and in that second, my life changed forever. My dream life was about to transform into an utter nightmare.[213]

The manager of the apartment block told Cliff that the police were at his door with a warrant to search his property.

I said let them go in. They're not going to find anything.[214]

Cliff couldn't figure out or comprehend what was going on. He called Malcolm Smith, his manager, but at that point Smith didn't know anything about what was going on either.

With his mind spinning, Cliff decided the short break with John, Joan and Martyn should continue and they set off for the drive up to Alentejo. Arriving at the lunch venue shortly before 1 p.m., John McElynn received a call from Malcolm Smith, who told him that a criminal allegation had been made dating back to 1985 relating to Sheffield and a male under sixteen. Cliff was horrified, he couldn't believe this was happening.

Minds elsewhere, they continued with their lunch date. Cliff was not only distracted by thoughts of what was happening in Sunningdale, what could have prompted this, and what the potential outcomes were, but by the constant ringing of the mobile phones around their lunch table. Both McElynn and Cliff's sister began getting calls from people saying that had they heard what was happening at Sunningdale. Then one call came in to McElynn that caused Cliff to abandon the lunch altogether.

The BBC were reporting on the police raid live. And, as it went on, they were filming the outside of my apartment from a helicopter.[215]

The fact that the police were inside Cliff's apartment, searching through his belongings as part of an investigation into a historic sexual assault allegation, was shocking to Cliff. Although he was aware of the Jimmy Savile investigation, the subsequent Operation Yewtree arrests and the public outrage towards historic sexual abuse by celebrities, in his mind he knew he was innocent, the police would find nothing. But he was also aware of the arrests of fellow public figure such as Jimmy Tarbuck, Paul Gambaccini and Freddie Starr.

Cliff also knew that, as well as constantly fielding questions about his own sexuality during his seven-decade career and addressing rumours of homosexuality, there were other more unsettling rumours about him floating about in the dark recesses of the internet, rumours about a connection with a paedophile ring consisting of high-profile politicians, entertainers and judges in south-west London centred around a place called Elm Guest House.

A large, imposing Edwardian house, Elm Guest House was a hotel in Rocks Lane near Barnes Common. In the early 1980s it was run by husband and wife Haroon and Carole Kasir and was advertised as a gay guest house in *Gay News*.[216] Over the course of their proprietorship, the Kasirs had established a small but flourishing industry with Elm House where male prostitutes would take their clients and where gay men could safely retreat at a time when homosexuality was still risky in a deeply homophobic society.

Rumours of sexual abuse at the property began to simmer and

in June 1982, the house was raided by the police. It had been under observation due to reports that it was being run as a brothel, but police interest in what was going on there also focused on reports of there being a number of 'vulnerable' children on the premises. It appeared that at least one boy, aged ten, had been sexually abused on the premises. During the police raid, twenty people were arrested including Mr and Mrs Kasir, who were subsequently convicted of running a disorderly house, fined £1,000 each and given suspended nine-month sentences at the Old Bailey. None of those arrested were high profile politicians, judges or entertainers. However, rumours of a so-called VIP paedophile ring connected with Elm House continued.

In June 1990, Carole Kasir was found dead. Before her death Chris Fay, an employee of the National Association of Young People In Care, alleged that he had spoken with Mrs Kasir alongside his colleague, Mary Moss. Fay claimed that three months before she died, Kasir had shown him compromising pictures of a former Tory cabinet minister in a sauna with naked boys.[217] While the photos of what allegedly went on in Elm House never emerged, Chris Fay and Mary Moss produced a handwritten list of high-profile names that they claimed visited Elm House. Moss published it online in 2013 and the thirty-eight names included Harvey Proctor, Anthony Blunt, Leon Brittan, Cyril Smith, Jess Conrad, Chris Denning and Sir Peter Bottomley, amongst others. Alongside some of them were the nicknames used within Elm House. 'Kitty' was one nickname.

It was, according to the list, the nickname of Cliff Richard when he visited Elm House.

It was disturbing, and a great example of the bad side of the internet, and yet I wasn't worried about it. I'd never ever heard

of that guest house in Barnes, so what did it have to do with
me? It was clearly all a load of spurious rubbish, and I assumed
it would just go away.[218]

But it didn't go away. Internet rumours tend to have a life of their own, spread maliciously by anonymous keyboard conspiracy theorists. And once online, they stay online. A quick search at the time of writing sees unfounded claims referencing the Cliff Richard/Kitty/Elm House connection on sites such as X (formerly Twitter), Tik-Tok, Tattle Life, Facebook and even Mumsnet where someone calling herself ShirleyPhallus (enough said!) wrote, 'I find the elm house / kitty allegations very easy to believe, especially given the allegations against similar, high profile men that turned out to be true.'

In fact, none of the allegations against any of the high-profile names on the list, Cliff Richard included, were true. The Elm House list, such as it was, turned out to be a complete work of fiction.

Chris Fay was discovered to be a convicted fraudster, who had been sentenced to a year in prison for conning pensioners out of almost £300,000 in 2011.[219] During the Independent Inquiry Into Child Sexual Abuse instigated by the Home Office, DCI Paul Settle, Head of Metropolitan Police's Operation Fairbank, which looked into claims of VIP abuse at Elm House and elsewhere, said in his witness statement that the 'infamous "guest list" proved to be a work of fiction created by Christopher Fay, Mary Moss and Carol Kasir.' He continued, 'Christopher Fay has admitted writing that list. When I investigated Elm House, we interviewed Chris Fay a number of times and his story changed each time he told it. I don't view him as a credible source.'[220]

However, the Elm House list remains visible on the internet

today. Cliff Richard's name can be found online next to the nickname 'Kitty', so when his house was raided by South Yorkshire Police in 2014, those who wanted to, clearly had ammunition to connect the two. And still can to this day.

Thereby, in their minds, proving him guilty.

After all, for some there's no smoke without fire.

Even if the evidence – or lack of it – proves contrary.

Back in Portugal, Cliff had somehow got through his lunch with all of this on his mind while fielding urgent calls from management and lawyers. At some point around 1.40 p.m., Philip Hall telephoned Cliff and spoke to him directly about the urgency of what was happening, what he knew and the need for them to draft a response immediately. They talked through the wording and it was decided that the statement should also reference indirectly the spurious online nonsense about Elm House, and within the hour Philip Hall had done just that on behalf of the singer. It said:

For many months I have been aware of allegations against me of historic impropriety which have been circulating online. The allegations are completely false. Up until now I have chosen not to dignify the false allegations with a response as it would just give them more oxygen. However, the police attended my apartment in Berkshire today without notice, except it would appear to the press. I am not presently in the UK, but it goes without saying that I will co-operate fully should the police wish to speak to me. Beyond stating that today's allegation is completely false, it would not be appropriate to say anything further until the police investigation has concluded.

This statement was included in the BBC news report at 2 p.m. on 14 August and again at 3.30 p.m. By this point other news organisations had got wind of the story. The *Mail Online* ran an article about the raid and at 1.30 p.m. the first ITV broadcast relating to the 'breaking news' of the search of the singer's home was aired. By the end of the day the story had been picked up by Channel 4, Sky, numerous overseas broadcasters, websites and had been broadcast on BBC television forty-four times,[221] each similar to the last but with developing snippets as the story unfolded.

Flushed with their scoop, the BBC's Richard Clark sent an email to Dan Johnson with just the subject heading, 'Good work, Dan. Well done, R.' Dan replied with, 'Thanks, Richard, it was just old-fashioned journalism, not just a gift from the cops.'[222]

But interestingly, during the first Channel 4 broadcast on their 7 p.m. news programme on 14 August, the reporter was asked by the presenter in the studio how 'Sir Cliff's name got into the public domain so quickly?' The reporter responded by saying there had been a leak to a media organisation, which 'goes directly against' the Leveson recommendations and that the name of the suspect should not have been publicised save in exceptional circumstances. He continued by suggesting that now the claimant's name was in the public domain, he might find himself the subject of further allegations. As Justice Mann concluded, 'This was a prescient remark, and turned out to be true, as will appear.'[223]

Watching from his holiday in Wales was South Yorkshire's Chief Constable David Crompton. 'I managed to watch the television coverage of the search and I became very concerned that it was something more than I expected to see. I had thought that there may be some limited footage of my officers going into

Sir Cliff Richard's property. What I saw was much more extensive and I thought it was intrusive,' he said.[224]

Cliff Richard only appreciated how intrusive the coverage was when he arrived at his hotel in Évora later that day.

> *There was a TV in one of the rooms, so we looked at the TV and that's when I saw the raid. I saw that helicopter outside the apartment block. It was a horrible, horrible time.*[225]

The original plan had been for Cliff and his three friends to stay in Évora for four days, but that was impossible with events happening in the UK. Cliff was in 'catatonic shock'[226] as he watched the news, aware that it was being broadcast across the world.

> *Before I had a chance to defend myself, or even learn what I was accused of, people all over the globe had seen the news report: Sir Cliff Richard, Police Raid. Historic sexual abuse. A young boy under sixteen . . .*[227]

Next morning, following a sleepless night, the plan was made to head home, back to his villa in Guia where they would work out what they were going to do.

> *People close to me would know I was innocent, of course. But what of the others? What if most people thought: There's no smoke without fire?* [228]

CHAPTER 14

THE DAY AFTER

On 15 August 2014, the UK newspapers hit the shelves with graphic headlines focusing on the raid on Cliff Richard's Sunningdale apartment.

'Cliff Accused', said the *Sun* over a photo of a gaunt-looking Cliff, with an inside spread headline of 'Sir Cliff molested boy at Christian concert'. 'Sir Cliff Richard Insists: I Am Not A Paedophile', proclaimed the *Daily Telegraph*, a completely false and unfair summation of what Cliff's statement of 14 August actually said and, in the words of Roy Greenslade writing in the *Guardian*, 'a nasty, inappropriate spin and just the kind of tabloid-style sensationalism the *Telegraph*, in its former pomp, would have criticised.'[229] The *Daily Mail*'s 'Cliff: I'm Totally Innocent' was more accurate, as was the *Daily Mirror*'s 'I Didn't Do This' and the *Daily Express*'s 'I'm Innocent'. Cliff, meanwhile, was making his way back to his villa in Portugal after abandoning his short break in Évora.

I can't begin to tell you, we had a terrible drive home. And when we got back, that place was surrounded by paparazzi. They were everywhere. There's three entrances to the house and they were all crowding around everything.[230]

Arriving back, they swept through the waiting paparazzi and holed up in the house for two weeks away from prying lenses and the attention of the world's media. Cliff even closed all the blinds in the house to prevent any unscrupulous voyeur getting an unwanted photo.

He was back home, but his world had collapsed.

That night I was in the kitchen of my house, the press were on three different gateways and that was the lowest moment of my life . . . I suddenly found that I couldn't stand up and I fell onto the floor and I was weeping and, again, the first thought was that I was in this hole and I thought how was I going to get out of this. Somebody, anybody, could say something about anybody and you never know until it's passed in court whether you're guilty or not.[231]

Cliff revisited that moment again in 2020 on BBC Radio 4's *Desert Island Discs* telling host Lauren Laverne that:

I was never suicidal, but I thought a couple of times I might die, because I used to wake up with my pulses, you know, on your wrist, the head, the heart thumping like crazy. And I'm thinking, oh, I don't want to kill myself, but this could kill me.[232]

Fortunately for Cliff, those closest to him – Team Cliff, if you will – provided unwavering support. John McElynn, who had seemingly taken the place of Bill Latham in Cliff's life, was holed up in the villa alongside him and was the person who found the singer collapsed on the floor.

Thank heavens it was John that came in and he got on the floor and said he was a priest. So, he obviously has a way of dealing with things like that. He just said to me, 'Did you do this?' And I said, 'Of course not.' He said, 'Have you ever done anything like this?' I went, 'Absolutely not.' He said, 'Then I believe you, God believes you, stand up. You can do this.' It gave me strength. I stood up. But I knew that torment lay ahead.[233]

How right he was. Now the alleged historic sexual abuse case involving Cliff was public, others would likely come forward with similar allegations. The term is 'bandwagoning', where a person who learns that a complaint has been made decides to support the original complaint (true or false) with a false complaint.

And the police were counting on it.

While Cliff sought sanctuary within the walls of his Portuguese villa, back in the UK the BBC were finding themselves in a bit of an awkward spot.

In a BBC Radio 4 broadcast at 6 p.m. on 14 August, there was a piece by a BBC journalist, Danny Shaw, which was reproduced shortly afterwards on the BBC website, in which Shaw reflected on 'how it was that the BBC came to be outside the gates when the police arrived for their search'. The irony of it: that one BBC department was questioning the behaviour of another department within the organisation.

Shaw continued by referring to a previous practice of police tipping off reporters and the observations of the Leveson Inquiry that such activities should be more tightly controlled. He continued: 'Since then, tip offs have dried to a trickle despite a series of high profile arrests. The media presence at Sir Cliff Richard's home, therefore, was highly unusual, it appears to be a deliberate attempt by the police to ensure maximum coverage.'[234]

Maximum coverage within the media would create an environment where others might come forward. South Yorkshire Police suspected, indeed perhaps hoped for this. The Jimmy Savile case is a prime example where this can work effectively. Following the broadcast of the ITV documentary *Exposure: The Other Side of Jimmy Savile* on 4 October 2012, which featured five women recounting being abused by the TV presenter during the 1970s, hundreds of people came forward in the days and weeks following the broadcast to say that they had also been abused by Savile and others.

Operation Yewtree was launched on 5 October 2012 in response to the broadcast and the sustained media interest and coverage in the days and weeks afterwards encouraged approximately 600 people to come forward to provide information to the investigative team, with 450 relating to Savile and alleging sexual abuse.[235]

As news of Savile's depraved actions came to light, public outrage grew and there was a sudden scandal amplification within the British press aimed not only at Savile, but other celebrities and various police forces deemed not to have been doing their jobs.

Within a month, BBC's *Newsnight* had suggested a leading Conservative politician was part of a paedophile ring in Wrexham. Although they didn't specifically name the politician, Lord McAlpine was wrongly linked by internet rumour following the

BBC broadcast. He strenuously denied the allegations, saying he had only ever been to Wrexham once in his life and the allegations were 'wholly false and seriously defamatory'.[236]

McAlpine successfully reached a settlement with the BBC over the false allegations and was awarded £185,000 as a result of being wrongly implicated in child abuse. Lord McAlpine said 'there is nothing as bad as this that you can do to people'[237] and was later to tell BBC Radio 4 that he believes he will never fully clear his name, adding, 'This is the legacy that sadly the BBC have left me with.'[238]

Others, as we have seen, suffered from having their names wrongly implicated, their names freely bandied about in mainstream and social media while their accusers remained anonymous. Obviously, the police are correct in taking seriously the investigations of sexual abuse, particularly when minors are the victims, but the 'bandwagoning' that followed Savile and others was bound to implicate the innocent as fantasists and conspiracy theorists made spurious allegations.

At its height, Yewtree identified over 2,000 suspects and 30,000 victims and in 2015, one of the officers in charge of Yewtree perfectly summed up the approach of the police to the claimants – and by extension to the idea of justice itself – when he said, 'Not all these people are lying. They can't all be making it up.'[239] But some were, and that ruined innocent lives of celebrities who, like Lord McAlpine, would suspect that their legacies were tarnished forever, regardless of their innocence.

There seemed to be an air of titillation in the over-zealous policing of celebrities in the wake of Savile, a witch-hunt where bandwagoning was simply one of the tactics used to cast a net wide and snare their prey. Talking about the research period in the writing of his Channel 4 series *National Treasure* – a drama about a celebrity (played by Robbie Coltrane) accused of historical sex crimes – a police advisor told scriptwriter Jack Thorne that 'before interviewing celebrities accused of sex crimes, she would spend some time on *YouTube* watching their greatest hits. Why? So that she could appear to be a fan. So that, during the walk to the interview room, she could flatter them. She felt that flattery was the best way to disarm a celebrity.'

Tipping off the media was the first step on this slippery slope.

Not only was Danny Shaw's piece awkward for the BBC, it also posed problems for South Yorkshire Police. They were not the force that tipped off Dan Johnson, they had merely felt compelled to cooperate with him to avoid Johnson publishing his story too early and therefore jeopardising the raid on Cliff Richard's apartment and prejudicing their investigation.

Despite being on holiday in Wales, Chief Constable David Crompton was keeping abreast of developments. 'Later that day I became aware of a commentary by a BBC journalist called Danny Shaw in which he expressed the view that SYP were seeking to maximise publicity,' Crompton said. 'I was angry that the BBC had taken this step. I felt that the BBC had initiated the chain of events which had led us to this position and I felt it was deeply unfair that they now appeared to be trying to create a false and misleading narrative about events. I was aware that Carrie [Goodwin] and Matt [Fenwick] were making efforts to get the BBC to retract this article but the BBC had refused to do so.'

At 7.22 p.m. on 14 August, Carrie Goodwin texted Dan Johnson to complain about Shaw's piece saying: 'Just seen Danny Shaw's report suggesting we tipped you off and it was to maximise coverage. Not happy about this at all. This wasn't the case and brings the force into disrepute.'[240] A few minutes later Goodwin sent an email to South Yorkshire Police's media department, copying in DS Matt Fenwick, referring to the Danny Shaw piece and saying: 'We need to challenge this as it implies firstly that we leaked it and secondly that this was to maximise coverage. I've challenged Dan Johnson on this. I'll draft a letter to Sir Bernard Hogan Howe[241] addressing this from the Chief as it was Met officers that informed Dan.'[242]

The source of the leak and who said what to who was becoming pivotal in the strained relationship between South Yorkshire Police and the BBC in the immediate aftermath of the raid, and within days the force had complained to the BBC and accused it of breaching its own editorial guidelines.[243]

An agreement was later reached between the BBC and South Yorkshire Police whereby the broadcaster would make it clear that South Yorkshire Police was not the original source of its information. The BBC tweeted: 'Lots of q's re original source of @BBCNews story on Cliff Richard. We won't say who but can confirm it was not South Yorks Police.'[244]

It does appear that South Yorkshire Police were not band-wagoning specifically. In one of his emails, Dan Johnson suggested he had South Yorkshire Police 'over a barrel because of the tip off I received',[245] which would be consistent with South Yorkshire Police feeling obliged to offer Johnson, and therefore the BBC, something to prevent the story coming out.

By default, though, this media interest would naturally bring the case to the wider public and create a bandwagoning effect without being categorically greenlit by South Yorkshire Police. It could, therefore, serve them a valuable purpose. After all, they couldn't, for a moment, expect the raid to go ahead in the glare of TV cameras without other people coming forward with allegations, particularly in the Savile zeitgeist.

In their defence, South Yorkshire Police never released Cliff Richard's name on the day of the raid, that was a decision made and undertaken solely by the BBC and which included using an image of the singer during early broadcasts and footage of him during later broadcasts. There was never any doubt to viewers watching whose apartment was being raided and on what basis. The allegations were out front and centre with key words – sex abuse, boy, under sixteen – all echoing prominently and, therefore, in a trial by media, finding the accused guilty without fair trial or hearing.

In an article published in *Spiked*, sociologist Frank Furedi suggests the whole raid on Cliff's apartment was carefully stage-managed by South Yorkshire Police and the BBC saying: 'The very public police raid on Cliff Richard's home was a grotesque example of the pernicious inquisitorial spirit at the heart of today's historic investigations of child abuse. The entire event was carefully stage-managed by the BBC and the police for the edification of the British public. The South Yorkshire Police performed this piece of reality TV in the full knowledge that Richard was abroad on holiday. They could have organised their spectacle when the former pop star was at home – but no, they decided their actions would have a more dramatic impact if they had the whole stage to themselves. For them, what really mattered was that the live performance enacted at Richard's home got as much media publicity as possible. This manipulative "reality-policing" is fundamentally about impression management, about sending a message about the police. It has nothing to do with fighting or solving crime, whether present-day crimes or past ones. Rather, it is a form of visual entertainment which preys on the public's sense of insecurity and seeks to channel our anxiety into an obsession with the omnipresent paedophile. So, it isn't surprising that this raid was executed with the collaboration of Britain's main broadcaster, the BBC. The cameras were already rolling when the five police cars arrived. The helicopters hovering above helped to give the impression that this was serious business, on a par with busting a Colombian drug baron or arresting a serial killer.'[246]

On 15 August, Thames Valley Police, who assisted South Yorkshire Police officers in the search, put out their own statement to deny any leak. 'Thames Valley Police did not speak to any media outlets prior to the warrant being executed in Sunningdale, Berkshire, yesterday. This is a South Yorkshire police investigation and local officers from Thames Valley Police assisted South Yorkshire officers in their search of the property.'[247]

As we now know from facts laid down in the Closing Skeleton Argument of the First Defendant, Dan Johnson's original source was not from *within* Operation Yewtree and was not a police officer, but his source *had* received their information from within Operation Yewtree but Johnson did not know or believe this to be the case at the time.[248] Neither South Yorkshire Police nor Thames Valley Police, as they categorically stated, were the source of leaks.

Whoever was the leak to the BBC – and we'll probably never know the true identity of the source – and whether or not South Yorkshire Police used the opportunity that landed in their lap to bandwagon, what is indisputable is that Cliff Richard's world – like that of Paul Gambaccini and others before him – had been turned upside down. He knew nothing of his accuser, was certain beyond doubt of his own innocence, and was gathering a team around him to fight the accusations.

In the meantime, the damage to his mental and physical

health was becoming overwhelming. But perhaps worse for Cliff, was the damage it was doing to his career and legacy that really mattered.

CHAPTER 15

Remarkably, after failing to barely trouble the UK charts in 1984 and 1985, Cliff found himself at Number 1 again in 1986, the fourth decade in which he'd had a chart-topping single, and he did so with a new version of his first ever Number 1, 'Living Doll'.

Comic Relief was launched live on Noel Edmond's *Late, Late Breakfast Show* on BBC1 on Christmas Day 1985 from a refugee camp in Sudan. The brainchild of comedy screenwriter Richard Curtis, comedian Lenny Henry, and charity worker Jane Tewson, it was set up in response to the devastating famine crippling Ethiopia. Pop stars had already done their bit with Live Aid in July 1985, however Cliff wasn't one of them. Although Bob Geldof can't remember inviting him to be one of the performers,[249] Elton John had requested Cliff join him for a duet. Cliff declined, as he already had two charity bookings that day, but he did turn up later at Legends nightclub in Bond Street, London, to sing as the Wembley event ended and the whole Live Aid event moved to the USA.

'I remember Cliff Richard coming down to sing and to be

interviewed,' recalled Paul Gambaccini, who had been part of the BBC covering the event and had gone to Legends after. 'He had done more charity work, quietly, than many of the people on the Live Aid bill, but wanted to show his support, despite not having been asked to perform.'[250]

Now it was the turn of comedians to make the public laugh while raising money for those in desperate need. One idea was to create a charity single to raise money and in January 1986 Cliff went into the studio with the cast of *The Young Ones* to record a version of 'Living Doll'.

Bringing alternative comedy to television, *The Young Ones* was an anarchic, offbeat, surreal sitcom that ran on BBC2 for two series in 1982 and 1984. The four main cast members were Adrian Edmondson, Nigel Planer, Christopher Ryan, and Rik Mayall, who played a hypocritical, radical, attention-seeking and self-proclaimed anarchist who just also happened to be a huge fan of Cliff Richard. Throughout both series there were many references to the singer, with the finale seeing the characters killing themselves off by crashing a London double-decker bus (as seen in Cliff's film *Summer Holiday*) through a giant poster of Cliff's face and over a ... cliff.

A collaboration for Comic Relief seemed inevitable.

I didn't mind the Cliff Richard jokes. It was quite flattering to be filtered into the scripts.[251]

Stuart Coleman, who had previously produced Cliff on 'She Means Nothing To Me', his 1983 duet with Phil Everly, was brought in to produce the single and to try and keep some form of order in the recording studio.

'After I'd worked with Cliff on "She Means Nothing To Me",

I was approached by the Comic Relief team to discuss doing a single with *The Young Ones*,' recalled Coleman. 'Richard Curtis and Ben Elton came up with both the concept and the song. I remember very well the afternoon we all got together to discuss the outline, and we never stopped laughing at the prospect of how the imagery 'twixt Cliff and these snotty yobs would work out. Richard and Ben wrote the basis of the new lyric and I added bits along the way. Having worked with both Cliff and The Shadows, I suggested that Hank Marvin was involved, and it all fell into place very quickly. *The Young Ones* were more worried about working with Cliff, than he was with them. They were in awe of him and he was a true professional. Everybody had a ball and we loved every minute of making it, although it was one of the most complicated records I have ever made.'[252]

'I thought I was going to be embarrassed,' remembered Rik Mayall. 'You know, we'd taken the mick out of him quite a bit so we didn't know what to expect and, after all, I was aged one when "Living Doll" came out. But he was terribly nice. He's a very nice, straight person – open and friendly. He just seemed to find the whole thing funny.'[253]

With an accompanying video featuring Cliff trying to keep a straight face in the recording studio as the four *Young Ones* create mayhem behind him, the song was Number 1 in the UK for three weeks. At the time it gave Cliff the accolade of being the only solo artist to have the same song in two different versions reach Number 1.

During this period Cliff was wrapping on rehearsals for his newest adventure, which would see him fulfilling his dream of starring in a musical in the West End. *Time* was a ground-breaking sci-fi theatrical production by Dave Clark, David Soames and Jeff Daniels about a contemporary rock musician, Chris Wilder, and his band transported from a concert to the High Court of the Universe to defend their planet.

Dave Clark wanted Cliff to play the role of Chris Wilder. 'When I was writing *Time*, I didn't have Cliff in mind at all. When I came to thinking of the musical opening in England, Cliff became an obvious choice because he is such an institution,' said Clark. 'I couldn't think of any other major star who had lasted so long and who had attracted generation after generation.'[254]

Ever since I had played Ratty in Toad of Toad Hall *for Jay Norris in Cheshunt, I had harboured a secret desire to star in a West End play. What was more, the plot's Good versus Evil morality play aspect appealed to me. I made a snap decision – OK, I'm in!*[255]

With a cast including a 'virtual' Sir Laurence Olivier, *Time* opened on 9 April 1986, and a year of sell-out shows followed, even though the musical was savaged by the critics. 'It's like a science-fiction Sunday school lesson,'[256] said one, while another wrote that Olivier's speeches as the Time Lord sounded like 'Captain Highliner after transcendental meditation'.[257] A concept album based on the musical was released in 1986, featuring contributions from Leo Sayer, Dionne Warwick, Julian Lennon, Stevie Wonder, Murray Head, Freddie Mercury and, of course, Cliff. It failed to trouble the UK Top 20.

Two tracks from the album by Cliff were released as singles, but neither broke into the Top 40. Only his duet with Stevie Wonder, 'She's So Beautiful', was mildly successful, reaching Number 17. The only true chart success from the album was 'In My Defence', sung by Freddie Mercury and a posthumous Top 10 hit for the Queen frontman. Although he wasn't in the production, Mercury did make one appearance on stage in the musical on 14 April, when he joined Cliff to duet the show's final number, 'It's In Every One of Us'. It was the last time Freddie Mercury ever performed live in public.

Cliff did *Time* for twelve months, leaving in April 1987, whereupon David Cassidy took over the role of Chris Wilder.

When it was all over I missed Time *terribly. Straight away I went on holiday to the Caribbean and found that I was in bed for about 10 or 11 hours a day. I didn't know I was that tired.*[258]

Cliff had every reason to be exhausted: not only had he been doing two shows of *Time* every day for six months, before switching to evening performances only for the final six months, he had also recorded a duet with Sarah Brightman of the song 'All I Ask Of You' from Andrew Lloyd Webber's musical, *Phantom of the Opera*, which became a Top 3 hit in the UK as well as reaching Number 1 in Ireland and South Africa. He had also recorded a duet with Elton John titled 'Slow Rivers', and then returned to the studio to record his own album, the twenty-eighth of his career, *Always Guaranteed*, which renewed his working relationship with Alan Tarney.

At this point in his career, Tarney was riding the crest of a wave owing to his collaboration with the Norwegian band A-ha and producing their hits 'Take On Me' and 'The Sun Always Shines On TV'.

'I felt that I had never recorded the definitive album with Cliff,' says Tarney. 'So, I got together with David Bryce on a casual basis and we started discussing it. Cliff at that time had gone off to work with Craig Pruess. He does this from time to time. He goes off and makes his own records with a producer he feels he can dominate. He then chooses his own material which, quite frankly, always sounds a bit inane. The idea with *Always Guaranteed* was to do something a bit more special.'[259]

Recorded over three months, *Always Guaranteed* proved to be a huge hit for Cliff and marked yet another strong chart comeback. It sold over 1.3 million copies worldwide, reached Number 5 in the UK album charts and spawned two Top 10 singles in 'Some People' and 'My Pretty One', his first solo records to break into the Top 10 since 1983. Not only was it a huge commercial success for Cliff, but he's also gone on record as saying that *Always Guaranteed* is 'my favourite album of mine'.[260]

Flushed with success, and celebrating thirty years in pop, Cliff embarked on a world tour playing concerts in Australia, New Zealand, Europe and fifty shows in the UK, which sold out in seventy-two hours. Conspicuous by its absence on this world tour, however, was the USA. Cliff hadn't had a Top 10 hit there since 1980's 'Dreamin'' and regardless of whatever he had released subsequently, success in the States eluded him.

America has been very difficult for me . . . About ten years ago, my record company here said to me, 'EMI America is not excited by Cliff Richard material and that's why there's no support' . . . When I was told that, I thought it's no wonder. I really didn't stand a chance of cracking the States.[261]

While Cliff felt he couldn't rely on the American branch of EMI, back in the UK it was a very different story, with the record label fully behind him, as former EMI producer, Tris Penna, recalls: 'I worked for over a decade at EMI Records at the end of the last century so observed Cliff and the music and entertainment industry's reaction to him close up. For starters he was never considered a joke or mere flim-flam. If anything, we all admired his stamina, talent, and ambition – and alongside Queen, the Beatles, Pink Floyd, Kate Bush, etc., he was seen as part of the very fabric and essence of what EMI was.'[262]

In November 1988, EMI released the album *Private Collection 1979–1988*, a compilation of his hits since – and including – 'We Don't Talk Anymore'. There was one new track recorded for the album, a song that would be Cliff's ninety-ninth single and his twelfth Number 1: 'Mistletoe and Wine'.

The origins of this song, which would become the biggest-selling single of 1988, a perennial classic and win an Ivor Novello award, had its roots in a jazz-rock band called Swegas, formed in 1971 at the London School of Fashion. Two of the band's members were students Leslie Stewart and Keith Strachan. When Swegas disbanded not long after they had started, Stewart and Strachan continued their relationship as songwriters and initially explored musical theatre.

They began working with Jeremy Paul, a writer who would go on to have great television success with shows such as *Upstairs Downstairs*, *Van der Valk* and *Lovejoy*. One of their early productions was an adaptation of Hans Christian Andersen's *The Little Match Girl* for the Orange Tree Theatre in Richmond, called *Scraps*. Rather than using an existing carol in the production, the team wanted something written specifically for the play.

'I thought we'd written the whole [show already],' recalled Leslie Stewart. 'I took my little boxer dog for a walk as I was a bit cross about the situation, and this line just came to me – "It's a time for giving, a time for getting, a time for forgiving and for forgetting" – and I thought, "That's it!" I rushed home, sat down, and wrote it in about twenty minutes. I've often found writing hard work, but this just came to me.'[263]

Lyrics were read down the phone to Keith Strachan, who composed the music in just thirty minutes. 'I knew it was good, as it was one of those songs where you want to hear the chorus again and again – that's the key to a hit song,' says Strachan. 'It had a harmony that worked well and I just couldn't get it out of my brain. If that's the scenario, then you know it's great.'[264]

Strachan was always convinced he had a hit on his hands, but couldn't get the right performer to sing it. 'I asked Dennis Waterman if he fancied doing it. Val Doonican sent me a very nice letter saying "thanks but no thanks", and I thought, maybe this is not as good as I thought it was.'[265]

Fate intervened when *Scraps* was adapted for television in 1986 as *The Little Match Girl*, starring Twiggy and Roger Daltrey. Its director was Michael Custance, who just so happened to be a neighbour of Terry Britten, the guitarist in Cliff's band. 'For a Christmas song to work, you have to have someone of a suitable profile to perform it,' says Strachan.[266] Michael Custance offered to get the song to Terry Britten who would, he hoped, get it to Cliff. Strachan duly sent off a more poppy demo to Custance, sung by Jeremy Paul's twelve-year-old daughter, and within days it was in front of Cliff.

> *I got a phone call from my then manager, Peter Gormley, who died some years back now, and he said that I want you to come and listen to a song. I think this is a smash hit record. And it came from a show called* The Little Match Girl, *and it had lyrics like a smile and a joke, a hug and a smoke. It was a sort of a pub song, but it had this mistletoe and wine chorus.*[267]

Cliff admired the melody, but was less keen on some of the lyrics, perhaps unsurprisingly as the original themes of the song

MATT RICHARDS & MARK LANGTHORNE

centred around the neglect and hypocrisy of the middle class. 'The story is about a kid who freezes over the Christmas period, who imagines herself in a better world,' explained Strachan. 'The sentiment of the song was meant to be that people didn't care about the poor – it's a socialist Christmas song. It was a song about the middle class's lack of concern.'[268] The writers didn't object when Cliff asked to change a few words and he added a couple of Christian references to the song before going into a studio in Wimbledon in July 1988, hanging a piece of tinsel inside, and recording his version of the song.

As soon as I added those lyrics, that made it a Christmas song.[269]

'Mistletoe and Wine' was released on 21 November 1988, and by 4 December was sitting on top of the charts, where it remained for four weeks to become the Christmas Number 1 of 1988, selling over 750,000 copies in the six weeks after its release. Despite hitting Number 1, winning an Ivor Novello Award for Best Selling Single of 1988 and earning £100,000 annually in royalties,[270] the original writers appear less keen on Cliff's version of their song. 'I hated it,' said Leslie Stewart. 'I found the lyrics offensive. I'm not a practising Christian. I didn't really know about it until I heard the demo, and then I heard about the verse he wanted to do. But, to be fair, he made it his song.'[271]

Cliff's resurgence continued through 1989. His album *Stronger* entered the Top 10 and went platinum, producing two Top 3 singles in 'The Best of Me' (Cliff's one hundredth single) and 'I Just Don't Have the Heart', an upbeat track written and produced by Stock, Aitken and Waterman, a trio who had dominated the charts for much of the eighties with light dance-pop hits for artists such as Jason Donovan, Kylie Minogue, Mel & Kim, Bananarama and Rick Astley.

They seemed unlikely bedfellows for Cliff and although the song may have been a commercial success, it was panned by the critics. 'I Just Don't Have The Heart: And it sounds like it Cliff,'[272] wrote Stephen Duffy in *Record Mirror*, while David Giles of *Music Week* said, 'Having barely put a foot wrong (musically) in over thirty years, Cliff crashes to earth with a bump,' before continuing, 'The result is a standard SAW stomp, putting one of pop's great legends on a level with Sonia.'[273]

In 1989 Cliff was also part of another unlikely musical pairing – perhaps an even greater clash of musical cultures – when he joined forces with Irish singer-songwriter Van Morrison for the song 'Whenever God Shines His Light'. Five years younger than Cliff, Morrison came to prominence in the sixties with the band Them before launching his solo career with 'Brown Eyed Girl' and the critically acclaimed album *Astral Weeks*. However, as he got older, Van Morrison gained the reputation of being curmudgeonly, temperamental and difficult to work with, a notoriety that started to outstrip his reputation as a musical genius.

For the pious Cliff, although he liked the song when Morrison sent it to him, the outcome of the collaboration was uncertain. The omens certainly weren't good when Cliff turned up at the studio on time to find Morrison absent. After a couple of hours hanging around, Cliff was fed up and simply recorded his vocal. Just as he was about to leave, Morrison arrived and the completed track was laid down. It became a Top 20 hit, resulting in the odd couple appearing on BBC's *Top of the Pops*, where the *Guardian*'s Greg Freeman observed: 'Cliff capering around in his Peter Pan way, as only he can, while Van looks to be considering if he should shortly punch his lights out.'[274]

'That was a very weird thing,' remembered Van Morrison, talking about the whole Cliff collaboration in a rare interview. 'I didn't know what the hell I was doing on that [*Top of the Pops*]. That was bizarre, especially when he span around.'[275]

Having collaborated with Van Morrison, Elton John, Sarah Brightman, and the cast of *The Young Ones*, as well as with the production team of Stock, Aitken and Waterman during the latter half of the eighties, Cliff was keen to continue and reinforce his resurgence as a solo artist that the success of the albums *Always Guaranteed* and *Stronger* had provided, and this would mean surrounding himself with producers he trusted.

Paul Moessl joined Cliff Richard's band at the age of nineteen as a keyboard player and soon became Musical Director. At just 21-years-old, he co-produced 'Mistletoe and Wine' with Cliff, so when Cliff went into the studio to record two new tracks specially for inclusion on his 1990 album, *From A Distance: The Event*, a live album from his 1989 Wembley Stadium shows, Moessl was back behind the desk. One of the tracks they recorded was a song Cliff had been presented with at his office's Christmas party by Chris Eaton.

'I went down to a Christmas party at Cliff's office in 1989,' recalls Eaton. 'He had done "Mistletoe and Wine" for Christmas in 1988 and in 1989 he had done the song with Band Aid[276] and one with Van Morrison. He was talking about "From A Distance"[277] as his Christmas record for 1990. I played him "Saviour's Day" in his Rolls-Royce and told him I felt strongly about it. After he'd heard it, he turned round and said, "This is a number-one song."'[278] Recorded in the summer of 1990, 'Saviour's Day' was released on 26 November 1990. On 23 December it topped the singles chart, thereby giving Cliff his second coveted Christmas Number 1.[279] When asked which of his two Christmas chart-toppers Cliff preferred, he answered:

Oh, I think 'Saviour's Day' would be my favourite; it's just a better song with better production, although it just didn't sell as many copies.[280]

Cliff was becoming a ubiquitous presence at Christmas and, riding this wave, he recorded a Christmas album in 1991, *Together With Cliff Richard,* an album of popular Christmas songs such as 'White Christmas', 'Silent Night' and 'Have Yourself a Merry Little Christmas', as well as his two big Christmas hits, 'Mistletoe and Wine' and 'Saviour's Day'.

The first half of 1992 saw Cliff throw himself into his Christian projects, travelling to Uganda with Bill Latham and making a promotional film for Tearfund, a Christian charity that tackles poverty through sustainable development, responding to disasters and challenging injustice. Cliff had a long association with Tearfund, having performed at their first *In The Name of Jesus* charity concert at the Royal Albert Hall in 1975 and eventually becoming a Vice-President of the charity.

Returning to the UK, Cliff began recording his thirty-first studio album. Imaginatively titled *The Album,* it was released to positive reviews, with *Music Week* saying it was 'Cliff's strongest album in years due to the inclusion of quality songs by quality writers,' before continuing with 'impeccable production that will spin off many hits and become a strong seller for months to come.'[281] Prophetic words indeed as the album became Cliff's first non-compilation or non-film soundtrack album to reach the top spot since 1961 and also featured two top ten singles.

CHAPTER 16

It would be another five years before Cliff released an album of new studio material due mainly to the fact that he had another obsession that was to dominate his life, one based on the book *Wuthering Heights*. It had been his favourite book at school and, enjoying his period on stage in *Time*, Cliff was eager to do something similar.

> *Starring in* Time *– The Musical had ticked one box for me, but I had started to realise that there was one dream role that I longed to play above all others. I wanted to be Heathcliff.*[282]

An enigmatic character, Heathcliff is a dark antihero, an outsider who is the embodiment of a Byronic character, troubled and conflicted, walking the line between good and evil. His life is defined by his intense love for Catherine Earnshaw, which results in his subsequent descent into vengeful darkness, finally destroying him and all those around him.

Cliff knew that there was little chance of anyone casting him in the role of Heathcliff – after all the character was almost twenty years younger than him – so, if he wanted to play the part, he would have to create the production himself. Undeterred, he sank five million pounds of his own money into making it happen, hiring director Frank Dunlop to co-write the book with him, and his old collaborator, John Farrar, to write the music. For the lyrics, Cliff went to the very top of the tree and enlisted the services of the recently knighted Sir Tim Rice, the man behind the words of *Jesus Christ Superstar, Evita* and *Chess* amongst others.

'I was thrilled to have been asked to write some songs by Cliff,' says Sir Tim. 'I really took orders from Cliff and the writer of the book, Frank Dunlop. At times I worked together with John Farrar if I was in LA, but at other times he would send me over a tape of a tune and I would fax him back a lyric.'[283]

The whole venture was an enormous risk for Cliff, not only financially but professionally. His pop career had enjoyed something of a resurgence and, even though he remained an object of ridicule for some, he had a huge and loyal fanbase. Would they be turned off by this new project? Would he become an even greater object of fun for pursuing this folly, if that's what it turned out to be? Could a dramatic West End flop be the final nail in the coffin of a career that had been reborn – against the odds – a number of times?

The odds were stacked against Cliff: data from Broadway shows that of the original musicals produced in the last thirty years, 30 per cent were open for less than a month and seven closed in less than a week, while another report claims that 80 per cent of musicals fail to recoup their costs.[284]

As soon as Cliff announced the project, the press ridiculed him, suggesting he was too prim and proper to play the character, that he was too old to play the part, and that he should simply stick to what he knew best, singing middle-of-the-road pop songs for an ageing female fanbase.

I've loved Wuthering Heights *since I read it at school. And loved Olivier in the film. He looked big and strong, which I think Heathcliff should be . . . It will be hard for people to accept me as Heathcliff, I know that, after thirty-six years with my image, living the life I've lived. But why should I play angelic parts all the time? Acting is acting. You don't need to have killed someone in real life to know how to knife them on stage. I've had negative comments in the press all my life, and it hasn't made me give up. So tough luck to them. I'm going to do it.*[285]

Undaunted, Cliff threw himself into rehearsals, no doubt spurred on by £2.5 million advance bookings for the show on the first day ticket sales opened.

Financially, there should be no danger. I know I have 430,000 fans out there – well, that's how many saw my last tour. But it is dangerous artistically. I am leaving myself open to ridicule.[286]

Following previews at Earl's Court in London, the production opened at the National Indoor Arena in Birmingham on 16 October 1996. Box-office records were broken as the show toured Birmingham, Edinburgh, Manchester, and London, but reviews for the show were horrific with comments such as 'this wretched show', 'it was like watching the Pope smoke dope', 'the bad taste theatre event of the decade', and 'withering rather than Wuthering'.[287]

Sir Cliff (he had been knighted by Her Majesty the Queen

in 1995) didn't read the reviews on the advice of Bill Latham. Instead, he authorised stunned promoters to advertise the 'stinker' reviews that the show and his performance received, saying he wanted all advertising to contrast the loathing the critics felt for the show with the acclaim of the fans.[288] By now half a million tickets had been sold and box office takings were £8.5 million.[289]

The press were wrong about Phantom of the Opera, Cats, Les Miserables *and* Starlight Express; *three of those musicals are the longest running shows in the West End! It's obvious to me that the critics have no concept of what the public actually wants and therefore they don't know what we're trying to do.*[290]

By the time the tour had completed its run, finishing at the Hammersmith Apollo in London in May 1997, Cliff had had the last laugh, particularly if financial gain is the sole reward. It had been a massive financial success, Cliff's investment had paid off handsomely, a filmed recording of the show was released on DVD and topped the charts for eight weeks, while an album of the original cast recording hovered just outside the Top 40. For all the critics' negativity, Cliff was immensely proud of *Heathcliff*. He had backed himself and had succeeded.

I do Heathcliff *and it's a huge success and I'm thinking, it's easy to stop there. That's the biggest and best thing that I've ever done.*[291]

But Cliff couldn't stop. His ambition remained and, with no family as such, his career continued to be the main driving force in his life.

However, in the background, there was a shift that was

beginning to evolve slowly, almost imperceptibly at first, but one that would manifest itself later and threaten Cliff's career with the potential to drive him out of the industry once and for all. It was first noticed with the release of four singles from his album *Songs From Heathcliff*, which featured ten songs from the musical. Unlike the original cast recording, this album broke into the Top 20 album charts, but all four singles performed poorly with only one, 'A Misunderstood Man', scraping into the Top 20.

For the first time in his career, Cliff was experiencing a lack of airplay on radio, particularly BBC Radio 2, and television. The singles from *Heathcliff* just weren't getting any exposure. Worse was to follow with his next album, *Real As I Wanna Be*, his first studio album for five years, when Chris Evans – the owner of Virgin Radio at the time and its most popular DJ on its high-profile Breakfast Show – publicly vowed he would never play one of Cliff's records again, saying he was 'too old'. He even went so far as smashing the station's collection of Cliff Richard vinyl on air. Despite the station being besieged by irate fans, other radio stations quickly followed suit and Cliff found himself unofficially blacklisted.

I was officially too old for Radio 1 and even Radio 2 were now loath to put me on their playlist. It really is so frustrating. What's the point of making a record that nobody gets to hear?[292]

The lack of airplay had a dramatic effect on record sales, with the album spending only one week in the Top 20 and shifting only 40,000 copies, when EMI had budgeted for sales of half a million. The shortfall caused executives at EMI to consider not renewing his record deal. 'Even though Cliff can sell out the Albert Hall at the drop of a hat, it's no secret his last album was a major disappointment sales-wise,' one confided. 'These days shifting records from the shelves is what the music biz is all about – there's no room for sentiment. In the past, negotiations over Cliff's new deals have been fairly relaxed, but now they seem non-existent.'[293]

With earnings and royalties dwindling because of this unofficial ban, Cliff took extreme measures. He released the song 'Can't Keep This Feeling In' from his *Real As I Wanna Be* album as a pre-release white label under a pseudonym, Black Knight, suggesting it was a hip new artist. The track was originally a rhythm-and-blues ballad sung with a lot of falsetto, but was now a heavily remixed dance version and it would be unlikely anyone could pick up on the singer's real identity.

The track was sent out to over 200 radio stations and was played on Climax Radio, Choice FM and BBC Radio 1 amongst others to favourable reviews, with the song getting to the top of the rhythm and blues charts, featuring in three soul charts and making the Top Ten in the *Music Week* charts. Without any reference to Cliff anywhere on the record, it proved that radio stations and DJs had a playlist policy of ignoring his songs. Once Cliff had been outed as the singer behind Black Knight, most stations stopped playing it.

London-based Choice FM DJ Jerry Bascombe said, 'It is a great record and it took about four days to realise the identity of the artist. I suppose, to be honest, if we knew it was by Cliff we would have never played it, so it proves his point,' while Simon Sadler, head of music at London's Kiss 100 FM, said, 'I have to say that if I did see his name on a record I'd find it very difficult to play,' and Manchester station Key 103 said they would 'never knowingly play a Cliff record'.[294]

He might not have been getting airplay or selling records,

but Cliff could still sell out concert venues such as the Royal Albert Hall where, at the end of 1998 and into 1999, he sold out thirty-two shows, a record for the venue, as he celebrated forty years in the business. Television still offered him the occasional primetime outlet with ITV recording *An Audience With Cliff Richard*, an hour-long special during which he performed some of his best-known songs, told industry anecdotes and answered questions from the array of showbiz stars in the audience, people such as old flame Una Stubbs, comedians Bobby Davro and Les Dennis, actor Sir John Mills and, conspicuous by his presence in the light of what was to come years later, Rolf Harris.

More concerts kept Cliff working throughout 1999, including three open-air gigs in London's Hyde Park, and August saw him back in the recording studio to lay down a track that would, once again, see him at the receiving end of an unofficial boycott of his music as the millennium drew to a close.

The song, written by Paul Field and Stephen Deal – with Jesus also given a songwriting credit – merged 'The Lord's Prayer' with 'Auld Lang Syne'. It was not originally intended as a single, but was initially composed as part of the Christian musical *Hopes and Dreams* in 1999. 'We never anticipated what would happen with 'The Lord's Prayer' from *Hopes and Dreams*,' recalls Paul Field, 'but my wife did suggest at the time that it would make a great Christmas single for Cliff.'[295]

Cliff was aware of the song and felt it deserved greater exposure.

If someone said to you there was the 'Lord's Prayer' set to 'Auld Lang Syne' you'd want to puke. But when I heard it, I thought that the most simple ideas are strokes of genius when they work, and this to me is a stroke of genius.[296]

But, having left EMI, Cliff didn't have a record label. Out of courtesy, he went back to EMI and offered them the renamed song – 'The Millennium Prayer' – but they declined, saying it didn't have commercial potential. Cliff then took the song to the independent label, Papillon, a short-lived company formed in 1999 by the Chrysalis Group with British rock band Jethro Tull. They were interested in signing 'heritage acts' and when they heard 'The Millennium Prayer' they were ecstatic, jumping at the chance to release it, with the proceeds going to the charity Children's Promise.

Cliff performed the track for the first time on his ITV *Audience With...* programme and on 15 November it was released to the world. Immediately there was a backlash with many mainstream radio stations refusing to play it, including BBC Radio 2, who said they wanted to appeal to a younger audience, and Capital Radio, the UK's largest commercial radio station, who also refused to play it on their traditional sister station, Capital Gold. There were even people appearing on TV and radio telling the public not to buy the record, singer George Michael being one of them, saying, 'I think everyone listening to this show should buy [John Lennon's] "Imagine" just to make sure they don't have this heinous piece of music on the radio as we go into the next millennium.'[297]

Cliff had his army of fans though, and a group of women, mostly middle-aged, gathered in protest outside Radio 2's London HQ, as fans logged on to the BBC website to vote overwhelmingly (82 per cent) in favour of the song being played on the radio, while a Christian radio station, Premier Radio, promised to play the song regularly. All around the country Christians joined *en masse* to buy the record, almost in protest at it being banned rather than any musical validity.

The fact that many saw the record as an example of Cliff exploiting people's faith for his own gain garnered additional controversy, with George Michael again weighing in: 'I think the single and the way it's been dealt with has been vile. Just knowing there has been a Christian campaign for it – I think it is so exploitative of people's religion, it really is. I think there are people out there who feel it is their duty to buy this record on the eve of the millennium. That is a really horrible reason for a number one record.'[298]

Regardless of what George Michael or others thought, 'The Millennium Prayer' entered the charts at Number 2 in November 1999. A week later it was Number 1, where it remained for three weeks, although it was replaced by Westlife's cover of Abba's 'I Have A Dream' in the week leading up to Christmas, thereby denying Cliff another Christmas chart-topper. 'Through all the controversy and adverse press that raged at the time,' remembered songwriter Paul Field, 'I was just thrilled that the words of Jesus were in some way able to reach millions of people at the turn of the millennium.'[299]

A lot of people want to buy 'Millennium Prayer' because they genuinely feel that this is a Christian celebration. It's a great shame that George feels that the marketing of the record has been 'vile', because ultimately that casts a shadow over a lot of people who've bought it. 'Millennium Prayer' has defied every marketing rule in the book, because of the genuine groundswell of support for all it stands for.[300]

Selling 600,000 copies, the song won an Ivor Novello Award for Best Selling Single of 1999, but has since become a much-ridiculed track, with VH1 voting it the Worst Number 1 Ever in a 2004 hall-of-shame poll, ahead of such delights as Mr Blobby, and 'Teletubbies Say "Eh-oh!"' by the Teletubbies.

Not that Cliff was worried. As the new millennium dawned, he was approaching his sixtieth birthday, he was riding high in the charts, and life was rosy.

What could possibly go wrong?

CHAPTER 17

'...an everlasting funeral marches round your heart.'
'The Crucible' Arthur Miller

Portugal. Friday 15 August 2014. The day after the raid.

Cliff had arrived back at his Quinta, just south of Guia, to find himself a prisoner in his own home. Paparazzi were gathering outside the estate's gates, while across the world, lurid headlines connected him to an alleged case of sexual abuse with a boy aged under sixteen. While internet trolls and conspiracy theorists wasted no time in taking to social media to act as judge and jury and find him guilty, without the hint of a fair trial or the chance to defend himself, droves of devoted fans back in the UK and elsewhere countered with messages of undying support, but it was already too late. Mud sticks, as the saying goes. The enormity of the position Cliff found himself in truly hit home.

I couldn't imagine what depression was like, but I have an idea now. I felt as though I was in this hole and I had no means of getting out. I didn't know how I could face the future or face my friends or face my family. I was in tears, I have to admit.[301]

But those close to Cliff rallied round him. Broadcaster Gloria Hunniford called him up and suggested Cliff get in touch with lawyer Ian Burton, founder and senior partner of BCL Burton Copeland and someone whom Chambers UK, the guide to barristers and solicitors, described as 'undoubtedly a star', adding: 'Ian Burton knows everyone and has seen it all before, which is very comforting to clients.'[302]

Elton John was another quick to get in touch with Cliff.

Elton was one of the first people that called me. He actually, I can't use the language he used, but he said, 'Go for their "rotten" throat. And I got a call from Tony Blair, who I hadn't seen for ages and ages, and he called me just to comfort me. Cilla [Black] *was right there.*[303]

But for all their support and sympathy, Cliff's closest friends couldn't disguise the fact that while he was innocent until proven guilty in the eyes of the law, as far as the baying public were concerned, he was most likely guilty. After all, it's that phrase again: no smoke without fire. And all this stems from the fact that the singer was afforded no privacy, that the search (and his name) was publicised, and it came from a tip-off that should never have happened.

'Notwithstanding Cliff's strongly worded statement that the allegation being investigated was "completely false", one of this country's most successful popstars is now the object of the scorn and derision that comes with an allegation of child abuse,' said Dominic Crossley, a privacy lawyer and partner at the law firm Payne Hicks Beach.

'No doubt his lawyers will be working overtime, but it's a damage limitation exercise from the time the police search was reported in the media, and this most abhorrent stain on his character will exist in some form whatever happens from here. Remember, neither Cliff Richard nor anyone else have been arrested or charged by the police in connection with this investigation, let alone tried and convicted. Unless he is convicted, he must be presumed innocent – which is all very well for me to say, but hopeless wishful-thinking when it comes to managing the mob's response on Twitter and other social media platforms.'[304]

As rumour and counter-rumour swirled, Cliff laid low in his Portuguese villa. With friends around him or calling him with support, he could cope. But when they had gone or when the phone didn't ring, loneliness set in, dragging him down to the lowest depths of despair. He found himself unable to sleep, his mind spinning in the pitch-black of night with thoughts of his career ending in shame, of questioning what he had done to deserve this. He prayed, God being somebody to talk to in those endless drawn-out nights. And he thought about his accuser – the nameless, faceless individual who, for whatever reason, had laid these allegations at Cliff's door.

In the end, only people who go through this can possibly know. I can't possibly describe it. I've done my best to describe what it's like. But it's never gonna actually get through the total loss of everything for yourself, there's just nothing you can do.[305]

Up until this point, with good reason, Cliff hadn't made any moves to contact South Yorkshire Police. Meanwhile, back in England the force said its officers were 'still seeking to speak to him. However, it seemed likely that the force will delay any interview with Sir Cliff until it has had a chance to evaluate and assess the phone calls it has had since carrying out the raid [by which we can only assume any other allegations that might have arisen]. Several items were taken away from Sir Cliff's £2.5 million flat in Sunningdale which will also need to be examined.'[306] These items included a computer drive, a CD of warm-up exercises, a book that Billy Graham had signed for him, several postcards his mother sent him, and a personal note from Princess Diana.

It is curious to note, also, that in the statement on 15 August, South Yorkshire Police said that: 'Since the search took place a number of people have contacted the police to provide information and we must acknowledge that the media played a part in that, for which we are grateful.'[307] Repeatedly South Yorkshire Police had denied that their tip-off to the BBC was to maximise coverage and to enable bandwagoning. This statement appears to fly in the face of such assertions and gives an indication that South Yorkshire Police were aware that, by giving the tip-off to the BBC, bandwagoning would result, even if by default. They could get what they wanted without appearing to blatantly seek it.

Frank Furedi suggested that, 'It was very obvious that the police raid on Richard's home was not about finding evidence that might link Richard to the allegation of sexual assault made against him. After all, that allegation concerns something that allegedly happened a quarter of a century ago, very far from Richard's current home. What could the police possibly have been looking for in relation to that allegation?'[308]

He continued: 'South Yorkshire Police have justified their public humiliation of Richard on the grounds that since the airing of their raid-as-spectacle they have received a number of calls from people with more information on this case. From their point of view, aside from the publicity value the main point of the raid was to encourage, if not incite, others to come forward and make allegations against Richard. In this era of Operation Yewtree (though the investigation into Richard doesn't yet fall under the Yewtree remit), policing depends less on evidence than on increasing the number of people making allegations. Such an approach is based on the assumption that the greater the number of allegations, the stronger the evidence and the likelihood of conviction. Reality policing considers itself most successful when it has created an atmosphere in which a contagion of allegations can flourish.'[309]

Eventually, after Cliff's legal team had flown out to Portugal, South Yorkshire Police reached out and requested they speak to Cliff in person in Yorkshire on 23 August.

His legal team confirmed their client would attend the interview.

Getting back to the UK would not be easy. Paparazzi were outside his gates, they would most likely be at the airport when he left Portugal and they would definitely be at the airport in England when he landed, all seeking out that elusive photo of Cliff Richard about to face the music.

A plan was hatched: Cliff's neighbour and business partner, Nigel Birch, would smuggle Cliff out as he lay down and hid in the back of Nigel's Range Rover the day before any paparazzi expected the singer to leave. Cliff would then spend the night at Nigel's house before flying back to England on a private jet with his manager, Malcolm Smith, to avoid the stares of curious onlookers.

Landing at Robin Hood Airport near Doncaster, Cliff was driven the twenty-seven miles to Sheffield and a South Yorkshire

Police training centre. It was Saturday 23 August and for the first time face-to-face, a police officer informed Cliff of the specific detail of the accusation made against him. Cliff remembers the moment as being both 'frightening' and 'vile' – especially when they read out the precise details of the sex crimes he was accused of committing.

It was also at times laughable:

> *It was the sort of thing if I'd been up on a murder charge, they would have asked: 'Do you murder often?' and I'd be replying, 'Only at weekends."* [310]

An intense period of questioning followed relating to Cliff's movements at the Billy Graham rally at Bramall Lane in June 1985. It was almost thirty years since the alleged assault and Cliff cast his mind back as best he could, but was floored by the allegations being made against him and the details of the abuse. As the questioning continued, Cliff felt he was going mad at the sheer repetition:

> *It must have been so boring for them to listen to. Every single answer started: 'I have never, ever molested a boy, a girl, a man or a woman. I never would. I never could. I never will.* [311]

Cliff knew the accusations were outrageous and nonsensical, but this didn't mean he could disprove them. It was beginning to dawn on him that it would likely be his word against his faceless, anonymous accuser. And to make matters worse, he was feeling that the very basic tenet of UK law – that an individual is innocent until proven guilty – was seemingly being cast aside by South Yorkshire Police in their hunger for a high-profile prosecution.

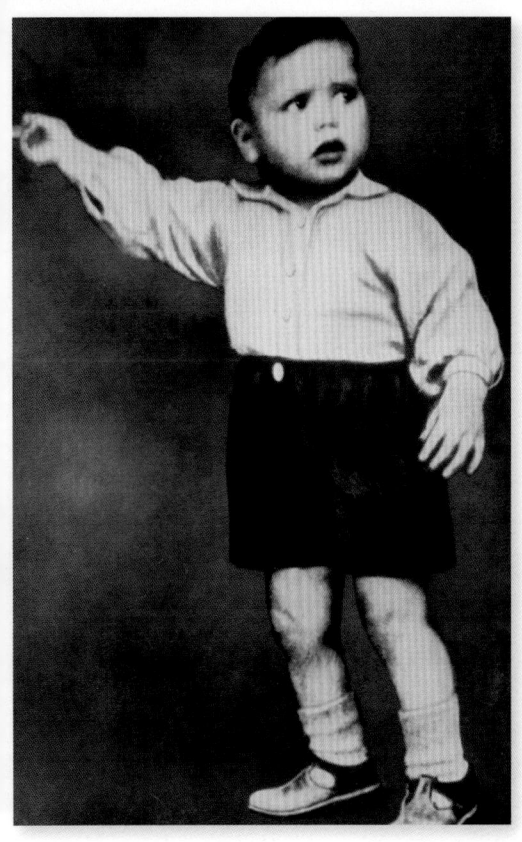

Cliff Richard photographed as a child in India, where he lived until the age of eight.

Cliff aged 19, saying goodbye to his sister Joan at Heathrow Airport, before boarding the plane to New York.

Left: Cliff Richard with The Drifters in 1959 before they became The Shadows.

Right: By the end of 1959, Cliff was a bona fide pop star and mobbed everywhere he went.

Left: From pop star to film star: Cliff as Don in *Summer Holiday*. The soundtrack had three Number One songs, all sung by Cliff.

Right: Cliff receiving a gold disc for Bachelor Boy from his manager, Norrie Paramor.

Above: Cliff toured the USA in 1962. Despite huge success at home, he failed to emulate his popularity across the Atlantic.

Above right: Cliff with Bill Latham, a man who was a central figure in Cliff's life for over 30 years.

Left: Cliff's announcement in the 1960s that he was a Christian was a very real proclamation of faith, although it was seen by some as a PR exercise.

Above left: As record sales declined in the 1970s, Cliff turned to TV and became more variety performer than pop star.

Above right: The late-70s and early-80s saw a revival of Cliff's pop career following the success of 'We Don't Talk Anymore'.

Below: Cliff with the evangelist Billy Graham. It was decades after Graham's 1985 rally in Sheffield that Cliff was accused of sexual abuse.

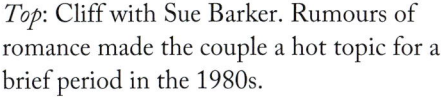

Top: Cliff with Sue Barker. Rumours of romance made the couple a hot topic for a brief period in the 1980s.

Above left: Speculation surrounded the relationship between Cliff and singer Olivia Newton-John but Cliff was always adamant they were simply good friends.

Right: Cliff with two of his closest friends, Cilla Black and Gloria Hunniford.

Above: Receiving his knighthood at Buckingham Palace in 1995, with his three sisters Donna, Joan and Jacqui.

Below: Cliff became synonymous with Christmas following a string of seasonal chart-toppers.

Above: Cliff on his 50-year anniversary tour, Time Machine, in 2008.

Below: Performing at the Diamond Jubilee concert at Buckingham Palace in 2012.

Above: Cliff in happier times at his Portuguese vineyard.

Below: The estate in Berkshire housing Cliff's penthouse, which was raided by South Yorkshire Police in 2014.

Left: Cliff immediately after winning his High Court Action against the BBC.

Below: Cliff in 2025.

They made me feel as it I was having to prove myself, rather than them trying to find that I was definitely guilty. I was not accepted, I don't think, as innocent. They assumed I was guilty. After the first interview I said to the officer: 'You guys have got a difficult job because there is never any proof in these cases.' My lawyer said: 'The police use the accusation as evidence.' I was thinking, 'I'm not an expert, but an accusation can never be evidence in my book. It can't be, or I could say what I wanted about anyone.' [312]

Rather than remain in the UK, Cliff flew straight back to Portugal after the interview, with his spokesperson releasing a statement saying: 'Today Sir Cliff Richard voluntarily met with and was interviewed by members of South Yorkshire Police. He was not arrested or charged. He cooperated fully with officers and answered the questions put to him. Other than restating that this allegation is completely false and that he will continue to cooperate fully with the police, it would not be appropriate for Sir Cliff to say anything further at this time.' [313]

South Yorkshire Police put out their own statement confirming a 73-year-old man had been spoken to in relation to an allegation of a sexual nature dating back to 1985: 'The man was interviewed under caution but was not arrested. He entered South Yorkshire Police premises by arrangement.' [314]

As Cliff beat a hasty retreat back to Portugal, the full ramifications of the BBC broadcasting images of South Yorkshire Police searching his Berkshire home began to take on a menacing life of its own. Once the images had been reported and re-reported and shared globally, the Cliff Richard investigation brought the defence of historic sexual abuse well and truly into the spotlight, and in the days and weeks that followed it rarely escaped the public's attention. The tree had been shaken.

Within a short period of time, and as yet unbeknown to Cliff, eight more complainants would come forward, all more than thirty years earlier, each in some way accusing Cliff of sexually abusing them when they were boys, with one exception who claimed sexual assault in his early twenties.

CHAPTER 18

'I cannot sleep for dreaming; I cannot dream but I wake
and walk about the house as though I'd find them comin'
through the door for me.'
'The Crucible' Arthur Miller

Having returned to Portugal, Cliff bunkered down in his villa, which remained under siege from legions of paparazzi. Broadcasters, TV stations, newspapers and magazines all sent in requests for interviews; some of the same media outlets that were vilifying him around the world. All were swiftly turned down. Elsewhere, social media continued to proclaim Cliff guilty without trial, accusers hiding behind their keyboards convinced he must be the next Jimmy Savile or Gary Glitter, and spouting their ill-founded diatribe across the anonymity of the internet.

Throughout, Cliff maintained a silence, a 'dignified silence' as described by his lawyers.

I couldn't say that I felt terribly dignified, but I was certainly keeping silent.[315]

Under such public scrutiny, Cliff felt obliged to withdraw from charity events previously scheduled. One such event was at Canterbury Cathedral, where he was set to perform as part of the fortieth anniversary celebrations of the Canterbury Cathedral Trust. His spokesperson said Cliff did not 'want the event to be overshadowed by the false allegation' before adding, 'He is sorry for any disappointment or inconvenience caused.'[316]

Closer to home in Portugal, the singer also pulled out of a ceremony where he was to be handed the keys to his adopted Portuguese home city, Albufeira. It is the city's highest civic honour, but Cliff felt his participation would overshadow the event owing to the allegations he faced, especially as other local individuals and organisations were also set to receive awards.

Holed up in Portugal, awaiting his fate, Cliff found himself facing sleepless nights, his mind in turmoil night after night. Who was his accuser? Why was he doing this? Why was he trying to damage him personally and professionally?

When he could get to sleep, he would suddenly wake with pulses racing and fearing he would die of a heart attack.[317]

The nights were the worst. Each night, I'd fall into a shallow sleep but wake up at 3.15 a.m. – always 3.15 a.m. – and lie awake for the rest of the night. I'd get three hours' sleep, at most. It was the last thing I thought about as I fell asleep, the first thing when I woke up.[318]

An uneasy mind is difficult to quiet.

In the lonely sanctuary of his bedroom, Cliff would turn to the faith that had supported him for almost fifty years.

*My faith, my fans, friends, my family – they never left me alone.
I was never ever alone all that period, so I survived a lot of it
because of that. There's no doubt, when your friends stay and
they all go to bed, you go to bed and suddenly you're on your own.
But I never felt alone. I was always able to speak to God, pour
my heart out, and I think that was very good for me.*[319]

At this point Cliff still believed he had only one accuser. He
was totally unaware of the other eight complainants who had
come forward. And early on, during another restless night and
after talking to God, Cliff decided he must take action towards
his sole accuser.

'I can't survive like this,' I told Him [God]. *'I'm beginning to
hate the person who is doing this to me. I can't live with this
hate. I need to forgive him.' I took a deep breath and addressed
my unknown tormenter: 'I forgive you. I don't know who you
are or why you are doing this to me – but you must have a
reason. I forgive you.' It was the same as the night I became
a Christian. There was no divine reply, no angelic trumpets
sounded. Nothing happened. All of my frustrations remained –
but at least I had lost the hatred. It gave me a small comfort.
It helped . . . a little.*[320]

Faith had sustained Cliff through the first few horrendous days
and nights of the allegations, as it had sustained him in the
decades since he first became a Christian. He is open in the fact
that had he never found God, he may not have survived the first
few days of the sex abuse ordeal.

Cliff's relationship with God has always been seen as something of an oddity to the onlooker. Very much the poster boy for

Christianity, the constant questioning about his sexuality and his refusal to acknowledge rumours that he is gay – thereby to many a tacit confirmation by silence that he is, or must be, homosexual – puts him in an awkward, contradictory position.

Christianity's stance on homosexuality remains divisive despite a seismic shift in legal reforms worldwide over the last forty years, leading some Christians to come to uneasy compromises, while others remain rooted in ancient theological texts and beliefs. The traditional Christian view remains that homosexuality is sinful and that sexuality is properly expressed only between a man and a woman within the confines of marriage, with punishment taken to the extremes if the Book of Leviticus is to be followed: 'If a man lies with a male as with a woman, both of them have committed an abomination; they shall surely be put to death.' (Leviticus 20:13).

In some of the letters of St Paul included in the Bible, he condemns homosexuality as 'unrighteous' and claims that men who practise homosexuality will not inherit the Kingdom of God. The Church of England, at the time of writing, do not permit same-sex marriages but will, instead, perform special church services to bless same-sex couples (although gay couples will still need to undergo a civil ceremony to be legally married).

Similar blessings can take place within the Catholic faith, but the Vatican clarified that imparting blessings to same-sex couples was 'not a justification of all their actions, and they are not an endorsement of the life that they lead.'[321] This is the same Vatican that, in 2008, declined to sign onto a UN declaration that called for the decriminalisation of homosexuality, complaining the text went beyond the original scope.[322]

Cliff has occasionally touched on the church's attitude to homosexuality. In 2005, he told Sky News:

I'm sad because we have to learn to deal with everything. Everything has changed. The church has got to come to terms with the fact that things have changed since even Jesus has died. It's only a mere 2,000 years. I mean slavery was an in-thing at one time. We were told to deal with it. And we've dealt with it. And we've got to deal with every aspect of life. There are gay people in this world. Some of them are very talented. Some of them could be great priests.[323]

In 2008, he told the *Independent*:

I think the Church must come round and see people as they are now. Gone are the days when we assumed loving relationships would be solely between men and women. It seems to me that commitment is the issue, and if anyone comes to me and says: 'This is my partner; we are committed to each other,' then I don't care what their sexuality is. I'm not going to judge; I'll leave that to God.[324]

And in 2011, speaking to BBC Radio 4 he said when commenting on whether the Church should accept same sex marriage:

I don't see why gay people shouldn't be married. I have got friends, same-sex couples, who have been together for decades. So, for them, it's marriage even though they can't call it marriage. It probably isn't marriage as such because we recognise it as a man and woman and having babies. [But] that's neither here nor there for me.

Cliff's tolerance and acceptance, as seen in these comments from the 21st Century, are strangely at odds with his participation in the 1971 National Festival of Light, a short-lived grassroots right-wing Christian movement formed by British Christians concerned with the rise of the permissive society and social changes in UK society by the late-60s. It promoted family values and set out to oppose 'pornography and moral pollution' which, in their eyes included the growth of sex outside marriage, the proliferation of sex in films, abortion, and homosexuality. One of the aims of the organisation was to offer the teachings of Christ as the key to 'recovering moral stability in the nation.' Amongst the leading lights in the movement were Malcolm Muggeridge, a British journalist and social critic, actress Dora Bryan, Lord Longford, a politician and social reformer, moral campaigner Mary Whitehouse and Cliff Richard.

I was a hundred per cent part of it at the beginning and its impact, under God, was colossal.

The foundations for the Festival of Light were rooted in the return to England in November 1970 by a young couple, Peter and Janet Hill, who had been travelling for four years as evangelical Baptist missionaries in India. The culture shock they sensed upon their return, particularly when they saw that sexually explicit content was more prevalent in mass media, led to them founding the National Festival of Light. Peter Hill was determined to bring this to the nation's attention and began planning a march on London culminating in a public rally in Trafalgar Square and an open-air concert of Christian music in Hyde Park. It would be held on 25 September, 1971. The call to arms went out under the banner 'Moral Pollution Needs A Solution'. A working committee was formed to organise the main event as well as the lighting of three hundred beacons across the country to symbolise Christian unity (Cliff Richard would light the one in Sheffield) and grassroots support came from Anglicans, Baptists, Plymouth Brethren and Pentecostal church denominations.

The first major rally was scheduled to be held at Westminster Central Hall on 9 September, 1971, but, already, the counter-culture movements of the time were beginning to rise up against this overtly Christian proselytising, amongst them the relatively recently-formed Gay Liberation Front. They saw the National Festival of Light rally at Westminster Central Hall as the perfect opportunity for disruption, especially considering the National Festival of Light's dim view of homosexuality despite its recent decriminalisation and so set in motion Operation Rupert. Su Small was one of the Gay Liberation Front's activists: 'I was getting more interested in general politics and personal politics and I'd become involved with gay liberation. I found myself at this meeting to discuss how we could combat the Festival of Light. A guy from Monty Python, Graham Chapman, was there and he said, "I've got a bob or two, so if anyone's got any ideas . . ." and the plan was that we were going to do a whole series of things. The first was to infiltrate the first big Festival of Light rally at Westminster Hall. The plan was that A and B were going in full drag and they'd stand up and shout, "Say it out loud: I'm gay and I'm proud!" Then we'd leave it a few minutes and so-and-so would let out the white mice and they'd all scream and stand on the chairs. We had about seventeen different things planned so that if some of us couldn't get in, something would still happen. We also had someone working inside the Festival of Light office keeping us abreast of things.' Pink Fairies drummer, Russell Hunter, was another activist involved: 'It was a time when Cliff Richard was giving out. And Mary Whitehouse, Malcolm

Muggeridge, Lord Longford and so on. They had this big rally for what they called the Festival of Light at the Central Hall, Westminster. Su Small, Rose, Sandy, Debbie Knight, and myself decided to dress up as nuns to infiltrate it. They'd certainly have never let us in dressed normally. Su Small was the Mother Superior, cos her habit was a different colour, and we passed straight through with no problems. They were vetting everybody at the door and they turned away a lot of people: obvious hippies who were there to make trouble. But we went straight through. At a certain point in the proceedings, we all stood up, started heckling and throwing the cushions. Then we did a conga up the middle aisle. We all lifted our skirts and started making obscene gestures until the Christian bouncers turned up and beat us up, especially me, when they discovered I wasn't what they thought.' Gay rights campaigner Tim Clark was also there: 'I remember all the mice being released. Two elderly women holding on to each other suddenly unfurled a banner from the balcony saying, "Cliff for Queen". It became total mayhem as the incidents started to pile up into each other. We deposited fake religious literature around which had religious covers, so they would be picked up and taken away to be read – only inside it was porn.'

The press covering the event were swift to highlight the disruption and it was a serious blow to the National Festival of Light, undermining their attempt to be taken seriously and opening the gates for other protestors to disrupt future events. Naturally, opposition began to mount up across the country but the climax of the Festival, the rally at Trafalgar Square and concert in Hyde Park, did take place and it is estimated some 45,000 turned up – somewhat less than the 100,000 expected. There was some heckling at Trafalgar Square but the rally passed off peacefully before the crowd wound their way through the streets to Hyde Park where Christian music groups performed. Cliff was also on the bill and artist and gay rights campaigner Stuart Feather was in the crowd watching. 'Cliff Richard, once Britain's Elvis and now a convert to Christ, came out and plugged in. "If we get honest with ourselves," Cliff is saying on stage. "Be honest, Cliff," someone shouted. "Admit you're a homosexual … Come out, Cliff."'

Cliff has never come out as gay. There have been rumours – and they are just that, rumours – throughout his career. But if he wasn't gay, he could quite easily quash these with a firm statement, though admittedly, he has twice denied it. Instead, he comes out with quotes like, 'If I was gay would it make any difference,' and 'As for my sexuality, I am sick to death of the media's speculation about it. What business is it of anyone else's what any of us are as individuals?'[325]

In a *Loose Women* interview, he answered his close friend Gloria Hunniford's question about his sexuality by saying, 'I don't mind talking about things, but there are things that are mine. That will go with me to my grave.'[326] Of course, it is his own business, but the paradox is that the speculation he has faced throughout his career – speculation he insists he hates – would disappear in an instant if he simply addressed the issue head-on.

Coming out as a gay pop star in the sixties and seventies, and even more so in the eighties, was likely career suicide. Coming out as a gay *Christian* pop star . . . unthinkable.

When he first burst onto the scene in the late fifties, Cliff was seen as a rock 'n' roll rebel, he was criticised in the press for sexual exhibitionism on the ITV show *Oh Boy!* and was chased down streets by throngs of girls following concerts. He had scant few, if indeed any heterosexual relationships and those that he did have played second fiddle to his burgeoning career.

His eighteen-month romance with Delia Wicks, one of his backing dancers, when he was nineteen ended with a curt *Dear John* letter written by him from Australia – with her name spelled incorrectly – saying he was 'confused' but had come to make 'one of the biggest decisions I'm ever going to make.' He said that if he was to be a 'Pop singer' then 'I have to give up one very priceless thing – the right to have any lasting relationship with any special girl.' A brief passionate but seemingly sexless affair with Una Stubbs followed before he supposedly lost his virginity to Carol Costa, the girlfriend of his bandmate, Jet Harris. In the sixties, he considered marriage to the dancer Jackie Irving, but there were no sexual relations with her despite them being virtually inseparable during a summer season in Blackpool. She ended up marrying Adam Faith. In the early seventies, there was tabloid speculation about a relationship with Olivia Newton-John with rumours that he had proposed to her, which resulted in Cliff going so far as putting out a statement to deny it. In a later interview he referred to their relationship:

> *The first time I met Olivia she was free. But very, very soon she wasn't. Our relationship is special, but it's never been a romantic one. I never proposed to Livvy and we never went on a date. When we went out, we always went as a team. We never got into the dating mode, and we might never have, I don't know . . .*[327]

In the 1980s, Cliff had a well-publicised tabloid relationship with Sue Barker, the former French Open tennis champion and Wimbledon semi-finalist, after they first met in 1981. 'I met Cliff through Alan Godson of Christians in Sport, whom I'd been put in touch with through the commentator Gerald

Williams,' remembers Barker. 'Alan gave Cliff my number and I think I spoke to him for the first time the night after I won the Brighton Tournament in October 1981.'[328]

I felt quite besotted with Sue almost immediately. I just like her as a person, admired her as a tennis player and found her very attractive physically. Funnily enough, I have never usually liked blonde girls.[329]

Their romance, if that's what it was, gained considerable attention in the media at the time and there were even rumours of Cliff considering a marriage proposal to the golden girl of British tennis, which Cliff was happy to entertain. 'He spoke about "getting married" in articles about us,' recalls Barker, 'but we certainly never discussed it. When I read these comments, they came as total news to me.'[330]

Just as he had dumped his girlfriend Delia Wicks with a letter in the early sixties, Cliff got a friend to tell Sue the relationship was over. 'I got a call from one of Cliff's friends, on his behalf,' Barker recalled, 'saying that Cliff just wanted to cool it. Our relationship was over. Really? He'd asked his friend to pass on this message over the phone?' Sue was fuming, insisting that she and Cliff had not passed the point of being just friends. 'It felt to me like a friendship,' she added, 'that had the potential to develop, rather than a significant romantic relationship, because we hadn't taken it far – and I'm not just talking about sex.'[331]

Cliff would later say he 'didn't love her enough to propose' and 'I didn't love her quite enough to marry her,'[332] which riled Barker some forty years later. 'If someone had told me that my relationship with Cliff would last a few months but I'd still be hearing about it forty years later, I wouldn't have gone near him,' she says. 'Frankly, it looks silly now that he's still talking about a relationship that was never really more than a friendship.'[333]

There appears little substance to any of these relationships. They are brief, fleeting, opportunistic or, perhaps in the case of Sue Barker, convenient. Mark Griffiths, who spent ten years playing in Cliff's backing band, observed the singer and tennis star together.

'I read into it at the time that it was good for Cliff to have a famous person on his arm,' Griffiths says. 'If it had been Tracy from Dagenham, it might not have happened. Sue's a great girl and I know they got on really well.'[334] Another band member, Graham Todd, said, 'I think it was useful for his career to apparently have a girlfriend. I think Sue was a lot more earnest and sincere about it than Cliff was. I always felt he was leading her on a bit. She was such a nice girl.'[335] The musician, impresario and former manager Tito Burns observed, 'All the talk about Sue Barker was a lot of rubbish. But it was understandable. It's show business. You've got to make the man seem macho. There's nothing wrong with that.'[336]

These comments certainly make the relationship appear, from Cliff's side at least, more convenient and strategised than a full-blown romance. The relationship with Barker also occurred during the period when the emergence of a new disease was being reported in the USA. The disease would officially be named AIDS in 1982, but unofficially it had become known as the 'gay plague', and its spectre produced misinformation and stigma that promoted fear and ignorance which, in turn, led to prejudice and increased homophobia.

If gay pop stars were nervous about coming out in the sixties and seventies, the hostility towards homosexuals in the wake of AIDS in the early eighties made it more impossible than ever. For

Cliff, with speculation about his sexuality constantly following him, a high-profile heterosexual 'relationship' that whipped up a media frenzy in 1981 and 1982 would be timely, to say the least.

It seems curious, also, that Cliff doesn't appear to have had a whiff of a heterosexual relationship since Sue Barker. Is he really that married to his career? Of course, suggestions of him being gay cannot be backed up with evidence other than a lack of heterosexual relationships and his living arrangements with Bill Latham followed by John McElynn and, frankly, no jury in the land would find him guilty as charged on such flimsy testimony.

Richard often declines discussion about close relationships and when asked about suggestions that he may be homosexual has stated, on the rare occasions he's offered a response that, categorically, he is not. When the suggestions were put to him by a London evening paper in 1976, Cliff replied:

> *It's untrue, but I have given up talking about it, because I think nothing I will say will change anything. People are very unfair with their criticism and their judgements. I know I catch the brunt of it but I don't give two hoots . . . I'm not going to get married just to prove it. I'm damned if I am. Of course I've heard the rumours, but I know what I am and my friends know what I am. What the mass public thinks doesn't bother me as long as they buy my records.*[337]

Acclaimed singer and session musician Bryan Chambers worked with Cliff for the whole of the *Soulicious* tour in 2011 and went to dinner with Cliff and John McElynn. 'Cliff was an absolute professional, incredibly generous and a gentle person, great to work with, but he was a closed book,' Chambers says. 'In honesty

I just always assumed he was gay. Spending time with him and John, it never occurred to me otherwise.'[338]

Cliff can come across as prickly and over-sensitive at times – but then, who wouldn't, when subjected to so much sneery condescension? The Bachelor Boy evidently has secrets, by his own admission. But whatever drives Cliff may well be the engine that keeps him feeling he has something to prove.

Over 100 pages and we are still none the clearer whether Cliff Richard is gay, or bisexual, or know much at all about him. Officially he is 'sexless', like Sir Edward Heath – a condition perhaps unique to England, or at any rate to our quirky libel laws. Despite regular interviews, and occasional revelations, Cliff is careful about what he shares with the press.

'None of us are open books,' he told the *Evening Standard*. 'There are things that go through my head which I wouldn't share with anyone. And no one will ever get them out of me, because that's my choice.'[339]

Watching him on stage, when he gyrates and thrusts, it seems like an imitation of sexiness. But then to understand what is sexy, you need to have had sex, and maybe he hasn't. It's possible, even probable perhaps, that he is and likely always has been a celibate homosexual who is trapped in an image of his own creating. And likely his steadfast belief in his faith means suppressing his sexuality was never an issue. God created us all, gay or straight. But it is up to each of us whether we choose to sin. As with any sinful behaviour, it's not about being *tempted*, but about wilfully engaging in activity that goes against God's law. Anybody who wants to follow Jesus Christ needs to make it their goal to stay away from sexual practices that the Bible says are sinful.

CHAPTER 19

After a month or so as a virtual prisoner in his Portuguese villa, Cliff looked out of the window one morning and saw that the paparazzi had vanished. There were new scandals to follow up, other celebrities to hound, more privacy to pry on. For the first time he could walk the length of his drive safe in the knowledge that no lenses were capturing his every move. Reaching the gates, Cliff found devoted fans and locals had tied or pinned notes of support to them. He read them and was overcome with emotion, breaking down at the kindness of strangers during his period of turmoil. His fans had sustained him during his career and now, in his hour of need, they were sustaining him again.

It didn't mean he was off the hook, however. The police were continuing to investigate the allegations, and rumours and conspiracy theories were still swirling about the internet with most, if not all of them, condemning him as a guilty man without giving Cliff the opportunity to protest his innocence.

There was no indication how long the investigation would take, let alone what would happen if it resulted in a court case.

In the meantime, Cliff could remain in Portugal, in a sort of judicial limbo, or he could find a distraction, something to take his mind off the madness going on around him. Easier said than done. As it happened, Cliff had booked some studio time in Nashville prior to the abuse allegations and house raid taking place. Perhaps recording an album might provide some sort of diversion.

Cliff had recorded his previous album, *The Fabulous Rock 'n' Roll Songbook*, at Nashville's famous Blackbird Studio, where artists such as Taylor Swift, John Mayer, Dolly Parton and Keith Urban had recorded. The album consisted of fourteen covers of classic rock 'n' roll songs as well as one new song, 'One More Sunny Day', composed by Cliff.

I like Nashville. It lives for its music. When you go to a restaurant, all the waiters and waitresses are singers, writers and players. They're just waiting to get started. I always look at them thinking, will I remember them when they get famous? There is a different feeling towards music that I like in Nashville. For my last album The Fabulous Rock 'n' Roll Songbook *I wanted to do it live and if you want get it a live excitement, Nashville is the place to go. These men and women they live to play music, they just have to play.*[340]

The last thing Cliff wanted to do in the autumn of 2014 with the allegations hanging over him was to make music, but a trip to Nashville to record the follow-up to *The Fabulous Rock 'n' Roll Songbook* might provide the opportunity for him to take his mind off things, and allow him to escape the intense media scrutiny he was being subjected to in the UK and Europe. Reunited with producer Steve Mandile, who had overseen *The Fabulous Rock 'n' Roll Songbook*, thanks to modern recording techniques, the sessions would also allow Cliff to 'duet' with his idol, Elvis Presley – if he could get permission from the Presley Estate.

Priscilla [Presley] *said to me, 'If it was up to me, I would say yes.' She said, 'Elvis knew all about you,' and I went 'Me?' and she said, 'He keeps up with all his competition, keeps an eye on all his competition,' so I thought, 'Oh my God, Elvis actually thought of me as competition.' I phoned Sony, who own all the rights to Elvis, and they said, 'Look, we'll let you choose one song. Which one would you choose?' And I chose 'Blue Suede Shoes'.*[341]

First recorded by its Tennessee composer Carl Perkins on 19 December 1955, at Sun Studios, Memphis, at little over two minutes in length 'Blue Suede Shoes' is a song that forms the cornerstone of rock 'n' roll history, becoming the moment, perhaps, when rock 'n' roll found its voice. Perkins' version, beginning with the lines, 'One for the money, two for the show,' from an English-language nursery rhyme dating back to the 1820s, wasn't polished, but producer Sam Phillips recognised that the pauses in the song's intro (due to the fact that drummer Fluke Holland was unused to counting in) were the secret ingredient in rockabilly.

Released on New Year's Day in 1956, it shot to Number 2 on the Cashbox chart, but tragedy struck Perkins as he travelled to promote and perform the song on Perry Como's TV show. Involved in a terrible road accident that claimed the life of a truck driver, Perkins was hospitalised with serious injuries and was pipped to Number 1 by Elvis's 'Heartbreak Hotel'. That same month, Elvis recorded 'Blue Suede Shoes' as the opening track for his debut album and his record label wanted to release it as a single.

Presley was reluctant for the release, loath to compete with his friend for sales, but once he realised songwriting royalties would support Perkins as he recuperated, Elvis agreed to the release and his version charted at Number 20. Elvis's version was a Top 10 hit in the UK in 1956 but, already, the teenage Cliff – then still Harry Webb – was transfixed.

> *Immediately, he obsessed me. I started trying to find out everything about Elvis that I could. When I first saw a photograph of him, I couldn't believe how cool he looked – that quiff! That curled lip! And when I realised that he had an album out already, I absolutely had to have it. I got a holiday job picking potatoes on a local farm. There I was, all day long, bent double and yanking spuds out of the dirt for a shilling an hour. The boredom and backache were all worth it when I had saved up the cash and was back down Marsden's to buy Elvis Presley. 'Heartbreak Hotel' wasn't on the record, but I didn't mind: there were so, so many new songs to love. I loved the opener, 'Blue Suede Shoes', with its urgent vocal and frantic rhythms.*[342]

Now, almost sixty years later, Cliff was in Nashville recording 'Blue Suede Shoes' as a duet with his idol, albeit thanks to technology.

> *I listen to this record and it's me singing with Elvis, the guy that gave me my career. If there had been no Elvis there would have been no Cliff Richard, because I was totally influenced. I also believe there may not have been a Beatles, either 'cause although they started five years after The Shadows and I did, we were all the same age, so they would have been listening*

to Elvis, Ricky Nelson, Little Richard, Buddy Holly, the Isley Brothers, all of those people and, you know, I just got lucky. I sang with Elvis and it's fantastic.[343]

With recording completed in Nashville, Cliff opted not to return to the UK, instead flying to his opulent villa in Barbados, where he hoped the winter sun would wash away his worries. There was no such luck. The dark cloud continued to hang over him. He could only stew and fret, unable to be involved in the investigation going on thousands of miles away in England. Every eventuality swirled around his head as he walked on the sands, every dark horizon loomed as the Caribbean sun set. He was in limbo; he couldn't write his forthcoming book, he couldn't release any recorded music, for as far as those who weren't his dedicated fans were concerned, Cliff Richard was a tainted brand.

For a man whose career and public persona was everything, this was unimaginable and, perhaps, unsurvivable. He was suffocating under the allegations.

And if Cliff thought things couldn't get any worse, he was in for a rude shock.

In February 2015, David Crompton, the Chief Constable of South Yorkshire Police, wrote an open letter to Keith Vaz, the Chair of the Home Affairs Committee, informing him that the investigation into Cliff Richard had 'increased significantly in size' and 'involves more than one allegation.'[344] In the letter it also said the force was in regular contact with Cliff's lawyers. 'We have not written directly to Sir Cliff Richard,' wrote Crompton. 'It is the responsibility of his lawyers to ensure he is fully briefed on the conversations which have taken place with investigators.'[345]

Two sections of the letter were heavily redacted, but regardless, the open letter, published on its website by the Committee, was swiftly picked up by national and international media, shaking Cliff to the core.

Of course, I knew the police had to talk to the people making these allegations. I've never disputed that sexual abuse, and paedophilia, are incredibly serious crimes that must always be investigated. Yet it was to transpire that my new accusers were desperate, troubled fantasists. Somehow, it seemed, the police just couldn't see that.[346]

Cliff's lawyers wasted little time criticising the open release of the letter and the fact that it publicly revealed that the singer was facing fresh historic assault allegations. Writing to Keith Vaz on behalf of their client, Gideon Benaim of Michael Simkins Solicitors said:

Plainly, it was not necessary for the SYP [South Yorkshire Police] letter to be published on any urgent basis, if at all. The SYP letter appears to have been in the hands of the Committee for a period of two weeks or more before it was proactively sent to media organisations, presumably to encourage widespread publicity. There was ample time to properly consider whether the SYP letter ought to have been released before it actually was. As a direct result of the decision of the Committee to publish the SYP letter, and to proactively send it to media organisations, our client has been exposed to a further round of unnecessary and extremely damaging media coverage, with no due process. Our client had no opportunity to comment or make submissions to the Committee in advance of publication, but had he been able to do so, the damage that has since been caused by the Committee's actions and by the SYP letter would, most likely, have been avoided. It is the Committee who have acted as enablers to the media so that they could report on claims of new allegations about which our client has been given no or very little information; about which he has yet to be questioned; for which he has not been arrested; and of course, over which he has not been charged. The Committee have, through their actions, facilitated coverage which would not have otherwise occurred.[347]

Benaim continued by issuing a strongly worded critique of these developments while also taking aim at Keith Vaz for his media appearances over the issue:

Extensive media interest was hardly dampened by the chairman of the committee who appeared on television to discuss the contents of the SYP letter on the same evening of its release. It is manifestly unfair to our client that he has again been put in a situation where speculation and rumours are rife, where he cannot defend himself because he is the subject of an investigation, and, where third parties appear to know more than he does. It is not how a criminal investigation should be conducted.[348]

Benaim also described the original letter from the police force as 'poorly worded' and 'at certain points unnecessarily emotive', while including a 'number of significant points which could be misinterpreted.' He said the police's letter 'has the appearance of being written without the level of care and attention that such an important communication demands' and 'disputed some of its contents,' before continuing to state that the singer has not been actively updated with 'substantive information' relating to the investigation, claiming that 'in the main it is his solicitors, BCL, who have contacted South Yorkshire Police for updates.' Benaim's letter added: 'That said, SYP and BCL have co-operated on several aspects of the investigation, for which our client has been grateful. He remains very keen to co-operate fully and for the investigation to be resolved swiftly.' The letter also addressed the police's disclosure that there is 'more than one allegation', saying the 'information that has been provided to our client about the new allegations is so scarce it is difficult to comment meaningfully.' It went on: 'Late on Friday 6 February, we telephoned one of the lead officers on the investigation. During the course of that call, the officer told us that there was now more than one complaint (albeit a small number). Very little substantive detail was disclosed.' This led them to question the claim that the investigation has 'increased significantly', saying: 'This phrasing is curious and seems to us to be – at best – a loose use of language and at worst to be unnecessarily emotive. In the current climate, the phraseology deployed was likely to lead both readers and members of the press to jump to exaggerated conclusions, as indeed it has.'[349]

In addition, Cliff released a statement: 'I have no idea where these absurd and untrue allegations come from. The police have not disclosed details to me. I have never, in my life, assaulted anyone and I remain confident that the truth will prevail. I have co-operated fully with the police, and will, of course, continue to do so. Beyond stating that the allegations are completely false, it would not be appropriate for me to say anything further until the investigation has concluded, which I hope will be very soon. In the meantime, I would, again, like to thank everyone for supporting me through this unbelievably difficult period.'[350]

It is interesting to note that the man leading the Committee which openly published the letter from David Crompton, Keith Vaz, was, himself, no stranger to scandal. In 1999, Vaz was appointed to be Europe Minister, but just a year later he was investigated for allegedly taking payments from a solicitor whom he had recommended for an honour. He faced eighteen separate allegations of wrongdoing but denied them all. Only one minor allegation was upheld. In 2001, as he stepped down from his ministerial role for 'health reasons', Vaz was subject to another investigation for allegedly using his position of power to help the Indian billionaire Hinduja brothers gain British citizenship, although an official inquiry cleared him of wrongdoing. Then in 2009, he was named in the MPs' expenses scandal exposed by the *Daily Telegraph*.

To cap it all, in 2016, while the Cliff Richard allegations were being investigated, Vaz – a married father of two – was accused in a tabloid exposé of posing as a washing machine salesman named Jim to pay two male escorts for sex and offering to provide class A drugs. The parliamentary standards commissioner concluded it was 'more likely than not that Mr Vaz has engaged in paid sexuality' and expressed 'willingness to buy cocaine' while handing him a six-month ban from the House of Commons.[351] For Sir Cliff, whose career had been built on a whiter-than-white persona, Vaz seemed the complete opposite, and perhaps not the person Cliff would want in charge of the Committee.

With the letter from Crompton now out in the open, the following morning's headlines were blatant in drawing attention to the fact the singer was now facing further allegations. It was an opportunity for the 'no-smoke-without-fire' brigade to say, 'I told you so.'

But the allegations were simply that: allegations.

And when South Yorkshire Police finally passed the details of them to Sir Cliff's lawyers, it took them barely a minute to see that these accusers were not remotely credible.

CHAPTER 20

What did the new millennium hold for Sir Cliff? He had finished the old one on a high with his The Millennium Prayer topping the charts, meaning he'd had a Number 1 hit in the fifties, sixties, seventies, eighties and nineties, a remarkable achievement. But he would be celebrating his sixtieth birthday in 2000; how much longer could he realistically go on? There was already a backlash towards his music on radio stations, he had not cracked America and had pretty well given up on the idea that he ever would, he was ridiculed by many, had been dropped by EMI, and the music scene was shifting rapidly around him, leaving him behind.

But he had been cast adrift before and always made a comeback. Could he continue to do so in his sixties and beyond? After all, rock 'n' roll is really a young person's game. As historian and journalist Nigel Jones comments: 'Its sounds, lyrics and themes are all about the joys, insecurities and embarrassments of youth,' before suggesting that ageing stars are 'pretending to suffer the pangs of unrequited love, when their contemporaries are more concerned about getting a GP's appointment or losing their winter fuel payments.'[352]

There were others around Sir Cliff still flying the flag for old-school rock 'n' roll, his contemporaries from the sixties still touring or making albums. Tom Jones, a few months older than Cliff, had enjoyed a career resurgence in the 1990s, Paul McCartney was exploring classical compositions while continuing to record albums that were hits in the UK, and the Rolling Stones had ended the 1990s with the *Bridges To Babylon* world tour which, at that time, was the second-highest-grossing tour of all time. Meanwhile Elton John was conquering musical theatre, writing Oscar-winning soundtracks as well as touring and recording, while across the pond, Bob Dylan was winning Oscars and Grammys, and Paul Simon was releasing a critically acclaimed album. There seemed no reason why Cliff should stop. But stop he did.

I had a few reasons. It wasn't just to jump off the treadmill. I wanted to have a good old rethink about my career; my work routine; my life. Did I want to keep going at the workaholic pace that I had always set? Or did I want to slow down a bit? [353]

Cliff's initial plans had been to take a year out and do a road trip across Australia in a Winnebago from Perth to Sydney, but these plans were shelved and he decided to head west instead, to America via Barbados.

Before he could depart, however, he had an important date at London's Savoy Hotel, where he was honoured with the prize for Outstanding Achievement at the South Bank Awards. The award, presented to him by Cherie Blair, the Prime Minister's wife, recognised Cliff's lifetime of contribution to the world of arts and entertainment. As well as winning the award, the evening provided yet more gossip about Cliff's private life when he was seen at the ceremony with PR executive Karon Maskill.

The BBC ran a story shortly after the pair were spotted together saying, 'Speculation has surrounded the couple since the 59-year-old pop legend was spotted in public with Ms Maskill, with whom he has become increasingly affectionate.'[354] Cliff's lips remained tightly sealed over whatever was or, more likely, wasn't going on between the couple and left it to Maskill's employers to release a statement and shoot the gossip swiftly down: 'Press speculation over a "special friendship" between Karon Maskill and Cliff Richard is entirely unfounded,' the statement said. 'Karon has forged a friendship with Sir Cliff as a result of her professional input as leader of the team which has publicised Cliff's work during the past year.'[355]

From London, Cliff flew to Barbados en route to America. It was on this trip that he was introduced to an architect, and he began planning the property that would eventually become his six-bedroom house on the island and lead to Cliff being granted Barbadian citizenship in 2010. Next stop was California, where he caught up with his old friend Olivia Newton-John, as well as staying with John Farrar, who had been a member of The Shadows from 1973–76 before going on to be a successful songwriter with credits such as 'You're the One That I Want' from the movie *Grease*, as well as collaborating with Tim Rice on Cliff's musical production *Heathcliff*.

Leaving California, Cliff headed for New York and it was here that an old friend introduced Cliff to the Catholic priest John McElynn, who would later become his live-in companion and advisor. 'In finding John, I think Cliff found a family,' says the actor Nigel Goodwin, a friend of the singer. 'There was John, his mum and his sisters and I think that was very important to Cliff.'[356]

Music was very much on hold for Cliff in 2000. He was

travelling, meeting new people, and planning his Barbados development. Life seemed good. But behind the scenes not all was rosy. Bill Latham had moved out of Cliff's house the previous year, which meant the singer was living alone for the first time since 1965. Cliff was lonely, perhaps another reason he took a year out travelling, he needed the company of people; not necessarily a relationship, but certainly a friendship. With that missing, there was a huge void in his life. At the same time the health of his mother, Dorothy, was deteriorating after having been diagnosed with Alzheimer's in 1998.

At first we thought she was just belligerent, as mothers can be, but then it became obvious to the family that something was wrong.[357]

Cliff had a bungalow built next to his sister Joan's house so their mother could retain a level of independence, but also be kept an eye on as the disease progressed.

Whenever Mum needed help, Joan was there and I thought, fantastic, we can all rest easily.[358]

But when his mother was found wandering in the local village, Cliff and his sisters realised they had no option but to put her into a home where she could receive care twenty-four hours a day. It was a heart-breaking decision for Cliff and the family, but the decline in her health left them little alternative.

She has pretty much no memory and no interest in herself whatsoever. We have to come to terms with the fact that this is not the woman we knew as mother. This is a different person now, a simpler person.[359]

In October 2000, Cliff Richard turned sixty and celebrated with a lavish week-long cruise around the Mediterranean on board the *Seabourn Goddess*. The eighty guests, who were piped onboard by Cliff while dressed in a naval uniform, included Shirley Bassey, Olivia Newton-John, Gloria Hunniford and John McElynn, who flew over from New York specially for the event. The cruise departed Monte Carlo and took in St Tropez, Barcelona and Las Palmas before ending in Malaga.

> *The people onboard are all very special in my life. That may be unimportant to anyone else, but it's my birthday and it was important to me to surround myself with people who have meant a great deal to me over the years.*[360]

With celebrations over, Cliff took the remainder of the year off before returning to what he did best, making music. At the beginning of 2001, he reunited with producer and songwriter Alan Tarney and went back into the studio to record tracks for his thirty-fourth studio album, *Wanted*, which comprised mostly covers of songs such as 'All Shook Up', 'Somewhere Over the Rainbow', 'And I Love Her' and 'What's Love Got to Do With It?', the international hit for Tina Turner but a song that was, in fact, originally written specifically for Cliff.

> *The song was written for me by Terry Britten, who wrote 'Devil Woman' and a bunch of other songs. And somehow or another, the demo that he sent to my office got sent back to him with a little message saying, 'We don't think this is right for Cliff.' So, he gave it to Tina Turner.*[361]

Cliff's new album, *Wanted*, reached Number 11 in the UK, and was promoted by twelve shows at the Royal Albert Hall as well as a world tour that took in Europe, Australia, New Zealand and the Far East.

By now, John McElynn had taken a sabbatical from the Church and had moved into Cliff's house to provide company, companionship and help. With Bill Latham having moved out and Cliff's mother in a home, McElynn alleviated the loneliness that was creeping in on Cliff as well as helping out with the singer's charitable organisations.

Our arrangement has worked out really well. John and I have over time struck up a close friendship. He has also become a companion, which is great because I don't like living alone, even now.[362]

The presence of McElynn, however, and the fact that he was living with Cliff and referred to as a 'companion' once again fuelled online and tabloid gossip about the singer's sexuality. Releasing his memoirs in 2008, Cliff spoke in relative detail for the first time about his relationship with McElynn, describing how he struck up an intimate (whatever that means in this context) friendship with the American former Roman Catholic priest.

They were introduced to each other in New York in 2000 by choreographer Pamela Devis who, knowing McElynn was keen on tennis as well as being a Catholic priest, was convinced the two of them would get on and passed McElynn's number to Cliff. Shortly after, the singer rang the priest and arranged to meet. Cliff, unsure how things would work out, had already booked himself into the grand Fitzpatrick Manhattan Hotel on

Lexington Avenue as an escape route, in case he didn't warm to the priest or like his family. Arriving in New York, McElynn wasted no time in picking Cliff up from the airport.

I breathed a little more easily when I met John and his family. We played tennis together – John, his sister, Janet and her husband Jack; they were very friendly and, as Americans do, immediately invited me to the family's home for dinner. I needn't have worried. The evening turned out really well and we've become very firm friends. I cancelled the hotel.[363]

Their friendship blossomed, part of the attraction for Cliff being that McElynn, thirteen years his junior, didn't seem aware or was influenced by the fact Cliff was a pop star. Being in America helped, where Cliff continued to remain relatively anonymous. 'This allowed him [McElynn] to be franker with him than most people feel they can be. I think Cliff found that very refreshing,' says author Steve Turner.[364]

When the singer left New York, the two of them kept in touch – McElynn flying to Europe for Cliff's sixtieth birthday cruise – and it wasn't long before McElynn took leave of the church and moved in with Cliff effectively taking over the role Bill Latham had had for thirty years.

'John once had a great ministry,' one of McElynn's former friends said, 'but now all of that is gone. He enjoys the fame, the first-class travel and the social world of the rich and famous.'[365] This is slightly unfair; for the most part McElynn stays in the background, he is rarely photographed at social events, and his dedication to Cliff's wellbeing, business and charitable affairs cannot be underestimated; often he will travel a day ahead of the singer to ensure hotels are prepared correctly for him or his properties are well-maintained. At airports, where Cliff feels especially vulnerable, McElynn will discreetly usher away fans, and at his office he looks after all communications for the singer.

McElynn has also become a spiritual advisor to Cliff and his influence appears to have spread to the singer's overall lifestyle. Those that know him suggest he is a changed man since McElynn came into his life, saying that while he used to be a man of humble and simple tastes, McElynn has seemingly given him the confidence to enjoy his wealth and the freedom offered by it.

'Cliff has started to spend money rather than save it. He's been doing a lot more travelling and seems to have a new sense of life,' says Steve Turner. 'It's clear that he's much happier in himself since meeting the priest. He's gone from someone who rarely invited friends to dine at his home to doing a lot more lavish entertaining.'[366]

As a Roman Catholic priest, McElynn would have taken a vow of poverty. Now he was sharing multi-million-pound properties across the world, travelling in lavish style, and enjoying the sumptuous social parties and associated wealth that comes with the trappings of fame. Rather than taking a sabbatical from priesthood, it appears McElynn has quit the clergy for good. There is no reference to him in the national US directory of Catholic clerics, while the religious order that ordained him says it now has nothing to do with him.

'He is now in England and is no longer a priest in our community. He's out of contact with us,' said a spokeswoman in America.[367] Inspection of the official Directory for the Catholic Arundel and Brighton diocese, which covers Weybridge – where the house that McElynn shares with Cliff is located – shows no record of John McElynn.

In 2006 the *Mail on Sunday* tracked down Betty McElynn, John's 85-year-old mother. She admitted he was no longer a priest and said, 'He left for the same reasons so many of them leave,' before adding, 'I know about his new life and Sir Cliff, of course. I hope they are happy. But I was surprised to hear that he was advising Sir Cliff on property. That was never John's thing, as far as I know.'[368] The newspaper also located McElynn's younger brother, Peter, who was discreet when questioned about the singer's relationship with the ex-priest. 'It's a personal matter,' said Peter. 'John is an incredible person, but you'll have to ask him and Sir Cliff about it.'[369]

Of course, Cliff is reluctant to provide any information about their relationship, declining to say whether their close relationship is a friendship or more than that, simply referring to McElynn as his 'companion' and 'blessing'[370] and repeating that speculation, gossip and rumour about his personal life and sexuality wears thin.

I am sick to death of the media's speculation about it. What business is it of anyone else's what any of us are as individuals? I don't think my fans would care either way.[371]

And when asked if the decades-long gossip-mongering about his sexual orientation hurt him, Cliff replied:

No, it did when I was young. It hurt my family a lot, of course. But who cares? It doesn't really matter to me anymore. I have got gay friends. Most people have gay friends. If I was gay would it make any difference? Would you not come to my concerts because I was gay? I hope not.[372]

When promoting his book, *My Life, My Way*, which detailed for the first time (to some extent) his friendship with McElynn, Cliff appeared on Sky News and was quizzed about sexuality by Kay Burley:

BURLEY: How do you feel when the press question your sexuality?

CLIFF: It's always been . . . for fifty years I have dealt with this. When I first started they tried to prove me out as some sort of sex maniac, then the whole gay thing came in. I'm thinking, do I really have to constantly spend my whole life justifying, qualifying? I don't have to do any of that, and now I don't. And in the book actually I, the title I wanted for my book, there's one line in the book where I talk about the press and I said, 'Do you know what? I'm an enigma,' and I am loving it. So now I'm thinking to myself, let them all do it, it doesn't really, who cares, my fans don't care, the public don't even believe it anymore.[373]

A year later, Cliff invited broadcaster Piers Morgan to his Barbados retreat for a special one-hour ITV documentary. Once again, the topic of the singer's sexuality was high on the agenda:

MORGAN: Cliff, what I'm curious about because I've known your career, I interviewed you on the *Wimbledon News* when I was nineteen, so twenty-five years ago, I've been fascinated by your success over the decades and everything else, but also I'm struck by the fact that of all the celebrities I've ever interviewed you've always been the most open and honest, of all of them. I can't think of anybody more frank about themselves, their deficiencies, their virtues, their success, their failures and so on, but the one area that you've allowed over the years, over the decades to continue to get this mythology around it is your sexuality and I'm curious why.

CLIFF: Well, it's not just my sexuality, I mean there are things I don't like to talk about publicly because I don't think they're anybody's business. I've never got that through to the press and they still ask me the question and I still don't answer them, because I've been asked questions I wouldn't ask my best friends; people I've known for years I would never dream of asking.

MORGAN: Like what?

CLIFF: I'm not going to tell you. You know what I mean, you know what I mean.

MORGAN: Do you feel uncomfortable talking about sex?

CLIFF: No. Not at all. No. I'm uncomfortable about talking about sex with people I don't know.

Later in the interview, Morgan tries to dig deeper.

MORGAN: How many people out there know the truth about your sex life? How many people do you trust to let them know?

Cliff pauses momentarily, perhaps slightly flummoxed by the directness of the question.

CLIFF: I wouldn't . . . I'd say that I would talk about that to almost . . . I can't think of anyone I would have spoken to that directly.

MORGAN: Really? Even closest friends?

CLIFF: My closest friends wouldn't even ask me about things like that.[374]

If Cliff is or was gay, coming out would put an end to all the speculation, all the tabloid gossip, all the rumourmongering. But let's be honest here, it could also prompt the loss of huge swathes of fans, particularly the hard right Christians. The career Cliff has chosen is one of sex and drugs and rock 'n' roll, but he has never been into drugs and certainly never appeared to be into sex, although he denies celibacy, telling BBC's *Woman's Hour* in 2002, 'Celibacy is a way of life, a vow. I have never vowed to be celibate, so I don't feel celibate.'[375]

So he only seems interested in rock 'n' roll and, if his fans were to desert him on the basis of him coming out as gay, then perhaps rock 'n' roll would disappear too.

That would have terrible consequences for a man who has dedicated his whole life to his career. Perhaps the only thing of equal interest to him is Christianity. He seems to have a genuine Christian belief, he's made no secret of the fact it's sustained him since the Sixties, and this in itself could be in direct conflict with the knowledge that he may be gay and, as such, he cannot – or is not able – to reconcile the two. Therefore, perhaps, he simply ignores it. Consequently, he is the eternal bachelor boy and a bachelor, especially one in his eighties, is a figure in today's society that can certainly get the tongues wagging as Michael Bywater in his book *Lost Worlds* describes: 'We can't be doing with bachelors now. Not bachelors; and their habits, no, their *ways*. You know how they are. We suspect them, especially Christian bachelors. The bachelor spiritual: Jesus and all his celibate followers, Sex has become so much the Greatest Good that we cannot conceive of anyone adjuring it without motive: nasty ways, inadequacy, small boys, little girls, simmering psychopathy. Those who have nothing to do with women we now prefer to consider as closeted gays, sexual uninterest beyond our hopelessly over-eroticized ken, and, perhaps, we so much fear and hate unfettered masculinity that we would rather it were corralled in the very homosexual relationships that a few generations ago we could barely imagine. Those same few generations ago, the bachelor, un-hamstrung by domesticity or the call of the bedsprings, was considered more of a man, freer to preach or fight or build or conquer. Now, he is less. So much less that we cannot acknowledge him as such. He is denied status, merely accorded a state. He is … single. And when he leaves the room, we glance at each other and the unspoken question hangs in the air. What, exactly, is he? He can't just be a bachelor.'[376]

There simply is no evidence that Cliff is gay. And neither is there any conclusive proof that his relationship with John McElynn is anything other than platonic. As Cliff says, it's entirely his own business as to what the nature of their relationship is. If it were two women in their later years, sharing a life and house, companionship, would anyone speculate about their sexuality?

The problem is that Cliff is a bachelor who has enjoyed, at the time of writing, an eight-decade career in pop music. For many of those willing to poke a stick at Cliff, being an elderly bachelor in pop music is simply enough to prove he's gay. Add in the fact he's lived with two men for the best part of fifty years, has barely had any heterosexual relationships, and that he refuses to categorically deny that he's gay by not talking about it, then the 'proof', for those that want to seek it, appears to be there.

Cliff's perceived homosexuality is simply an assumption by certain members of the public and, as a result, the rumour has taken on a life of its own over the decades. Cliff could have halted these rumours at any time by either coming out as gay or marrying a woman, Una Stubbs perhaps or Sue Barker. But his career came first to him, always has done and always will do. To have come out as gay – if indeed he is – would alienate a large proportion of one section of his fans, particularly the hard-right Christians, and to marry would alienate another large proportion of his fans. He cannot win. And all the while people snipe at him from the anonymity of their keyboards or smartphones.

We might ultimately conclude that the most significant aspect of Cliff's sexuality is his complete repression of it.

Maybe the last word on this should go to someone who has witnessed Cliff and John's relationship/friendship first-hand. Vicki Wickham was the manager of Dusty Springfield, Labelle, Morrisey and Marc Almond, amongst others, and once found herself on holiday with Cliff and John.

'I stayed with them at Andrew Lloyd Webber's house in Barbados. We were all guests. Cliff and John were there together. To everyone present there it was a given that they were together. That they were a gay couple. There was a closeness, a tenderness between them. I didn't think it was a sexual thing at all, so perhaps that doesn't make it gay in the defining sense, but in every other way it was. There was a deep love and respect.'[377]

CHAPTER 21

With the *Wanted* tour completed, Cliff rested for much of 2003 in Barbados, his six-bedroomed house construction having been completed in 2001 and becoming the biggest property on Sugar Hill, as well as the most expensive. Built on three levels in a traditional Caribbean plantation style, with a mosaic-tiled swimming pool and private tennis court, it faced due west providing an opportunity for him to soak up some evening sunshine and plan his next career move.

While the *Wanted* album sold reasonably well and reached Number 11 in the album charts, neither of the singles released from it performed outstandingly, both failing to break into the Top 10. Taking away 'Millennium Prayer', this meant that Cliff had only had one Top 10 single since 1993, the longest spell of his career without such a high-placed hit. For someone so career-minded and commercially and chart statistics-obsessed as Cliff, desperate to have a Number 1 single in the 2000s to secure a longevity unreachable by others, this mattered.

'Cliff's different from everybody else,' suggests producer

Pete Waterman. 'I guess he's very competitive. He doesn't want to become Des O'Connor, he doesn't want to become the Morecambe and Wise joke. Cliff sees himself as competing in every market for everyday record sales. He doesn't want to be thought of as an ageing pop star. He wants to be treated as a pop star, but I think even he has to accept at sixty-three there's very few eighteen-year-old and seventeen-year-old kids that are going to go into Woolworths on Monday and buy Blue and Cliff Richard.'[378]

More successful, perhaps, was his side venture as a winemaker. Having emulated the likes of Sam Neill, Greg Norman and Francis Ford Coppola by going into the wine business, his first vintage of Vida Nova had sold out in Tesco within twenty-four hours.

I'm overwhelmed by the reaction, because, just like music, wine is so subjective. It's a thrill that people like my wine.[379]

While his wine business flourished, Cliff headed back into the recording studio to lay down tracks for what was becoming a staple of his calendar, the Christmas record. *Cliff at Christmas* saw the singer reunited with EMI and the album consisted of nine previously released songs plus eight new tracks, including one written by Chris Eaton, who had previously written 'Saviour's Day'. It was called 'Santa's List', which would be released as Cliff's quest to hit the Christmas Number 1 spot in 2003.

I found a song that's never been recorded before, so you won't have heard it until I release it as a single. Obviously, I like my singles, but only time will tell whether or not it'll be number one

at Christmas. It's impossible to tell these days. And if someone's
got a better record, I'll have to be number two.[380]

Bookmakers had Cliff at 33/1 to hit the top spot at Christmas in 2003, but the favourites were The Darkness at 5/1, who were riding the crest of a wave and had specifically recorded '(Christmas Time) Don't Let The Bells End', complete with a tongue-in-cheek video. As it turned out, both were pipped by outsiders Michael Andrews and Gary Jules with their cover of the Tears For Fears track 'Mad World'; Cliff's effort peaking at Number 5.

Having reunited with EMI for the *Cliff at Christmas* album, the singer promptly left the label (again) and jumped ship to Decca, who had originally turned Cliff down in 1958. 'We may not have signed him back in 1958,' said Decca president Costa Pilavachi, 'but it's never too late to correct a mistake – and we're very excited to welcome Cliff Richard to the Decca family in 2004, Decca's 75th year, with his exciting new album of great songs.'[381]

Recorded in Nashville and Miami with a selection of new and established writers, including Barry Gibb of the Bee Gees, *Somethin' Is Goin' On* was Cliff's first new album of original music for three years. The chance to work with Barry Gibb, who wrote two tracks as well as appearing on the album alongside his brother, Maurice, was a dream come true for Cliff.

My favourite band of all time were huge in the mid-seventies . . . I loved the Bee Gees! They had an amazing wealth of songs and their harmonies were impeccable. People talk about how the Beatles revolutionised pop and they did. But the Bee Gees were not far behind them, and in truth, many times were a step ahead. Working with Barry from the Bee Gees, my

all-time favourite band, bar none. My dream just kept finding
more and more ways to come true.[382]

Released in October 2004, the album received generally positive reviews with Dave Simpson of the *Guardian* commenting
that the sessions in Nashville have '. . . stirred life into the old
fella' and contains '. . . slick songs about love and loving Him
upstairs. Many of us will still prefer Marilyn Manson, but
Cliff's army of fans might find this his best work in years.'[383]
Selling 150,000 copies worldwide and reaching Number 7 in
the UK album charts, the record produced one Top 10 and one
Top 20 single despite getting hardly any radio airplay, an issue
that continued to rankle with Cliff and led him to proclaim that
he would not be recording any new music, blaming an unofficial
boycott by radio stations against his music.

> *I just don't have the time to waste making a record that no*
> *one will play. As a musician you make a record for the radio*
> *so that the public can hear it, but my songs don't get played.*
> *It's not that DJs don't like them, it's that the stations have a*
> *policy that says, 'We don't play him'. I will be playing concerts*
> *until the day I die because I love the atmosphere – but I'll never*
> *make another record.*[384]

The previous year, radio station Classic Gold had implemented
a No-Cliff policy claiming he 'doesn't match our brand values',[385]
which led to one of its presenters, veteran DJ Tony Blackburn,
being suspended after he rebelliously played three Cliff records on
consecutive days. 'I'm not a mad Cliff Richard fan, to be honest,'
said Blackburn. 'I thought it was stupid from our point of view
because, basically, he's got such a big fan base.'[386]

The resulting publicity led to a reversal of policy with the station's chief, John Baish, saying, 'We've been overwhelmed by the support for Cliff. We should be playing him as much as the Beatles, and we play the Beatles quite often.'[387]

Classic Gold's policy of refusing to play Cliff records was not isolated and it was an issue Cliff's management certainly knew of, despite it being unofficial. 'This is a problem we've been aware of for some time,' said Bill Latham, Cliff's manager at the time. 'Radio stations do seem to find it difficult to include him [Cliff] on their playlists.'[388]

While he might have threatened never to record again and while radio stations unofficially banned him from the airwaves, Cliff was embarking on a new crusade that would have far-reaching effects on the music industry as a whole and benefit every generation of past, present and future hit-makers.

Every three months from the beginning of 2008, I will lose a song.[389]

Under copyright law in the UK at the turn of the century, performers received royalties from record sales and radio airplay for fifty years after a song was released. The composers of that song, however, were entitled to the exclusive rights to their composition and appropriate royalty payments for their entire life and a period of a further seventy years after their death.

This meant that while composers and their families and heirs could benefit from their works for their lifetime and well after their death, potentially lucrative recordings that reached fifty years old could be exploited without recompense to the performers, once that aspect of copyright had ceased after fifty years.

So, songs such as Cliff's 'Move It' would be out of copyright in 2008, Elvis's 'That's All Right' in 2004, the same year as Bill Haley's 'Shake, Rattle and Roll', while the Beatles' entire catalogue would start to become freely available on 1 January 2013 with their debut single 'Love Me Do' and album *Please, Please Me*. All these records, and those reaching their fifty-year copyright expiry, could be re-released freely by any organisation – with the owners of the rights up to that point, including performers, totally powerless to stop this. Therefore they would receive none of the royalties from any subsequent reissue, while the artist themselves lost the right to earn any further income from the record unless they actually composed it.

While the British Phonographic Industry (BPI) was spearheading a campaign to extend the copyright law and lobbying the government over its concerns, it found an unlikely political ally in Cliff Richard who, given his longevity in the industry, was beginning to approach the cut-off point where the other songs he performed in the 1950s such as 'High Class Baby', 'Living Doll' and 'Travellin' Light' would also see their copyright expire in the first decade of the twenty-first century. Cliff was adamant that performers should be given the same rights as composers.

It seems to me we should ask for parity. It doesn't seem just. We are as important to a song as the writer is, because we give it life.[390]

Despite Cliff's lobbying, however, an independent report led by former *Financial Times* editor Andrew Gowers ignored the music industry's pleas to extend the copyright length from fifty to ninety-five years. For some, Cliff's position as the spokesperson for the push to increase copyright length was seen as part of the reason why their calls were not heeded.

'He [Cliff] became the voice of the campaign. To some extent the industry was foolish for not preparing the case with somebody else, who needs the money more, but is going to be hit by exactly the same rules,' said Keith Harris, former manager of Stevie Wonder before becoming Director of Performer Affairs at collection society PPL, the UK's licensing company for over 140,000 performers. 'One example I'd like people to think about is that Cliff in his early years used an orchestra called the Norrie Paramor Strings. They did all the EMI stuff from the late fifties to the early sixties. Now these session players could use the money as well. What financial position are they in?'[391] Andrew Brown, writing in the *Guardian*, commented: 'It's not a coincidence that the most prominent campaigner for copyright extension in this country is Cliff Richard. He is the only British singer of the 1950s whose records still sell in significant quantities. How has he suddenly become a socialist cause?' Undeterred, Cliff continued the fight, speaking to European politicians in Brussels and joining 4,000 other performers, among them Paul McCartney, U2 and Peter Gabriel, in a full-page advertisement in the *Financial Times* calling for a copyright extension from fifty years to ninety-five years.

British Prime Minister Tony Blair appeared to pick up the baton on Cliff's behalf, according to a written record of an internal Labour meeting which saw the Prime Minister set out his 2006 priorities: 'At the meeting of the national executive committee on July 19 last year Blair said that, despite the "dominating global headlines" and recent terror attacks, Labour must not lose sight of the domestic agenda . . . Blair "addressed concerns" about copyright laws "whereby Cliff Richard and the Rolling Stones only receive fifty years' protection compared with seventy years in the rest of Europe.'"[392]

Revelations that Blair had suddenly taken up the singer's cause raised eyebrows when it emerged that Blair and his family had been holidaying at Cliff's Barbados villa for the past three years, suggesting a significant conflict of interest and, perhaps, a breaching of ministerial rules, which clearly state that 'no minister should accept gifts, hospitality or services from anyone which would, or might appear to, place him or her under an obligation.'

Examination of the Register of Members' Interests show that in August 2005 alone the Blairs spent twenty-six nights at Cliff's Barbados villa free of charge, although they said they gave a donation to charity in lieu of rent, but declined to say how much or to which charity it went to.[393]

While there is nothing to suggest Blair broke any rules, other politicians expressed their feelings about his visit to Cliff's Barbados villa with the Conservative Shadow Culture Secretary at the time, Hugo Swire, saying, 'We're glad the PM is supportive of our calls for an extension of copyright laws, yet this is another example of a conflict of interests.' While the Liberal Democrat MP Norman Baker said, 'The Prime Minister has crippled himself by accepting hospitality from someone with a vested interest in Government policy.' Two Labour ministers, who were present at the Labour meeting when Blair set out his 2006 priorities, were said to have expressed surprise that he seemed so well informed about the copyright issue.[394]

Cliff, one of the first artists who would benefit from such a copyright law change if it came into practice, insists the offer to the Blairs to use his villa as a holiday retreat had nothing to do with his lobbying for copyright change.

How dare people suggest I asked him to help me or spoke to anyone else. My very raison d'être is not to do anything like that. I've always been careful not to talk to Tony about politics, because that would spoil things. He must have great difficulty, in the same way people like myself do, in finding friends who want you for yourself. So, I wanted Cherie and Tony to think, they're friends of ours, they never ask us for anything.[395]

Perhaps it's simply a coincidence that in May 2007, the Commons Culture, Media and Sport Committee threw their support behind the call to extend copyright by at least twenty more years and challenge Andrew Gowers' earlier report by saying: 'We strongly believe that copyright represents a moral right of a creator to choose to retain ownership and control of their own intellectual property. We have not heard a convincing reason why a composer and his or her heirs should benefit from a term of copyright which extends for lifetime and beyond, but a performer should not.'[396]

It would not be until 2011, following more concerted lobbying by Cliff and others, that the copyright law would eventually be changed. Becoming known as 'Cliff's Law', copyright on music recordings would be extended from fifty years to seventy years and applied specifically to the performers of the music. It was a significant victory for performers, and Cliff was as its heart.

Of course I'm pleased for myself, but the relief will be huge for those performers whose pension is largely made up of royalties from perhaps just two or three recordings in the fifties or sixties. Well done and thanks to the lawmakers for a good and just decision.[397]

There was a sting-in-the-tail for Cliff, though. The new copyright law decreed that it would only apply to recordings made after 1963 (thereby protecting the Beatles' catalogue), meaning Cliff would lose the royalties to his hits such as 'Living Doll', 'Please Don't Tease' and 'The Young Ones' from 2008 onwards.

I think it's wrong and unfair. But there's nothing I can do about it.[398]

CHAPTER 22

Despite his 2004 threat to stop recording any new music, Cliff just couldn't stay away from the studio and 2006 found him laying down tracks for a new album called *Two's Company (The Duets)*, which saw him collaborating with artists such as Dionne Warwick, Brian May, Daniel O'Donnell and Olivia Newton-John on reworkings of classic songs like 'Anyone Who Had a Heart' and 'Fields Of Gold'. The album broke into the Top 10 and Cliff's reworking of 'Move It', with Brian May of Queen, was released as part of a double-A sided single in December 2006 along with Cliff's attempt at another Christmas Number 1 song, '21st Century Christmas'.

If it topped the chart, it would mean that the singer would be the first ever artist to have a Number 1 in every decade since the 1950s. His official website urged fans to 'buy copies for family and friends – let's all do our best to help him achieve that "No 1 in the sixth decade!",' although in an interview with the *Daily Telegraph*, Cliff claimed not to be interested in hitting the top spot.

The truth is, I don't think about hits anymore. I just look for great songs and put them out there and see what happens. I wasn't specifically thinking of doing a Christmas song this year but when I heard '21st Century Christmas', I just couldn't resist it. I love the idea of satellites tracking Santa and texting him your Christmas list, but it returns to the essential message of Christmas when I sing 'We thank Bethlehem and bless the Lord for love again.' Fashions change, but Christmas will always be special. I love everything about Christmas, and that includes Christmas songs. I don't think you should ever have to be embarrassed about your faith.[399]

In the same interview, writer Neil McCormick is quick to jump to Cliff's defence: 'There is a bah-humbug aspect people have towards Christmas records and Cliff has become very identified with that. I would say "Oh yes, let's have Cliff." He's our original rock 'n' roll star and he's still doing it and he has as much right to have a hit record as anybody else and he's slightly better tuned into what makes a hit. He's also one of the most overtly Christian artists and the Christmas slot is the place where Christianity and popular music come together with no embarrassment whatsoever, so it's the natural place for him.'[400]

Hopes of the top spot at Christmas were high as '21st Century Christmas' entered the charts at Number 2 on 17 December, but were dashed almost immediately when the *X Factor* winner Leona Lewis released her debut single, 'A Moment Like This', a week before Christmas. Lewis's single became a Christmas juggernaut, selling over half a million copies in its first week to secure the top spot over Christmas, Cliff's single having dropped down to Number 7. By the following week it had exited the Top 40 altogether.

Disappointment at not securing another Christmas Number 1 aside, Cliff hit the road again in 2007 resuming his *Here & Now Tour* in South-East Asia, South Africa, the United Arab Emirates, Europe and Iceland, highlighting his popularity outside of the UK. Despite being sixty-six years old, the concerts would often see him performing up to thirty songs as he showed few signs of slowing down, let alone retiring.

People often say: 'When will you retire?' but retirement is a dead end. I still feel I have something to offer, but if I can slow down and not need to do as much, that would be great. The ageing process does not stop for anyone, so I'm going to pull back slowly. I'm only going to go to places that I like.[401]

Of course, the places Cliff liked more than anywhere else were his villa in Barbados, his vineyard in Portugal, and the Wimbledon tennis championships, and he spent much of 2007 dividing his time between the three following completion of his *Here & Now* tour. An additional attraction to time spent in Barbados was that he could also record songs for his upcoming record, *Love . . . The Album*, at Bluewave Studios, a state-of-the-art recording studio built and owned by Eddy Grant. It was in one of the most culturally important properties in Barbados; a historic plantation house built in 1719 with views across the south-east of the island, and site of an uprising by 400 slaves in 1816 that served as a milestone in the fight for emancipation. Released in November 2007, *Love . . . The Album* hoped to benefit from an experimental marketing initiative whereby the maximum cost of the album, £7.99, would drop to just £3.99 if enough fans ordered it prior to its download release. Having taken on copyright laws, Cliff now showed that, despite being a pensioner, he was not going to be sidelined by technology or modern commercial platforms. Instead, he embraced it.

We either keep one step ahead of the technology which is changing our industry so radically – or we throw up our hands and quit.[402]

It was an initiative that worked: in only half the time expected enough fans had ordered the album to slash the purchase price to £3.99. However, the cut-price offer didn't entice enough people to make the record a Top 10 hit and it became Cliff's lowest-placed studio album release since 1984's *The Rock Connection*.

But however much his career meant to him, the performance of his latest album wasn't foremost in his mind towards the end of 2007. Instead, he was mourning the passing of his mother, Dorothy, who died after a decade-long battle with dementia.

It was a merciful release, but it still hit me, hard – harder than I'd expected it to.[403]

Throughout his career, Cliff's mother had been totally supportive of everything he did. Right at the very beginning in 1958, she lent her seventeen-year-old son and his friends Ian Samwell and Terry Smart the £5 they needed (the equivalent to almost £125 at the time of writing) to record their first demo above the HMV store in London's Oxford Street. It was a show of faith that bore fruit and led to one of the longest and most successful careers in British showbusiness. But her cruel disease had robbed Dorothy of the last decade of her life, and in a frank interview in 2006, Cliff revealed his heartbreak over his mother's illness.

My mother knows nothing about political uproars, about terrorists, she does not know what time it is, does not know what month it is, or how bad the weather is outside. She is living, but what it does take away is your life. My mother does not have a life. I have talked with my sisters and said I personally felt as though I have already mourned my mum, because the person we have with us is not the vibrant woman we all knew.[404]

After a Christmas in New York – he had no Christmas single to promote in 2007 – Cliff retreated to Barbados to grieve privately. It looked like his only opportunity, as 2008 would be his fiftieth year in showbusiness and, surely, there would be celebrations. As it happened, his fiftieth anniversary year proved to be a relatively low-key affair. It began away from the bright lights with Cliff focusing on Tearfund projects in South America, before joining Olivia Newton-John in China on her charity walk along the Great Wall to raise funds for her cancer hospital in Australia, which was followed by a summer at his Portuguese villa.

Later in the year he visited the UK to attend a gala lunch in his honour courtesy of the Variety Club and the EMI launch of *The 50th Anniversary Album*, a double album of forty-nine of Cliff's hits plus a new single, 'Thank You For a Lifetime', a tribute to his fans.

I think fans will receive it well, because it's really a song for them. It's really me saying – as the title suggests – thank you for a lifetime.[405]

As 2008 drew to a close, Cliff's mind was turning to another looming anniversary in 2009; the fiftieth anniversary of Cliff

Richard and The Shadows. They had officially broken up in 1968 and while there had been a few sporadic performances together in the years since, there had never been a full concert tour. A 'Final Reunion' arena tour (later renamed *The Reunited Tour*) was announced and Cliff and the band moved to a remote location near Killarney in south-west Ireland to rehearse for the upcoming shows.

In December 2008, as a 'taster' for their forthcoming tour, Cliff and The Shadows performed at the London Palladium in that year's Royal Variety Show, playing three songs, 'The Young Ones', 'Willie and the Hand Jive' and 'Move It'. It was the first time they'd performed together in almost twenty years.

> *They are sounding great. That sound will envelop people and I firmly believe they are so much better than they were. They were never bad, it's just that we were nineteen years old when we started, well, I was seventeen when I recorded and they were sixteen, so in those early years when they were recording they were barely twenty . . . we have grown in our own art forms and so therefore what we're presenting, I think, is much, much better than it was.*[406]

The *Reunited Tour* stretched into 2009, eventually playing thirty-six dates across three continents, and, as far as Cliff was concerned, it was a fantastic experience. However, one person missing from the lucrative tour was original bassist Jet Harris, who quit the band in 1962 and whose wife, Carol Costa, had had an alleged fling with Cliff behind his back. Harris's place in the band was taken by Mark Griffiths.

Commenting at the time from his home on the Isle of Wight, Harris suggested the tour organisers were acting as though he were dead. 'I'm not. I'm alive and well,' he said. 'Surely it's obvious that I should be there as one of the original members of The Shadows. This is supposed to be a bit of history. I even named the band. They will surely be playing the early songs which I put my stamp on. I think a lot of fans will frown at this. I could have done a cameo at least. But no one has called to explain why.'[407]

Cliff remained tight-lipped as to why Harris was excluded from the tour, with Bill Latham commenting on his behalf: 'There is no reason other than the fact that Jet left the group in the early days. He was one of the originals, but the line-up has changed a lot since then. Mark Griffiths has played with The Shadows many times.'[408]

A fiftieth anniversary album, *Reunited*, was recorded, featuring new recordings of all their hits and three additional songs they'd never laid down, although none of those performing ever spent time in the studio together. Cliff recorded his vocals in Miami, Hank Marvin recorded his guitar parts in Australia, and Bruce Welch and Brian Bennett recorded their contributions in London. It became Cliff's first Top 5 studio album in sixteen years, while The Shadows hadn't released an original album since 1990. The only single released from the album was 'Singin' the Blues'. It reached Number 40 in the UK and would prove to be the last time Cliff troubled the singles charts until 2018.

Despite the success of the tour and the album, it seemed that this was the end of the road for the collaboration, as Hank Marvin alluded to when asked the question whether it would be the last time they'd perform together. 'Well, I reckon it probably will be,' said Marvin. 'Notice the word "probably" crept into that. Listen, a tour of this size, it is a big tour, it's going to take us about four months. We can't really do anymore, this is for most of us the ultimate, the fiftieth anniversary reunion.'[409]

With any future tours or recordings with The Shadows seemingly remote in light of Marvin's comments, Cliff threw himself into his own recordings. In 2010, as he approached his seventieth birthday, he recorded an album of standards from the Great American Songbook, titled *Bold As Brass*. It was a recording strategy somewhat in vogue at the time; Rod Stewart had wrapped his sandpaper vocals around the Great American Songbook standards of Hoagy Carmichael, Cole Porter and George Gershwin for four multi-million selling albums in the first decade of the twenty-first century. Robbie Williams had already jumped on the bandwagon with *Swing When You're Winning*, which sold over two million copies in the UK despite mixed reviews. Cliff's album didn't achieve anything like the success of Stewart or Williams, but it did continue to demonstrate his love of American music and how it has influenced his career, whether it be the rock 'n' roll of Elvis or the melodies of Cole Porter. That influence was to help shape his next album *Soulicious*, which saw Cliff travelling to Memphis to work with American songwriting and producing legend Lamont Dozier, and duet with artists such as Roberta Flack, Candi Staton and Percy Sledge.

The idea really came from a guy called David Gest . . . [who] said, 'I've got this idea about you doing some soul music and maybe singing with some soul singers, make it a duet album,' and I thought, yes, please, I'd love this, and without David I couldn't really have done it. I didn't know Freda Payne, I didn't know Peabo Bryson or Roberta Flack and all these people that I sang with, the Temptations, the Stylistics, Candi Staton,

Brenda Holloway, Deniece Williams, I mean . . . it was an
absolute treat to find my dreams come true and to sing with
people like that.[410]

Released in October 2011, the album, Cliff's first of primarily new
songs since 2004, became a Top 10 hit and garnered reasonable
reviews, with Terry Staunton in *Record Collector* writing, 'Brace
yourselves, cynics, some of this is actually very good.'[411] A short
eight-date UK tour to promote the album followed, featuring
guest artists who had appeared on the album such as Percy
Sledge, Freda Payne and Jaki Graham. They would each come
out to perform a duet with Cliff and then sing a couple of their
own hits while Cliff went backstage to change costumes in a
revue-style format.

The crowds lapped it up, but a review in the *Guardian* of
the O2 shows in London leaves the reader in no doubt who
was the real star of the show: 'There were moments when the
guests had clearly misjudged the audience. Little wonder the
crowd tittered with embarrassment when James Ingram flung
himself to the floor and began dry humping the stage. But
there were moments of greatness, and they came when Cliff
left the guests behind and concentrated on the string of late
70s and early 80s MOR hits that posited him as a wholesome
answer to Fleetwood Mac: "Devil Woman", "We Don't Talk
Anymore"and "Carrie" sounded wonderful – clever and sparky
and so unlike the crooning of "The Young Ones", it's hard to
believe they are sung by the same man.'[412]

Cliff's next record, *The Fabulous Rock 'n' Roll Songbook*, recorded
in Nashville, wouldn't be released until November 2013. Until
then he kept himself busy with TV appearances, charity concerts,
carrying the Olympic Torch in Birmingham, performing at

the Diamond Jubilee Concert outside Buckingham Palace, and touring Australia and New Zealand with his *Still Reelin' and A-Rockin' Tour*.

Things were looking good for a man now firmly established as a national treasure and in the twilight of his career.

For some he remained an object of ridicule, someone to be lampooned. Did Cliff worry? Probably not: he knew his standing, he had developed a thick skin, and he knew he could count on *his* fans. After all, everything he had achieved in his career spoke for itself.

And surprises – and surprising fans – kept on appearing, none more so, perhaps, than former Smiths' frontman, Morrissey, who asked Cliff to open for him at his forthcoming Barclay Centre concert in New York. Initially, Cliff was wary, thinking it was some form of a prank.

> *About a month ago my manager rang me and said: 'I'm going to throw a curveball at you. Morrissey wants you in New York with him.' I said, 'My initial answer is yes, but can you check it's not a joke? Is there an ulterior motive?' He got hold of Morrissey's management and he said: 'No, Morrissey's a fan and he'd like you to be there.' So I said, 'Yes, please.' The chances of me singing for 15,000 people in New York are pretty well nil for me at the moment anyway. So I thought it would be great.*[413]

While Cliff would be the support act in New York, Tom Jones would perform the role in Los Angeles. When asked why he had chosen these 'veteran frontmen', Morrissey replied, 'Veteran is a gentle way of saying "old", isn't it? Well, it's only my view of course, but everything is a question of style, and Tom and Cliff qualify greatly in the style department, and age has nothing to do with it. There are millions of obese nineteen-year-olds who only buy clothes that blend in with the couch.[414]

Sadly, the much-anticipated concert never took place. Following a number of dates across North America Morrissey cancelled the tour before it reached New York, blaming a respiratory infection and acute fever. It was a great disappointment to Cliff, who was desperately looking forward to the show and the opportunity to play to thousands in the USA. He was also aware that a number of his own fans had bought tickets to the Morrissey show as well as booked flights and hotels so, ever the consummate professional and keen to ensure his fans didn't lose out, Cliff organised an alternative gig at the smaller Gramercy Theatre in Manhattan, where he would play an intimate show and hold a Q&A session.

> *I know that many fans were disappointed about the Morrissey concert being cancelled and I was disappointed as well. I've decided I'm going to go anyway to New York and I'm going to put on an evening. While it won't be the show I had planned to do with Morrissey, it will be a really nice, intimate evening with my fans and I'm looking forward to seeing everyone there.*[415]

The show, packed with hits from his career as well as some cover versions and performed with just a programmer and one backing singer was, as one reviewer noted, a masterclass in how to put a setlist together: 'There isn't a musician who couldn't learn how to put together a set list from this show. Early hits followed by later period hits, followed by newbies astutely placed among favourites, followed by an acoustic set followed by two of his biggest hits. Sure, it was Cliff's audience to lose but, still, that's the way it is done. Nothing is taken for granted.'[416]

Cliff was in high spirits as he headed back to Portugal via Wimbledon. He was looking forward to a relaxing summer in the Portuguese sun, drinking wine from his neighbouring vineyard and planning the next stage of his career. There was a new album to record in Nashville, an autobiography to write, tours to schedule.

In the summer of 2014, the future looked so bright.

Then it turned to darkness.

CHAPTER 23

It was 2015 and South Yorkshire Police had exposed the fact that Cliff was now facing more than one allegation. In fact, by April 2015 it emerged that a total of nine individuals had come forward to allege they had been molested or abused by Cliff in the past. And in one of these allegations, the past stretched way back to a supposed incident in Coventry in 1958, when Cliff himself was just seventeen.

Details of these allegations had been forwarded to Cliff's legal team and, at once, it was plainly obvious to them that the allegations were ludicrous. Yet the public weren't privy to this information, and all they knew was that Cliff was now under investigation for further allegations.

However, Cliff's fans stood by him regardless of what was being said, printed or broadcast. For many, they had already bought tickets for a series of concerts around the UK that had been planned for the autumn of 2015 to celebrate Cliff's seventy-fifth birthday. The tour would culminate in five shows at the Royal Albert Hall, including one on his actual seventy-fifth birthday, 14 October 2015.

But with the allegations hanging over him, no matter how much *he* knew they were untrue, Cliff was in a quandary: could he really undertake a tour, which was ultimately a celebration, in the current climate? A consummate professional, he wanted to give the fans his best – he always felt they deserved that – but would this be possible in the circumstances? Regardless of his physical fitness, he was mentally and emotionally drained, the trauma of the last few months having taken a huge toll on his wellbeing. Perhaps it was too much to ask. He suggested to the promoter that the tour be cancelled, but was told in response that the tour was virtually sold out and that there had been no noticeable returns since the allegations broke.

It seemed there were a lot of people out there who had kept their faith in me and who didn't believe a word of the innuendo and the rumours in the media. I've always loved my fans, but I don't think my love has ever been stronger than in that moment.[417]

Cliff decided the tour should go ahead and he returned to Killarney in south-west Ireland to rehearse with his band.

While his fans had proven their continued support for him, Cliff could also rely on those close friends who were standing by him. One of the most loyal was author and broadcaster Paul Gambaccini, who spoke to BBC Radio 5 Live shortly before Cliff's tour about their friendship and how he was convinced Cliff was innocent of all the allegations. 'He's keeping his wits,' Gambaccini said, 'and he knows of the love and support he's getting from the British public. We are in contact, and I'm glad to be able to be of support to him. If Cliff Richard is ever convicted of any criminal offence, I will eat mine, Paddy Ashdown and Alastair Campbell's hats.'[418]

Perhaps more than anyone, Gambaccini could relate to the situation Cliff found himself in. At 4.38 a.m. on 29 October 2013, Gambaccini was woken by a ring on his doorbell. Answering it, the man standing in front of him said, 'You are under arrest for blah, blah, blah, blah – and buggery.'[419] Eight Metropolitan Police officers stormed his apartment and arrested him in connection with allegations of historic sex abuse against two underage boys in the late 1970s and early 1980s. His possessions, including computers, cameras, phones and diaries were taken away by the sack load, and he was unceremoniously hauled down to Charing Cross Police Station where he was held in a cell for two hours before being questioned.

Aleksandr Solzhenitsyn wrote of his own arrest: 'It's a blinding flash and a blow which shifts the present instantly into the past and the impossible into omnipotent actuality. That's all. And neither for the first hour nor for the first day will you be able to grasp anything else. Except that in your desperation the fake circus moon will blink at you: "It's a mistake! They'll set things right!"'[420] But, of course, they don't.

As Gambaccini says about himself in his book *Love, Paul Gambaccini: My Year Under The Yewtree*: 'I have considered a visit from Operation Yewtree likely ever since I read on the BBC website that the Metropolitan Police, having failed to stop the serial offender Jimmy Savile in his lifetime, set up a dedicated phoneline and website and encouraged members of the public to accuse celebrities for sexual offences.'[421]

The irony here being that Gambaccini was one of the first to speak out about Savile. 'All it would need was a couple of fragile individuals to take up the Met's invitation, add two and two and get five. For several months I have been plagued by periods of darkness.'[422]

He was aware of Scotland Yard fishing for accusers who would make accusations and allegations against celebrities in the public eye, citing BBC colleagues Sandi Toksvig and Liz Kershaw as examples of people contacted by the police to see if they would make accusations of sexual assault against people.

'It is a tactic of the police to call out and ask if people would like to make accusations. This was brought to my attention by Liz Kershaw of 6 Music, two weeks before I was arrested she told me that [Operation] Yewtree had called her and asked her if she would like to accuse Dave Lee Travis. And she said, "No, don't you need evidence?" and they said, "No, we need people who agree." That's the premise under this mutation of the British justice system which has occurred from the centuries old, internationally respected, objective, evidence-based system, into the subjective, rumour and accusation-based system, there can be no evidence, only people who agree, and hence Sandi was called up and asked if she wanted to accuse anybody.'[423]

Over the next year, the successful and busy career that Gambaccini had cultivated over decades ground to a halt; the numerous good causes that took his money in happier times dropped him; friends – or those he thought were friends – shunned him and during the investigation he lost £200,000 in legal fees and lost earnings.[424]

His bail was renewed six times as the police and Crown Prosecution Service dithered and blundered over what course of action to take. Scotland Yard sent officers thousands of miles around the world at great expense to question those that knew Gambaccini, before it emerged that his two accusers were fantasists. According to his solicitor, Kate Goold, the police themselves seemed to have little belief in the allegations: 'Once Paul's case was dropped, we found out through a witness the police had spoken to that a couple of months after his arrest, the police felt there was a five per cent chance of a conviction. Yet, Paul was kept on bail for almost an entire year, unable to work.'[425]

Throughout the entire year he was under investigation Gambaccini's name was in the papers, great for press circulation, horrific for Gambaccini. Meanwhile his accusers remained anonymous – and continue to do so. And the more Gambaccini's name was circulated publicly, the more chance another accuser would come forward. It was a tactic the police were depending on, the flypaper theory as Stephen Fry called it, or bandwagoning as we've referred to it earlier. It was a tactic used – whether wittingly or unwittingly – by South Yorkshire Police when they released information to the BBC regarding the raid on Cliff Richard's Berkshire property. In doing so, South Yorkshire Police had played a part in the singer's name coming into the public domain hoping, much as the Metropolitan Police had done with Paul Gambaccini, that other accusers would come forward.

However, in Gambaccini's case it didn't work. So, the Met had to use a different approach. 'An allegation was made by one person [against Gambaccini] on 4 April 2013,' recalled Gambaccini. 'His case was investigated by many officers, because we have seen the names of the people who have signed in and out on this. They dropped the case in September and that was, of course, five months later. Then seven weeks later I am arrested and in between they had asked my accuser, "Is there anyone who can corroborate your story", and he said, "Well, go to my mate from the late 1970s", and they did. The police told me that this person accused me.' Gambaccini was later told through an intermediary that he [the 'mate from the late 1970s'] did not accuse Gambaccini and on the police log it never even says he was interviewed.

As far as the public was concerned, the police were giving the impression that by arresting high-profile celebrities they were cracking down on cases of historic sexual abuse. The truth was very different and they were simply using the bandwagoning technique to compensate for their own shortcomings in past investigations relating to sexual abuse. Those caught up in these travesties of injustice, accused by the fantasists, the delusional and the attention-seekers, were no more than collateral damage as far as the police were concerned. Gambaccini later said: 'I spoke with [a] person who was familiar with the case and he told me a couple of things about my accuser and his mate that made me realise, oh, okay, I get it now. It turns out that these two people had lived within walking distance of my flat in the late 1970s, so they knew the building in which the Radio 1 DJ lived. I was also told that my accuser had been expelled from school for making a false sexual allegation and, now that the police were asking people to accuse celebrities of sex crimes, he had returned to that kind of behaviour.'

He continued, 'Unfortunately, when money and attention are on offer, human nature is such that some people will respond to the offer of money and attention. So, we now have this unholy mix of the genuine victims who have needed and not received attention for many years and this other group, admittedly smaller, of persons who are falsely accused.'[426]

While current law states that lifelong anonymity must be bestowed on the victims and alleged victims of the majority of sexual offences, including rape, there is no such clause for defendants. Should defendants be granted anonymity between accusation and charge? There are calls for reform of the law: the trauma Gambaccini went through would later lead him to lobby for sexual abuse suspects to be granted anonymity until charged, unless there were exceptional circumstances.

But such calls polarise opinion, with opponents suggesting publicising the identities of defendants *encourages* other victims to come forward, for example in the cases of Stuart Hall and Rolf Harris. While those in favour of anonymity for the defendants question whether it is right that for the sake of mere suspicion, details of individuals' private lives are held up and subjected to public scrutiny for the possibility of attracting other accusers.

False allegations often, though not always, come from young, vulnerable people. Gambaccini's accuser certainly met that profile: 'I know his name,' Gambaccini said. 'I know where his mate lives, as the famous saying goes, but I am not going to show up because I know that my accuser's mate suffered incalculable personal tragedy and I think is a distressed individual.'

Gambaccini was cleared of any allegations of historic sexual abuse in 2014 and was awarded a five-figure settlement, way below the costs he had incurred and income he had lost during the battle to prove his innocence. Reacting to the verdict and the trauma he went through Gambaccini didn't hold back: 'I thought I must take action, because no one can acquiesce in his own attempted annihilation. The Metropolitan Police and [Commissioner] Bernard Hogan-Howe attempted to destroy my life and end my career for public relations purposes, in a 100 per cent fraud that was aided and abetted and encouraged by the Metropolitan Police. I can honestly say they are the most dishonest organisation I have ever encountered.'[427]

It wasn't so different for Cliff. Except he hadn't been arrested and charged.

'Two weeks shy of 75, Richard resembled a freeze-dried version of the pop icon who has strutted across the stage of British music for the past six decades. His skin had the aspect of bendable plastic and he appeared reluctant to make eye-contact with the uber-Cliff fans pressing close. He was here to perform, not to strike up new friendships.'[428]

It was September 2015 and Cliff was performing on the opening night of his *75th Birthday Tour*. After a period of rehearsals in Killarney, Ireland, Cliff kicked off the tour with a warm-up gig in the small town's three-thousand-seat theatre before heading out across the UK. Despite six decades of performing, stepping out on stage again was a fraught moment for the singer, being the first time he had performed in public since the sex abuse allegations had been aired. A media storm had followed and the police investigation was ongoing.

Nobody, least of all Cliff, knew what the crowd's reaction might be.

Would people not turn up? Would they boo? I was still getting very little sleep and I felt horribly, sickeningly nervous.[429]

He needn't have worried, the crowd on that first night – as they were throughout the tour – were adoring; at once revelling in his music while also appearing to send a wave of communal support, an energy that seemed to envelop the room and find its way on stage to reassure then reenergise the performer. One reviewer wrote: 'His voice was as tremulous as ever as he put it to effective use unloading endless payloads of pop perkiness. Time capsules from a more innocent age, "Summer Holiday" and "The Young Ones" read like chaste Valentine cards and a tilt at Jerry Lee Lewis's "Great Balls of Fire" conveyed much of the punch and swagger of the original.'[430]

Less than a week later, on the opening night of the UK tour

proper in Birmingham, Cliff received a standing ovation before he had even sung a note. It was repeated throughout the entire tour. For all the trials and tribulations he had faced in the past year, his adoring fans had stood by him.

In tribute to them Cliff performed 'Golden', a single written by Chris Eaton and dedicated to those fans who had supported him. It was a new song included on Cliff's triple album *75 at 75*, which was released to accompany the tour and celebrate the singer's seventy-fifth birthday. It reached Number 4 in the album charts; only one of his albums in the past eleven years had gone higher, proving that whatever allegations were facing him, as far as his fans and record sales were concerned, he still had selling power.

More good news emerged for Cliff in September 2015 with reports that the police investigation was floundering, amid claims that one of accusers had already been dismissed with detectives unable to find any evidence to corroborate the claim. It didn't totally exonerate Cliff, there were still other accusers' claims that the police were investigating, but it gave him hope, a beacon in the dark.

It didn't last long, however.

CHAPTER 24

In October 2015 it came to light that the police investigating the sex abuse claims against Cliff were poised to hand files of evidence to the Crown Prosecution Service (CPS) 'within the next two weeks'.[431] Based on this evidence, the CPS would then decide whether he should be formally charged. All doubts and worries resurfaced for Cliff; despite the fact he knew every allegation was false.

To make matters worse, no sooner had the dust settled on Cliff's *75th Birthday Tour*, than on 1 November 2015, with no sign of any evidence being handed over to the CPS, Cliff was summoned to a second interview by South Yorkshire Police. It had been well over a year since his initial interview, under caution, yet now Cliff found himself heading to the same training centre, accompanied by Malcolm Smith and his two lawyers, to be interviewed by the same officer whom he had met the first time.

At the second interview, which was about the other handful of accusations, there was a time when I had to say to them,

*'Stop referring to these people as victims. They're not victims, I'm
the one who is being victimised here.' I said, 'I don't understand
how you can possibly do this on the strength of this guy* [the
accuser].*' He* [the interviewing officer] *actually said, 'If you'd
met him, you'd understand.' And I thought, no I wouldn't, I
wouldn't understand.*[432]

In spite of co-operating at all times and calmly and confidently
giving his answers, eager to get the interview over and done
with, Cliff and his team were shocked when another policeman
entered the room and announced they would have to call a halt
to the proceedings, meaning they'd all have to return to continue
the next day.

*I found that really strange and it was just typical of the way
South Yorkshire Police seemed to like to work. It was a disgusting
thing. They don't seem to have any concern for us as human
beings. Where are the good old days where you could stop a
policeman? My mum and dad used to say, 'Ask a policeman.'
Well, would I now? No, I would not.*[433]

As after the first interview, Cliff's team put out a statement:
'Sir Cliff Richard voluntarily met with and was interviewed by
members of South Yorkshire Police. He was not arrested or
charged, nor has he ever been. He cooperated fully with officers
and answered the questions put to him. Other than restating that
the allegations are completely false and that he will continue to
cooperate fully with the police, it would not be appropriate for
Sir Cliff to say anything further at this time.'

Although not admitting publicly, Cliff and his team were
encouraged by the direction of the second police interview.

The singer had left the interview having not been charged or arrested, and chinks were beginning to emerge in the stories of the initial accuser.

> *The accuser got everything wrong. He got the year wrong* [the accuser claimed it happened in 1983]. *That* [Billy Graham] *rally wasn't until 1985. It* [the attack] *was supposed to have happened in a room that hadn't even been built then.*[434]

Cliff dared to hope that it would soon all be over. The initial accuser's allegations had been found to be seriously flawed. They appeared the work of a fantasist but the police, for whatever reason, had seemed to believe them, even when security officers from the event in question contacted lawyers independently in support of Cliff. They wanted to make a statement, saying they were at the rally, on duty, and that they didn't think the alleged sexual abuse was possible.[435] They were ignored by South Yorkshire Police.

The stress Cliff was under was intolerable. He knew he was innocent, those close to him knew he was innocent, but the police kept pursuing their investigations. It had been going on for well over a year now and it was beginning to take its toll. Cliff was seventy-five years old and had kept himself in good shape, but what he was going through now put an incredible strain on the singer's health, both mentally and physically.

There had already been warning signs following the initial raid, when Cliff found himself unable to lift his arm simply to play tennis. He thought he was going to die, but his coach reassured him by telling him, 'Your brain is just not working right and it's affecting your body.'[436] But following the second interview, Cliff had another terrifying health episode.

I'd bid for, and won, a week at a chateau in France at a charity auction and I went there with some friends, including Gloria Hunniford. On the first day I fell on some stone steps. My teeth went through my lower lip. I had to have eight stitches at the front, twelve on the inside . . . I think it was to do with the stress, I don't think I would fall over normally. After this I got shingles, too. I remember my doctor saying, 'Stress is a major factor.'[437]

As Cliff recuperated, the initial accusation against him appeared to be withering. However, there were still another eight outstanding allegations from other individuals who had come forward to allege they had been molested or abused by Cliff in the past. And in one of these allegations, the past stretched back to a supposed incident in Coventry in 1958. Details had been forwarded to Cliff's legal team and, at once, it was plainly obvious to them that the allegations were nonsense.

To prove the point, another of the accusations stemmed from 1981 and a seemingly innocuous video shoot in Buckinghamshire.

Penned by B.A. Robertson and Alan Tarney and released in August 1981, 'Wired For Sound' was an ode to the recently launched Sony Walkman and became a massive hit for Cliff across the UK, Europe, South Africa and Australia. The single was accompanied by a video that epitomised the early 1980s: Cliff, plugged into a Walkman, and a troupe of dancers, looking like they'd just stepped out of a Jane Fonda fitness video, roller-skating nonchalantly around the recently opened Central Milton Keynes Shopping Centre, weaving in and out of concrete structures against a backdrop of tropical plants and tiled walls.

The song reached Number 4 in the UK charts, the video

being a constant feature on BBCs *Top of the Pops* during the summer of 1981.

> *I spent a few hours skating around a plaza and, when it started raining, an indoor car park. We had a fabulous time – it was so enjoyable. I had no way of knowing this day would come back to haunt me, in a terrible way, more than thirty years later.*[438]

In 2015, thirty-four years after the 'Wired For Sound' video was filmed, an allegation was made that Cliff had sexually assaulted a man during the making of the video. The man, who was twenty-one years old at the time the alleged incident took place, claimed that he was working in one of the shops in Central Milton Keynes Shopping Centre on the day of filming when Cliff roller-skated alone into the store, sexually assaulted him, and roller-skated back out. That wasn't the end of it. Two hours later, he claimed, Cliff skated back in and assaulted him once more.

> *Have you ever heard anything so ridiculous? We fell about with laughter when we heard that. Surely if it were true, he would only have had to push me in the chest and I would have fallen over?*[439]

The allegations were ridiculous and absurd, the accuser 'clearly a fantasist'[440] according to Cliff's close friend Gloria Hunniford. It was later revealed the accuser had become a 'religious minister' since the alleged assault.[441] Despite the ludicrous nature of this allegation, it has never been disclosed if a file on this claim was or wasn't sent to the CPS by the police.[442]

If only the public knew how crazy these allegations were! But they didn't. And I knew only too well what some people would still be thinking: Yep! No smoke without fire.[443]

The roller-skating allegation wasn't the only fantastical one to be aimed at the singer as an assortment of rapists, blackmailers, attention seekers and even a dodgy 'minister' lined up to accuse Cliff with allegations of sexual assault. None of which should have stood up to any form of serious investigation unless, of course, they were made to a police force with an already bankrupt reputation ready to listen to anything.

One accuser, a man in his forties and said to have had mental health problems, contacted Cliff's PR team after watching the BBC footage of the raid on his Berkshire apartment and threatened to spread false allegations about the singer unless he was paid a sum of money. The man was subsequently arrested by police on suspicion of blackmail, told not to contact Cliff's team again and the blackmail charge dropped. This only led the man to go to South Yorkshire Police and make sexual abuse allegations against the singer again. South Yorkshire Police reportedly added them to their file being prepared for the CPS.[444]

It later came to light that another one of Cliff's alleged victims was himself one of Britain's most notorious sex offenders, who was serving several life sentences for a series of rapes and sex attacks. A paranoid schizophrenic with his identity protected by the Sexual Offences Act, although referred to as 'David' in media reports, he can never be formally named, but he had made a number of baseless and deeply damaging accusations against Cliff from the psychiatric hospital where he was detained,[445] including that the singer sexually abused him in 1982 and blamed the singer for turning him into a rapist.[446]

He told a national newspaper that he was interviewed around thirty times by the South Yorkshire and Metropolitan Police Forces concerning the Cliff Richard allegations[447] and claimed that Cliff had abused him in a room at the Elm Guest House in Barnes in front of other people.[448]

'David' had already been interviewed extensively by Detective Chief Inspector Paul Settle and his team from the Metropolitan Police. They had found 'David', who had learning difficulties and had been in care, to be a suggestible, vulnerable fantasist and, needless to say, all of his claims had no truth in them whatsoever.[449]

However, almost inexplicably, South Yorkshire Police seemed to take 'David' seriously even though the Met had decided he was not a reliable witness and the detectives from South Yorkshire Police investigating the Cliff Richard allegations seemed to treat 'David' as a victim.[450] Somewhat incredibly, Detective Chief Inspector Paul Settle's conclusion that 'David' was not a reliable witness was apparently not passed on to South Yorkshire Police.[451]

None of this was made public at the time, leaving Cliff hung out like live bait.

New Year's Eve, 2015. Another New Year under the dark shadow of allegations. It was difficult for Cliff to celebrate the end of one year, the beginning of another. Who knew what 2016 would bring?

Cliff spent New Year's Eve in Florida, and then travelled home for rest and relaxation in Barbados, which was only broken by a short trip with friends to Oman in March, before he returned to Barbados for some more winter sun.

Meanwhile, back in the gloomy depths of a British winter, the police were continuing to trawl through Cliff's past, searching for something – anything – that would enable them to prosecute the singer. And all the while, despite the media circus, the hundreds of thousands of pounds being spent on the investigation, and the whirlwind of internet theories and social media salaciousness, Cliff heard nothing from any of the officers in charge. Not a word. All Cliff and his team knew was that the investigation could yet drag on from many more months, and they only knew *that* information from newspaper reports.

By Valentine's Day, it had been 549 days since Cliff's Berkshire apartment had been raided by South Yorkshire Police in the full glare of BBC cameras. As veteran crime commentator Nick Ross coolly pointed out, that's three times longer than it took to bring Hitler's gangsters to trial at Nuremberg after the Second World War.[452]

Matters were made worse a few weeks later when, in March 2016, BBC *News At Six* broadcast archive footage of Cliff with the disgraced presenter and disc jockey Jimmy Savile on *Top of the Pops*, during a report about the inquiry into Savile's catalogue of sexual abuse at the BBC. In the archive clip that was broadcast, the DJ can clearly be heard saying Cliff's name and it was aired just after the reporter told of the 'missed opportunities to stop' Savile. This news item, on a programme regularly reaching almost four million viewers, focused on Dame Janet Smith's review into the culture and practices of the BBC during the 'monstrous' campaign of sex abuse by Savile and fellow TV broadcaster Stuart Hall while they worked for the corporation.

But Cliff was never once named in Dame Janet's report. Why would it, her report had nothing to do with the singer. The broadcast brought a stinging rebuke from Cliff's lawyers, who wrote to the BBC claiming it was defamatory: 'The libel complaint says the inclusion of archive footage of Jimmy Savile stating the words "Cliff Richard" is defamatory of Sir Cliff Richard, causing the viewer to believe that there were missed opportunities at the BBC to apprehend Cliff Richard for wrongdoing.'[453]

They threatened legal action if the clip was used again and it was understood that bosses at the BBC subsequently warned staff to no longer use the film. But why use it in the first place? It was totally unnecessary and always potentially libellous. There were countless archive clips of Savile on *Top of the Pops* that could have been used instead. It's impossible to know, but could the clip have been purposefully used to besmirch Cliff by association? Certainly, one viewer on Twitter had suspicions: 'Subtle of the BBC to show a clip of Savile introducing Cliff Richard on *TOTP*,' they tweeted.[454]

There seemed no escape from the glare of publicity for Cliff.

On 1 May his name was in the newspapers again when Cliff's original accuser publicly claimed the police hadn't spoken to him for three months. The accuser, a man who claimed he had been abused as a teenager by the singer at Billy Graham's rally, said that the detectives' handling of the case had left him 'unwell'. The last time he heard the voice of his police liaison, he claimed, was back in January – despite earlier complaints of being neglected. He continued to say he had only found out about developments in the case by reading newspaper reports.[455]

Speaking through former detective Mark Williams-Thomas, who acted as his adviser and who had been contacted by the accuser in the wake of the Jimmy Savile exposé in 2012, he said: 'I'm very, very angry with the lack of communication from South Yorkshire Police. I haven't spoken to anyone, I just get texts saying, "I'm sorry, it's ongoing. I can't tell you anymore."'[456]

The man, who can never be named for legal reasons, had

been interviewed twice by police since making allegations against Cliff. His last interview was a year earlier. Mr Williams-Thomas was also critical at the time the investigation was taking. He said: 'Looking at it from the point of view of the alleged victim and the alleged offender, I cannot see the logic in why it has taken so long to be dealt with. Whilst that goes on, both sides sit in limbo. The alleged victim does not want to do anything that would interfere with any potential criminal case.'[457]

So, what was causing this extraordinary delay in handing a file to the Crown Prosecution Service? This was never made clear. The police refused to say. When the full repugnancy of Jimmy Savile's actions emerged and police began their investigation into so-called VIP child abuse, we were told their actions from that point forward would be 'proportionate and consistent'. Cliff's treatment at the hands of the police seemed anything but. 'Cliff is said by friends to be suffering huge emotional distress as matters drag interminably on,' wrote Richard Madeley. 'That's not justice. That's dangerously close to something known as abuse of process. Abuse of process is not the same as malicious prosecution but part of its legal definition says: "Some act in the use of the legal process not proper in the regular prosecution of the proceedings." Unnecessary delay is not proper. Neither is a failure to provide some sort of account as to why it is taking so long. We employ the police, we pay their wages and we're paying for this inquiry too. Time for the cops to tell their bosses – that's you and me – what's causing this increasingly bizarre delay.'[458]

Finally, in May 2016, it was announced that detectives investigating the sex abuse claims against Cliff Richard had sent a 'full file' of evidence to the CPS. 'We have received a full file of evidence from South Yorkshire Police,' said a spokeswoman for the CPS. 'We will now carefully consider its contents in line with the Code for Crown Prosecutors, in order to establish whether there is sufficient evidence to provide a realistic prospect of conviction, and whether it is in the public interest to do so.'[459]

After two years of investigation, having exhausted all avenues and at great expense, South Yorkshire Police had whittled down the nine accusers to four that they believed the CPS might consider strong enough to prosecute.

A spokesman for Cliff said: 'It would be inappropriate to comment while the matter is under review.'[460]

For the singer D-Day was fast approaching.

CHAPTER 25

THE TOXIC LEGACY OF JIMMY SAVILE

To fully understand the ordeal that Cliff had been going through with South Yorkshire Police from the summer of 2014 onwards, we need to revisit the national hysteria that had enveloped Great Britain two years earlier following the revelations that were beginning to emerge and would eventually prove Jimmy Savile to be one of the most prolific and notorious paedophiles ever seen.

Savile had died in October 2011, the curtain finally closing on what most had seen as a triumphant career on radio and television and a lifetime of charity work that had raised over £30 million for good causes. Such was his reputation that he was knighted in 1990 after personal lobbying for the honour by none other than Margaret Thatcher and he was also given a papal knighthood the same year by Pope John Paul II. But throughout his life and career, there had been rumblings of a lurid, promiscuous and sordid lifestyle. Presenters and colleagues at the BBC had heard gossip and rumour about Savile for a number of decades. In 1980, journalist Roger Cook received an anonymous letter and telephone call alleging that Savile abused patients at Stoke Mandeville Hospital. DJ and TV presenter Nicky Campbell had also heard rumours that Savile was a necrophiliac, but considered them an urban myth, while during a conversation Sir Terry Wogan was asked by columnist Jean Rook, 'When are they going to expose him [Savile]?' Wogan is reported to have replied, 'That's your job.'[461]

It appears, despite all the gossip and rumours, nothing was acted upon during Savile's lifetime although a subsequent report by Her Majesty's Inspectorate of Constabulary set up after Savile's death, found that he could have been stopped as early as 1963, when a man from Cheshire was told to 'forget about it' and 'move on' by a police officer when he reported an allegation of rape by Savile. Another man, trying to report an assault his girlfriend had suffered at the hands of Savile during a *Top of the Pops* recording was told by police he 'could be arrested for making such allegations' and dismissed. The HMIC report investigated seven incidents – including five sexual assault complaints and two pieces of intelligence – and concluded that a failure to piece the dots together left police unable to stop Savile's reign of abuse over five decades.[462]

Upon his death Savile was venerated; obituaries praised him, the Prince of Wales led tributes, his gold coffin was visited by thousands of fans and mourners while displayed at the Queen's Hotel in Leeds, and his funeral took place at Leeds Cathedral before he was buried in Scarborough. Within a couple of months, the BBC had aired a show paying tribute to Savile, while also shutting down a BBC *Newsnight* investigation into historic allegations against him.

But the rumours wouldn't go away, and one man acting upon them was Mark Thomas-Williams, an ex-detective turned

TV journalist. Six months of intensive investigative work led to him and a TV producer uncovering a pattern of abuse that had Savile's fingerprints on them from the BBC to Broadmoor to Stoke Mandeville Hospital and Leeds General Infirmary. In doing so, Thomas-Williams identified five women who allowed their stories of abuse at the hands of Savile to be told. It culminated in the ITV documentary *Exposure: The Other Side of Jimmy Savile.*

It was preceded by a week of national headlines painting Savile as a paedophile and in the immediate aftermath of the documentary being broadcast at least eleven women came forward and the first of a number of other arrests, in this case Paul Gadd aka Gary Glitter, were made. Headlines surrounded the documentary and Savile dominated the national press for another forty days. As a result of the scandal, Operation Yewtree was launched.

Williams-Thomas suddenly found himself hot property, in demand with the media and with other investigations, as the true scale of Savile's crimes became apparent: a 2013 report by Scotland Yard in collaboration with the NSPCC found that Savile was a 'prolific predatory' sex offender with, at that point, 214 criminal offences across 28 police forces between 1955 and 2009.[463]

The scale of Savile's crimes shocked the nation and a moral panic engulfed society, Operation Yewtree giving rise to a sense of hysteria amongst the population where any ageing celebrity with even the faintest rumour of scandal in their past was fair game. The need to tackle historical sex abuse became paramount and police became determined they would pursue claims without fear or favour, no matter how powerful the suspects were.

Soon newspapers were full of speculation about 'who's next?', the wave of popular opinion being driven by a whirlwind of media frenzy. Dawn Neesom, formerly of the *Daily Star*, recalled playing 'paedo bingo on the news floor'. 'We were lapping it up,' she breezily confessed. 'It sold. That's why we kept doing it.'[464]

Before long the suspects were reeled in: Max Clifford, Rolf Harris, Dave Lee Travis, Chris Denning, all subsequently found guilty. But there were others, too, innocent others, victims of this new approach to justice – or injustice in their cases – which would ultimately ruin people's lives: Paul Gambaccini, Neil Fox, Freddie Starr, Jim Davidson and Jimmy Tarbuck, among others, were all arrested and subsequently not charged, their lives subsequently in financial, professional and personal ruin.

Just on these figures alone, Yewtree appears more miss than hit. However, Metropolitan Police Commissioner Sir Bernard Hogan-Howe dismissed claims that Yewtree was a witch-hunt against celebrities and sought to defend the operation: 'I don't think it's a witch-hunt at all, we're just going where the evidence takes us and victims are making allegations . . . Obviously, it's a serious issue for the suspect who's under investigation after that time, but we don't take these things on lightly, and we do try to keep it confidential. If you look at all the debate there's been about Jimmy Savile, for example, this man for thirty years appears to have attacked many victims and no one listened. Is it wrong to pursue it now?'[465]

The telling line in Hogan-Howe's comments is '. . . we're just going where the evidence takes us.' But all too often the evidence simply didn't stand up, *if* there was any evidence at all. As we have seen from the Paul Gambaccini case, allegations were being made by fantasists and, as far as Cliff Richard was concerned, even though he was still under investigation, he knew – without doubt – that he was innocent and the claims were from another fantasist or opportunist.

While we mustn't diminish the claims of the accusers of Savile and Glitter and the others found guilty, the investigation and justice process in their cases was long, detailed and thorough. Those people who came forward to accuse Savile were genuine victims. They suffered the most horrific abuse at the hands of genuine paedophiles and sex attackers and should be applauded for the courage they showed in giving evidence.

But all too often in other cases, the police were reacting to the groundswell of public opinion in the light of the Savile horrors, the overzealous prosecutions doing no more than protecting their own reputation. Collateral damage was simply an occupational hazard, as Mark Thomas-Williams, who was behind the outing of Savile, pointed out when asked about the falsely accused. 'Collateral damage,' he shrugged. 'It must be very difficult for those people to objectively see the bigger picture, but that's what this is about.'[466]

Collateral damage was prominent in another operation running alongside Yewtree. Operation Midland was set up in November 2014 and was based on claims from a single alleged victim known as Nick. He said he witnessed a group of powerful men in the 1970s and 1980s abusing young boys in central London locations, such as a flat in the Dolphin Square block near Westminster and at Elm Guest House in south-west London. Nick's allegations followed a claim in Parliament by Tom Watson MP, at the time the Deputy Chair of the opposition Labour Party. Watson claimed in 2012 he had seen 'clear intelligence suggesting a powerful paedophile network linked to Parliament and No. 10.'[467]

Nick had first made allegations of child abuse to the Metropolitan Police in 2012, shortly after ITV had broadcast its Jimmy Savile documentary. He reported sexual and physical abuse by his stepfather, Raymond, a military figure. The Met referred him to his local force, Wiltshire Police, where he repeated his claims, adding he was abused by a group of other alleged figures, all nameless except one, Jimmy Savile. He claimed that an unnamed driver would take him to London to abuse 'parties', but after examining the wider claims Wiltshire Police decided against any further action.[468]

Over the next couple of years Nick would blog of his experiences online, alleging he was among the victims of an 'establishment group' – including politicians and military figures – who kidnapped, raped and murdered boys in the 1970s and 1980s.[469]

The *Sunday People* picked up on the story and began running with it. Nick had a meeting with Tom Watson MP and would later tell police, 'Mr Watson formed part of the little group supporting me and putting my information out there to encourage other people to come forward,'[470] while Watson said of the meeting that it 'was solely to reassure him about the police's credibility, and I did do that.'[471]

In October 2014, Nick met officers from Scotland Yard and handed them a list of twelve establishment figures whom he claimed were part of the paedophile ring, among them former Prime Minister Edward Heath, former Home Secretary Leon Brittan, ex-MI5 chief Sir Michael Hanley, the then Chief of Defence Staff Lord Bramall, as well as the former Tory MP Harvey Proctor. Part of Nick's allegations was that he had personally witnessed members of the group murder three young boys.[472] Shortly after that Operation Midland was launched.

At this point, with Operation Yewtree also running and the nation in a state of shock with revelation after revelation and arrest after arrest following Savile, the police were adhering to a national policing policy of all victims must be believed. As a result, Nick's accusations were bought by detectives . . . hook, line and sinker. Before his team had even had a chance to investigate the claims properly, Detective Superintendent Kenny McDonald, the officer in charge of Operation Midland, declared: 'Nick has been spoken to by experienced officers from the child abuse team and from the murder investigation team and they and I believe what Nick is saying is credible and true.'[473] It was anything but true.

Nor was it credible.

Protected by lifelong anonymity because he was a sex complainant, Nick watched on as police began raiding the homes of suspects, even though they had no corroborating witnesses, no independent evidence and no records of missing children that fitted Nick's story. But it made good headlines for the newspapers, and conspiracy theorists on the internet revelled in the breaking news stories convinced they had been right all along.

No smoke without fire.

But slowly, Nick's allegations began to unravel. Nobody was coming forward to corroborate what he had said. Within a month the Metropolitan Police admitted that it should never have stated Nick's claims were true and credible – even though he had already been awarded £23,600 in compensation – and Detective Superintendent Kenny McDonald was taken off the inquiry.[474] The searches of the homes of Bramall, Proctor and Brittan had yielded nothing to corroborate Nick's allegations. Why would they? There was nothing to find.

Operation Midland was closed down in March 2016 with no arrests made during its sixteen-month investigation, which cost the public purse millions of pounds. A review, led by former High Court judge Sir Richard Henriques, was highly critical of the force for believing Nick too readily, and said that he should face criminal investigation for lying to police. Consequently, Northumbria Police began investigating Nick for perverting the course of justice.

In November 2016 they searched Nick's Gloucestershire home and seized a laptop, a MacBook and an iPad found in the front of his Ford Mustang (purchased with his compensation). On these they found a staggering 350 category A indecent images of children – the most serious – and in June 2017 he was charged with four counts of making indecent photographs of children, one count of possessing indecent images of children and one count of voyeurism. The offences took place from 2013 to 2016, coincidentally the time during which he had gone to the police and the media with his allegations.

In May 2019, Nick's trial for perverting the course of justice and fraud began at Newcastle Crown Court and during the trial the judge lifted an order barring publication of Nick's real name. With his anonymity removed Nick was exposed as Carl Beech, a fifty-year-old fantasist and paedophile, a divorced father of one, and a school governor who gave charity talks to children as young as five on behalf of the NSPCC.[475]

Beech pleaded not guilty to all charges, but during three days of cross-examination all his lies were exposed and, summing up the prosecution case, Tony Badenoch QC described Beech as a 'sophisticated paedophile for whom lying was as natural as having a morning cup of tea.'[476] In July 2019, Beech was jailed for eighteen years.'[477] Harvey Proctor, the only living victim of Beech's lies, broke down in court as the verdict and sentence was passed. He was later awarded £900,000 in compensation for victimisation.

The case of Carl Beech and his deceitful allegations against high-profile figures, made when he was under the protection of anonymity, highlights how a fantasist can ruin lives with a combination of lies with the subsequent media frenzy and the overzealous approach taken by the police a product of the zeitgeist following the Savile scandal. No celebrity was immune, they were all fair game. Cliff Richard was merely another name in a long line.

The former Prime Minister Edward Heath was another high-profile figure whose reputation was put under the spotlight as the result of malicious sexual abuse allegations, and the manner in which Wiltshire Police investigated posthumously the former Tory politician gives an indication of the tactics of the police at the time, and shows remarkable similarities to the tactics used to attempt to snare Cliff Richard.

Edward Heath, the UK's Prime Minister from 1970 to 1974, died in 2005 in Salisbury, Wiltshire. Rumours that he was involved in some form of sex abuse ring had been circulating since the 1990s, when a former prostitute's trial collapsed after it was alleged she had threatened to expose him as a paedophile.[478] In 2015, with the Yewtree/Midland operations in full swing, Heath's name again resurfaced, this time in relation to Heath abusing a twelve-year-old boy, and Wiltshire Police received a number of allegations against him thereby instigating an investigation.

The investigation, known as Operation Conifer, was led by the force's then Chief Constable Mike Veale. Right from the start, bias against Heath was evident when one of Veale's senior officers, Superintendent Sean Memory, spoke in front of TV cameras outside Heath's former home in Salisbury. The incident, likely totally unprecedented in police history, quickly became notorious as Superintendent Memory said, 'This is an appeal for victims: in particular, if you have been the victim of any crime from Sir Ted Heath or any historical sexual offence, or you are a witness or you have any information about this, then please come forward.'

And come forward they did: thirty-five fantasy allegations rained in against Heath, ranging from him being part of a satanic sex cult to murdering boys on his private yacht.[479] Over two years Wiltshire Police investigated forty-two separate allegations against Heath from forty individuals concluding that, had he still been alive, six of the allegations would have led to the former Prime Minister being interviewed under caution, although police stressed no inference of guilt should be drawn from this.

But Heath's reputation had been blackened, made worse by the fact he was not alive to defend himself. Like those before him, Proctor, Gambaccini, Fox, et al, mud sticks regardless of the evidence. And now Cliff Richard found himself in similar territory; although not facing accusations of paedophilia he was subject to an investigation into sexual abuse against boys, accusations made by faceless accusers, guaranteed a lifetime of anonymity while the shadow of allegations against him, regardless of their falsity, would follow Cliff to his dying day and, perhaps like Heath, long after. 'Paedophilia is a good subject for false accusations because it is so hard to disprove once the suspicion is aroused, and because it raises such strong emotions of disgust,' wrote Charles Moore. 'People who love denouncing others usually pick emotional subjects. They do not falsely accuse them of, say, supporting the Liberal Democrats or parking on a double yellow line. They falsely accuse them of murder, witchcraft, terrorism, blasphemy or even sex crimes. Because of public indignation against the misdeeds themselves, few dare resist the accusers.'[480]

There was also another aspect, one that unites Edward Heath, Harvey Proctor and Cliff Richard and which shines a murky light on the dark underbelly of this hysteria: 'the anti-gay aspect of the paedo panic', as Brendan O'Neill put it.[481]

In his press conference, Harvey Proctor suggested he was the victim of a 'homosexual witch-hunt'. Certainly, the investigations into Proctor, Heath and Richard cast lurid speculation about the lifestyles of these three 'bachelors' in the 1970s and 1980s, a period when the private lives of gay men – or bachelors – were routinely intruded upon by the law, which disproportionally criminalised sexual activity between men. The very phrase 'he never married', or 'confirmed bachelor', became a code phrase implying homosexuality.

Proctor, a bachelor, was openly homosexual; Heath, a bachelor who liked yachting and was christened 'Sailor Ted' by *Private Eye*, never came out but was dogged by rumours of being a homosexual all his life; and Cliff, who was the eternal confirmed bachelor and even wrote a song called 'Bachelor Boy', constantly denied being gay.

Many media outlets used the investigation into Cliff Richard as confirmation that he always has been a 'closeted' gay, simply because he never married. But that doesn't define his sexuality, and it is certainly no red light towards criminal behaviour. However, being unmarried – especially in the world of entertainment – has been endowed with unsavoury connotations made all the more sinister by the focus on Jimmy Savile, who was famously unmarried, and Cyril Smith, an unmarried Liberal MP, who was unmasked after his death as a serial paedophile that abused scores of boys.[482]

The cases of Savile and Smith lead to the generalisation that bachelors must be abusers, whether gay or straight and this simply feeds into the notion that although, in the overwhelming majority of cases it is close family members – primarily men who identity as heterosexual – who abuse and molest youth, the cultural perception persists that primarily gay and bisexual men – and by association, lesbians and trans people – prey on the young.

As Catherine Mayer wrote in *Time*: 'There are many things about Cliff Richard that some people find a little unsettling: his amortal determination to hang on to the appearance of youth, the bizarre calendar poses, the relentlessly chirpy public persona, the evangelistic tendencies. These do not mark him out as a guilty man any more than his evangelism.'[483]

Despite his constant public denials, and very public expressions of his Christianity, speculation continued about Cliff's private life – as happened with Ted Heath. It didn't matter if they were true or not. In fact, Heath's closest advisor, Lord Armstrong of Ilminster suggested that Heath was neither homosexual nor heterosexual. 'You usually detect some sense of sexuality when you are friends or work closely with them,' he said. 'I think he [Heath] was completely asexual. There are some people like that and I think he was one of them.'

The way in which Heath's name had been released to the public echoed with Cliff Richard's, when South Yorkshire Police's 'shotgun wedding'[484] relationship with the BBC revealed the singer's identity following the raid on his Berkshire apartment.

Bringing his name out into the public domain opened the doors to any fantasist to come forward with historic allegations, always protected by a lifetime of anonymity.

All it needed was that first allegation.

CHAPTER 26

The Crown Prosecution Service (CPS) functions as a non-ministerial department of the UK Government and started operating in 1986. It is responsible for public prosecutions of people charged with criminal offences in England and Wales with the exception of cases conducted by the Serious Fraud Office and certain minor offences. It is headed by the Director of Public Prosecutions (DPP) and in May 2016, the person holding that elevated role was Alison Saunders.

Saunders, who had replaced Sir Keir Starmer in the role in 2013, had already become a somewhat controversial DPP. Her policy towards the reporting of rape had led to criticism that a number of people had been wrongly imprisoned as a result of disclosure failings, or that rape trials had simply collapsed.[485]

As columnist Allison Pearson wrote: 'The problem is that our police have been brainwashed into accepting the Saunders' view of rape cases, which goes something like this: accusers are always telling the truth and allegations are the new evidence,'[486] before continuing in another column: 'Guilty until proven innocent.

The tenure of Alison Saunders at the Crown Prosecution Service will be remembered for a monstrous inversion of that fundamental principle of British justice.'[487]

Saunders had been the incumbent during the injustice faced by Paul Gambaccini. So she seemed hardly the person Cliff Richard needed adjudicating his own case. Even more so when part of her crusade seemed to be following in the footsteps of Sir Keir Starmer by 'seeing it as her role to atone for the CPS's historical mistakes'.[488] And one of the CPS's biggest historical mistakes was not prosecuting Jimmy Savile in 2009 after Surrey Police submitted a file to them containing references to four potential offences by the DJ and broadcaster.[489]

The over-zealous arrests, investigations and fly-papering that followed can only be as a result of this crusade and while there were guilty men arrested, the likes of Harris, Clifford and Hall, others were innocent and had their lives ruined.

Cliff Richard was next in the firing line as he waited anxiously for the CPS to make their decision.

He didn't have to wait long.

While South Yorkshire Police took two years to run their investigation, the CPS took just five weeks to deliver their verdict.

On Thursday 16 June 2016, prosecutors announced that no charges would be brought against the singer with a statement saying: 'The CPS has carefully reviewed evidence relating to claims of non-recent sexual offences dating between 1958 and 1983 made by four men. We have decided that there is insufficient evidence to prosecute. This decision has been made in accordance with the Code for Crown Prosecutors and our guidance for prosecutors on cases of sexual offences . . . The complainants have been informed and provided with a full explanation in writing.'[490]

Cliff had been at his villa in Portugal as he awaited the news.

Finally, after two years under investigation, Cliff was told that he would not be facing any charges.

After it was all over, I sat on the side of my bed and thought, this is so fantastic. And I wept. I couldn't help it. Then I drove up to Lisbon with some friends for the Queen's Birthday, where they wanted me to sing the National Anthem. They'd asked me weeks earlier. What I loved was they'd asked me before I was cleared, so they'd trusted me. So, I went to the garden party, had two glasses of champagne and sang two verses of 'God Save the Queen' at the Governor's residence.[491]

Naturally, those closest to Cliff were thrilled with the outcome. Gloria Hunniford, who had been by his side during the darkest hours, commented, 'It has been torture, personally I always knew he would be cleared. The relief of having it confirmed today is something. I saw him the other day just last week. Honestly, I gave him a hug and he was skin and bones. I think it has taken a big toll on him and the relief will be enormous.'[492]

The BBC were quick to make a statement:

The BBC is very sorry that Sir Cliff Richard, who has worked as a musician and performer for so many years with the organisation, has suffered distress. The BBC's responsibility is to report fully stories that are in the public interest. Police investigations into prominent figures in public life are, of course, squarely in the public interest, which is why they have been reported by all news organisations in this country. Once the South Yorkshire Police had confirmed the investigation and Sir Cliff Richard's identity and informed the BBC of the timing and details of the search of his property, it would neither have been editorially responsible nor in the public interest to choose not to report fully the investigation into Sir Cliff Richard because of his public profile. The BBC, at every stage, reported Sir Cliff's full denial of the allegations. The BBC, therefore, stands by the decision to report the investigation undertaken by the South Yorkshire Police and the search of his property.[493]

This statement from the BBC did not satisfy Cliff. Talking to the *Daily Mail*, the singer said he was:

Bitterly disappointed to see that while finally appearing to offer an apology for the distress I have suffered, the BBC do not acknowledge they themselves have caused it. They are at the same time undermining their own apology by claiming that they were acting in the public interest. I fail to understand how this so-called story was in the public interest and I believe that is a view shared by millions of fair-minded people. So, in due course we may have to let the courts determine this issue.[494]

There was something else rankling with Cliff. The statement from the CPS had been all well and good, but closer analysis revealed it failed to include the words 'not guilty' or 'cleared' or 'innocent'. It had simply mentioned 'insufficient evidence'. To all those saying there was 'no smoke without fire', the suggestion that the police did not have sufficient evidence appeared to support their claims that there must be some truth in the allegations.

They say 'insufficient evidence', which to the reader, certainly to me, suggests maybe there is some evidence, but not enough. That's ridiculous.[495]

Cliff needed more. He wanted his name cleared beyond all reasonable doubt. His reputation had already suffered enough and without a 'not guilty' outcome, the cloud would continue to linger over him, personally and professionally. So, in response to the comments from the CPS, Cliff issued his own statement:

After almost two years under police investigation, I learnt today that they have finally closed their enquiries. I have always maintained my innocence, co-operated fully with the investigation, and cannot understand why it has taken so long to get to this point! Nevertheless, I am obviously thrilled that the vile accusations and the resulting investigation have finally been brought to a close. Ever since the highly-publicised and BBC-filmed raid on my home, I have chosen not to speak publicly. Even though I was under pressure to 'speak out', other than to state my innocence, which was easy for me to do as I have never molested anyone in my life, I chose to remain silent. This was despite the widely shared sense of injustice resulting from the high-profile fumbling of my case from day one. Other than in exceptional cases, people who are facing allegations should never be named publicly until charged. I was named before I was even interviewed and for me that was like being hung out like 'live bait'. It is obvious that such strategies simply increase the risk of attracting spurious claims which not only tie up police resources and waste public funds, but they forever tarnish the reputations of innocent people. There have been numerous occasions in recent years where this has occurred, and I feel very strongly that no innocent person should be treated in this way. I know the truth and in some people's eyes the CPS's announcement today doesn't go far enough because it doesn't expressly state that I am innocent: which of course I am. There lies the problem.[496]

His statement concluded:

My reputation will not be fully vindicated because the CPS's policy is to only say something general about there being 'insufficient' evidence. How can there be evidence for something that never took place! This is also a reason why people should never be named publicly until they have been charged unless there are exceptional circumstances.[497] *To my fans and members of the public, to the press and media, all of whom continued to show me such encouraging and wonderful support, I would like to say, 'thank you' it would have been so much harder without you.*[498]

Cliff's next move was to grant close friend Gloria Hunniford an exclusive and frank television interview. Broadcast less than a week after Cliff had received the news that he was not going to be charged, the hour-long interview on ITV's *Loose Women* saw the singer not hold back in his criticism of the way the investigation against him had been run and also the role of the police. He was additionally critical of the continuing anonymity of his accusers while his own name had been circulated worldwide. It was to be a crusade Cliff would continue to forge in the years ahead.

Meanwhile, others were quick to offer their insight into the hounding of Cliff and the fact he had been, rightly, cleared. Amongst them was Matthew Parris, writer, broadcaster and former Conservative politician, who commented so perfectly in the *Spectator*:

Sir Cliff Richard will not be charged with historic sex offences. There is 'insufficient evidence'. Nobody, I suppose, thinks the way Cliff Richard has been treated has been fair. He says he was 'hung out like live bait' in order to attract further allegations, and we can see exactly what he means. Indeed the police (who called a press conference in front of Sir Edward Heath's house to announce similar allegations against the late Prime Minister) rather boast about what another victim, the broadcaster Paul Gambaccini, called their 'flypaper strategy'. Much of the disquiet we feel boils down to two complaints. First, that it's cruel and wrong for the police to name individuals unless or until they've been charged. Secondly, that when it is decided that no charges will be brought, the preferred phrase 'insufficient evidence' still seems to leave a stain on the individual's reputation.

Plainly this can be misleading as it covers the whole range of possibilities, from 'no evidence at all' to 'evidence leading to strong suspicions but nothing that can be proved'. But equally plainly, the authorities cannot announce that a suspect has been 'cleared' when he or she hasn't even been charged. Nor (as some have suggested) can they start describing anyone they don't charge as 'innocent' because they cannot know that.

I've toyed with 'inadequate' evidence and 'no useful evidence', but the latter may not always be strictly true, and the former, like 'insufficient', provokes speculation that there was indeed some evidence but not quite enough, or not usable in court. 'Insufficient' leaves the impression that there may well be more out there somewhere, but it has not proved possible to find it.

The problem is the word 'evidence'. Sometimes this amounts to mere accusation. I believe this has been the case in most or all of the recent investigations. Because the word 'evidence' itself covers a range of meanings, from 'something possibly indicative' to 'nothing but an unsupported accusation', the word should be avoided. I conclude that the stock phrase for police announcements should be 'found no basis for a charge'. I prefer this to 'no basis for a criminal charge', because the latter might be thought to hint that there could be a basis for some other kind of charge. I'm confident my proposed new wording answers the difficulties complained of.[499]

Cliff was desperate to return to making music, to getting his life and career back on track, but despite being told he would not be facing any charges, his lawyers had also warned him that there was every possibility that his accusers could appeal against that decision.

Sure enough, in August an application under the victims' right to review scheme was lodged by one of his accusers, challenging the decision by the CPS not to pursue a case against the singer. Cliff's lawyers informed him that the chances of the appeal against the decision being upheld was almost zero.

But almost zero isn't zero.

The appeal couldn't have come at a worse time for Cliff: at the beginning of August his eldest sister, Donna, had passed away at the age of seventy-three after battling ill health. It was another hammer-blow to the singer following his two years under investigation and, being close to all his sisters, Cliff was devastated by Donna's death. 'He's really been through it this year, poor Cliff,' said close friend Paul O'Grady. 'He's had a terrible time. He is absolutely devoted to his sisters. He will be at a complete loss.'[500]

Cliff didn't appear publicly for three weeks following Donna's death until he was greeted by 1,000 fans at his vineyard in Portugal. He had already organised an event there to mark a new red wine being released and, being the consummate professional, Cliff wasn't going to let his fans down. He was joined at the event by another of his sisters, Joan, and reassured his fans that he was 'back to his best'.

I'm OK, everything will be OK. I want to thank all my fans for being so amazing, they have been incredible.[501]

Of course, Cliff couldn't be certain that everything would be OK. One of his accusers was already challenging the CPS's decision not to pursue a case against the singer and in September, a second person came forward to challenge the decision. Prosecutors refused to confirm any further details regarding the second challenge, but a spokesperson for Cliff released a statement saying, 'Sir Cliff reaffirms his innocence and has every confidence the CPS will come to the right conclusion as soon as possible.'[502]

In a bizarre coincidence, this second appeal emerged just as Channel 4 was about to broadcast their drama series *National Treasure*, which starred Robbie Coltrane as a once-successful comedian from the 80s and 90s now hosting a TV quiz show and suddenly accused of historic sex crimes against women that were alleged to have taken place two or more decades previously. 'I never knew anyone who's been arrested,' said Coltrane.

'But day to day you'd open the papers and think, "Oh shit". Sometimes I'd say, "Oh I always fucking knew he was an arse". Other times you'd think, "He's a nice bloke".' Regarding Cliff Richard specifically, Coltrane added, 'It's not for the BBC to publish the police business. But they did. Of course, I feel for him. I feel for anyone who's innocent.' During an interview for *Huffpost*, Coltrane was pushed on the topic of anonymity for those accused: 'That's the big question – the fishing expedition as they call it. If you publish the guy's name, other people will come forward, the bravest person will come forward, as will several other people. In our drama, some are just going to the tabloids, some are delusional, but some inevitably might be true, and it's up to the cops and psychologists to work out who's telling the truth. Who do you want to protect here? The people who've been falsely accused, or the people who've been be-spoilt? At some point along the line, you have to choose between the two. They can't both be true. Of course, innocent people whose lives have fallen off a cliff should be protected, but more importantly, so should people whose lives, sex lives, self-esteem have been ruined, they must be protected more, that's what I would say.'

The first episode of *National Treasure*, which went on to win a BAFTA for Best Mini-Series, was broadcast on 20 September 2016 and watched by over five million viewers. By the time the second episode was transmitted on 27 September, the CPS had reached a verdict regarding the two challenges against the decision to drop the allegations against Cliff.

As the singer had hoped, the CPS had come to a swift decision and came down in his favour. 'In accordance with the scheme, a CPS lawyer who was not involved in the original decision-making process has completed a full review of the evidence and has concluded that the decisions not to charge were correct.'[503]

Cliff was quick to release a statement of his own:

As I have said previously, I'm innocent, so I'm obviously pleased with today's CPS decision and the speed with which they reached it. I hope that it brings this matter to a close.[504]

After two long and painful years, the allegations against Cliff had been thrown out, not once but twice. He could now get on with his life, get back to his career, perform once more, and record new music. In fact, the day after the CPS stated they were correct not to bring historic sexual abuse charges against the singer, Cliff announced a new rock 'n' roll covers album would be released on 11 November. It was the *Just... Fabulous Rock 'n' Roll* album he had recorded in Nashville with Steve Mandile during the earliest dark days of the investigation.

My new CD is another dip into an incredible period of our musical history. A happy, creative, and in many ways an innocent time. I will always love this music, but more importantly I hope you do too. Rock on! [505]

Cliff flew back to the UK from Portugal in late 2016 to do the obligatory PR rounds that accompanied the release of a new album. He was on familiar territory, this was his 102nd album so tours of TV studios, radio stations and newspaper offices didn't faze him but, of course, wherever he went, the interview always came round to the abuse allegations and how it felt to be finally cleared. In one interview with Celebrity Radio, host Alex Belfield asked Cliff how he must be looking forward to Christmas in 2016 with nothing in the back of his mind after all that had gone before.

I am actually, yes [looking forward to Christmas]. *The last couple of Christmases have been rather fraught, even though I've been surrounded by friends, absolutely surrounded by friends and constantly supported by fans. It's been quite an incredible learning process for me and . . . I'll say it to you now, the one thing I'm very grateful to the South Yorkshire Police for, they showed me I had more love than they did. I was more loved than they were. So it was a learning process to suddenly realise that even people who don't buy your record necessarily, even they were coming to me in the streets and airports and stuff and wishing me well and saying, 'Good on you, we're right behind you, mate'.*[506]

But the release of a new album wasn't the only thing occupying Cliff as 2016 drew to a close: ever since the police raid on his Berkshire apartment in August 2014, his team of lawyers had been readying legal actions and Cliff was about to go into battle once more.

This time *against* South Yorkshire Police.

And the BBC.

CHAPTER 27

Sunday 10 July 2016. It is the final of the Men's Singles at Wimbledon. Britain's Andy Murray against Milos Raonic from Canada. Scanning the crowd, BBC cameras pick out celebrities such as Bradley Cooper, Benedict Cumberbatch, Lily James and Hugh Grant, all trying to blend in inconspicuously, wearing dark suits, designer shades, discreet and demure dress. Then the camera fixes on a man wearing a bright red tartan jacket, yellow rose pinned to its lapel, bright red tie against a crisp white shirt. There's little hope of evading attention wearing this attire.

Perhaps Cliff didn't want to escape the cameras. Maybe he was keen for all to see he was there, one British institution in the greatest tennis institution of them all, Centre Court. That's why he was beaming. Or perhaps his appearance on Finals Day had something to do with the fact that it came just hours after he confirmed he would be suing South Yorkshire Police and the BBC. Just as Andy Murray was merciless in beating Raonic, now Cliff was being ruthless in taking on the two organisations that had threatened to ruin him.

As he attended Wimbledon, Cliff released a statement:

I confirm that I have instructed my lawyers to make formal legal complaints to South Yorkshire Police and the BBC so that in the absence of satisfactory answers a Court will determine whether or not their behaviour was justified and proportionate. It is important not only for me personally but much more widely. My life was effectively turned upside down and my reputation, worldwide, was unnecessarily damaged. I would not want the same to happen to others whether in the public eye or not. Whilst the police of course need to properly investigate allegations made to them, it is clear to me that questions need to be answered by both the police and the BBC about their initial handling of my matter, which has rightly been condemned from so many quarters, including the Home Affairs Select Committee, the broader press, and, even the police themselves . . . I firmly believe that privacy should be respected and that police guidelines are there to be followed. That means that save in exceptional circumstances people should never be named unless and until they are charged. As everybody has accepted there were no such 'exceptional circumstances' in my case.

A source close to Cliff said he didn't make the decision 'to take on two British institutions lightly', but felt 'no one else should suffer as he did'. The source added: 'The essence of this is that he does not want anyone who is innocent, like him, to go through what he has experienced in the past two years. He is in the fortunate position of being able to try to do something about this and we hope the judge in due course will find that there has been an unlawful misuse of private information.'[507]

Cliff's relationship with South Yorkshire Police had only

started the moment they raided his apartment, so he had little reason to worry about burning any bridges with them. The BBC, however, was a different story. Cliff had had a long-standing relationship with them that had gone right back to virtually the very beginning of his career, with him making his first BBC TV appearance on *Here's to the Next Time* in May 1959 (although he had actually first appeared on TV performing 'Move It' on Jack Good's *Oh Boy!* for rival channel ITV).[508]

Since then, Cliff had become a staple on the BBC, whether it be on *Top of the Pops*, the Eurovision Song Contest, or as a regular guest on chat shows. And, of course, beginning in 1963 with *The Cliff Richard Show*, he had fronted his own entertainment series and Christmas specials right up to 1997. While he hadn't been a fixture on any of the BBC Radio playlists for some years, he still had – or, at least up until 2014 – a presence on cosy BBC magazine, daytime and breakfast shows; the sort of shows his fans would typically watch.

Cliff possibly wouldn't want to admit it, but for his career and his continual albeit peripheral presence on TV, he needed the BBC more than the BBC needed him. So, to take them to court would represent a huge gamble for Cliff. Lose . . . and he would probably be ostracised from the BBC forever.

The financial risk was enormous, too. Cliff had already spent hundreds of thousands of pounds in legal fees defending himself against the false allegations, and in the run-up to taking on the BBC and South Yorkshire Police[509] his outlay would only grow. Not that Cliff was struggling for cash: in the 2016 *Sunday Times* Rich List he was said to be worth £58 million and so, when he put his Berkshire apartment up for sale, it was for reasons other than money.

I couldn't go back to live there. I probably over-reacted but that's the way it felt. I only went back there once to take my stuff out and I didn't feel comfortable. It suddenly became a place that they, the police, had gone into, you know, thinking those things.[510]

When the apartment sold in 2016 for £2.9m, it meant that, for the first time since arriving in the country from India in 1948, Cliff no longer had any property or family base in the UK and, for the foreseeable future, he would divide his time between his Portugal and Barbados homes with breaks in the USA in between touring. Later, he would spend most of his time in New York, eventually buying a one-bedroomed property with John McElynn for £800,000 'in the midst of Manhattan's coveted boutiques and shopping, finest restaurants, top hotels and museums',[511] thereby abandoning living in the UK for good.

'Cliff won't come back and live here,' said Gloria Hunniford. 'He has made that jump now. He was very disillusioned with what happened. He likes the anonymity in America. Some people recognise him, but he does not get it all the time like he does here. His place is in New York and he likes it there. He loves coming back to perform occasionally and is looking forward to playing summer shows this year. But I don't think he will ever live here all the time again.'[512] Cliff's disillusionment turned to satisfaction in May 2017, however, when he finally had an outcome that vindicated his decision to sue the BBC and South Yorkshire Police. Somewhat out of the blue, his action against SYP was settled quickly and out of court when the force apologised to the singer and agreed to pay him substantial damages.

The barrister who headed Cliff's legal team, Justin Rushbrooke QC, said, 'I am pleased to announce that South Yorkshire

Police has now recognised that its conduct was unlawful and has agreed to pay the claimant a substantial sum by way of general and aggravated damages to compensate for its conduct, as well as appropriate sums in respect of the financial damage and legal costs incurred by the claimant.'

Adam Wolanski, representing the force's chief constable, said: 'The force accepts that the claimant's private information should not have been disclosed to the BBC and that its reason for doing so, namely, to protect the integrity of its investigation, was not an adequate reason for doing so. It acknowledges that its conduct in this regard was unlawful and offers its sincere apologies to the claimant for the distress and humiliation he has suffered.'[513]

It was not revealed how much SYP would pay Cliff, but it later transpired they settled at £400,000 in damages and £300,000 in costs to the singer.[514]

In May 2017, I reached a settlement with the South Yorkshire Police out of court. As part of it, they agreed to pay me damages for the harm I had suffered, although that was never the main reason for my legal action. South Yorkshire Police made a public statement in court, and it meant more to me to be given their 'sincere apologies', along with a public admission that their conduct had been unlawful, than any amount of damages would.[515]

The BBC, however, chose not to settle and so Cliff's case against them remained ongoing. Reacting to the decision of SYP to settle out of court, a BBC spokesperson commented:

We've said throughout that the BBC's responsibility is to report news stories that are in the public interest. Against the extensive disclosure of historic child sexual abuse by figures of high public prominence, we consider that the report into the investigation into Sir Cliff for such an offence, and the decision by police to search his premises, was such a news story and that the BBC had a duty to report it. The police decision to settle the claim against them by Sir Cliff because of how they handled the investigation doesn't change the fundamental principle that journalistic organisations should be able to report on the police and police investigations into individuals. A search happened, and because it did, the BBC reported it – just as any other media organisation would have and did.'[516]

With neither Cliff nor the BBC backing down, there was no alternative but to move to trial.

CHAPTER 28

The High Court, London, 12 April 2018.

A nervous Cliff Richard arrives to begin his legal battle against the BBC: one Great British national treasure versus another.

The original writ, served against both the BBC and South Yorkshire Police, was issued in 2016. A legal source said of it: 'The writ runs to 26 pages and is utterly devastating. It represents total war between Sir Cliff and the BBC.'[517]

And Cliff had celebrity backers, with one of them, fellow veteran singer Rod Stewart, making his views abundantly clear: 'Pay attention, please, Cliff. You've been persecuted, mate, and we all know it. We are one hundred million per cent behind you. You sue those bastards. I'll give you half.'[518]

With South Yorkshire Police having settled with Cliff out of court in 2017, the singer and the BBC now came face to face in London a year later.

I would never have dreamed it [the BBC] *would do this to me. It would never have even crossed my mind. To me the BBC would absolutely stay by the rules. The new generation have come in, in all fields now, and they seem to have that lack of respect of what's happened before . . . A whole new group of people. They don't care what we've done in the past. For me, the BBC is Paul Gambaccini, Gloria [Hunniford] when she worked for them, all the DJs that I've met, all the people who work on the* Today *programme,* World At One. *That's the BBC. They are not to blame for what happened to me. It's the people at the top. Somebody at the top said: 'Good idea. Let's get this story.' And somehow they were able to get the police to tell them when they were coming. It shouldn't do that. I'm sure that was probably against the law. I always thought a police raid was supposed to be secret. Nobody should know. And yet the BBC were there. So, they have a lot to answer for and that was real intrusion into my privacy. To actually film my apartment, it's unforgivable.*[519]

As he arrived at court on that first morning, Cliff was photographed outside looking sombre and clasping his hands as in prayer, before entering the building without uttering a word to waiting reporters.

Cliff's case ostensibly was that the BBC's coverage of the search was a very serious invasion of his privacy for which there was no lawful justification. The fact and details of the investigation, which the BBC published, was private information and there was no public interest in its disclosure to millions around the world. This was therefore a claim for misuse of private information, a breach of Article 8 ECHR and breach of the Data Protection Act 1998.

The singer's barrister, Justin Rushbrooke QC, had already provided a written statement, which included: 'It is hard to encapsulate in words the sense of panic and powerlessness that must have been induced in him on 14 August 2014 when he realised that the BBC were relaying instantaneously and indiscriminately around the world highly sensitive and damaging information concerning himself – all based upon an allegation of serious criminal conduct which he knew to be entirely false.'[520]

He then went on to tell the court: 'No citizen should have to watch film footage broadcast on national and international television of police searching their home shot from a helicopter hovering just overhead . . . No citizen should have to learn from their friends that they are a person under investigation for a historic sex offence involving a child.'

As a result of this unlawful invasion of his privacy and breaches of his data protection rights, it was argued that the singer was entitled to substantial damages, including aggravated damages to reflect the flagrant way in which the BBC went about breaching his rights. In addition to his general damages claim, Cliff was seeking £278,261 for legal costs as damages, £108,500 for PR fees, and an undisclosed sum for the 'substantial non-recoverable advance' that had been agreed for his autobiography, which had been due to be published in late 2015.[521]

It was on Day 2 that Cliff took to the stand to answer lawyers' questions in court. But after swearing an oath on the bible, it didn't get off to a good start: upon being asked by his own QC whether he was content being addressed as 'Sir Cliff', the singer responded light-heartedly with the comment, 'Yes, absolutely! I prefer it to Mr!' It might have been a joke aimed at settling nerves, but the tabloid journalists wrote subsequently that the singer had taken the stand and had insisted on being referred to as Sir Cliff.

It was a lie, and it gave such a bad impression of me . . . but I'm afraid that's tabloid journalism for you. I expect no better from some of them by now.[522]

Later, Cliff recalled, with a wavering, emotional voice, watching a news item while at a hotel in Portugal and seeing footage of the raid on his apartment with police officers searching through his belongings.

I don't recall exactly what channel it was, but I could see the police going through the drawers in one of the rooms of my apartment. I felt confused; disturbed and very upset. It was like I was watching burglars in my apartment, going through my personal belongings.[523]

Occasionally sobbing, the singer went on to describe how he felt unable to return to his Berkshire apartment.

In my mind it had become contaminated. I didn't feel comfortable there any longer. I have in fact been burgled before, and this for me was a worse experience.[524]

And when the questioning turned to the impact the broadcast had on his reputation, Cliff answered:

I felt as though everything I had worked for during my life – trying to live as honestly and honourably as I could – was being torn apart. I felt forever tainted. I still do.[525]

Clips from the BBC's coverage was played in court – although Cliff turned away and didn't view them – and lawyers for the BBC said the raid was a 'matter of legitimate public interest', as was its coverage, and that the reporting contributed to public debate.[526] But Cliff was adamant, during his ninety minutes giving evidence, that the police search and subsequent publicity not only disrupted his personal life, but also his career and charity work.

Everywhere I have ever been, I felt my name was smeared. The police didn't do that, the BBC did.[527]

At the end of Day 2, Cliff left the court with Gloria Hunniford, who had been with him all day to offer support. Cliff and Gloria posed on the steps to the court, smiling and waving as photographers caught the image for posterity. The singer appeared much more relaxed compared to his appearance the previous day. Undeniably a great weight had been lifted from his shoulders; he had given his version of events, he had revealed how the allegations and publicity had impacted him, and he had cast the first stone in the battle against the BBC.

The trial was expected to last for ten days. Cliff was determined to be in court for the entire duration.

I wanted to hear all the evidence, and I thought it was important for the judge to see me there every day and realise the case meant a lot to me. That it was a very big deal in my life.[528]

The trial was also a big deal for the future of journalism in the United Kingdom, in particular the relationship between reporters and police and sources of information. Writing in the *Guardian*, Roy Greenslade, professor of journalism at City University, said, 'I sympathise with the singer, but were he to win, the media's role as public watchdog would be fatally compromised.'[529]

He went on to argue that the ramifications for press freedom following a victory for Cliff in court were 'awful to contemplate', creating 'a situation in which the media would be unable to report the early stages of police investigations, such as revealing the identity of arrested people. They would enjoy anonymity until and unless they were charged. This would be a fundamental change to custom and practice. It would have the effect of allowing police officers to operate in secrecy and would deny journalists the right to scrutinise the activities of the police. The media's role as a public watchdog, holding power to account and acting on behalf of the public interest, would be fatally compromised.'[530]

Tracey Singlehurst-Ward, a partner at law firm Hugh James, also saw problems ahead with a potential Cliff victory: 'If Sir Cliff Richard wins, it could change the manner of reporting by mainstream media in future police investigations and, arguably, "chill" free speech. Will the press be free to report upon investigations of any kind, or prohibited from doing so until there is an actual arrest or other balancing factor?'[531]

But, surely, naming the accused before they are charged, as happened with Cliff Richard and Paul Gambaccini, Harvey Proctor and others, breaches the rules of natural justice. It seems absurd that those who freely accuse others of a sex crime can retain their anonymity for life, as set out in the Sexual Offences Act 2003, while those being accused *can* be named and their identity distributed via global platforms almost instantly.

'The rule was introduced to meet plausible complaints that rapes were being severely underreported,' says columnist Simon Jenkins. 'There is evidence that accuser anonymity has indeed led to a rise in reporting sex crimes. But, as [Paul] Gambaccini said on Monday, the imbalance of denying anonymity to the accused has breached two cardinal rules of natural justice. One is that those accused of a crime should not be named until formally charged, to protect them from casual or malicious falsity. The other, given the inevitable publicity, is that innocence be assumed until guilt is proven. The casual dismissal of both principles in the 2003 act was extraordinary. Sex crimes are complicated by the fact that evidence is sometimes hard to come by. This is indeed an argument for making the accuser anonymous. But the case for instantly revealing the identity of the accused is poor. It is that other witnesses might recognise the name and come forward, thus aiding the prosecution in proceeding to a charge.'[532]

In Cliff's case, the revealing of his identity was more than simply tempting other witnesses to come forward; it was for the purposes of media viewership, for clickbait, for newspaper sales. The case wasn't advanced by Cliff's name being made public; it was never going to be, as there was never any case to answer in the first place. But that didn't stop South Yorkshire Police and the BBC revealing Cliff's identity.

As the trial continued, so the judge heard from all sides of the argument, each putting their cases forward. Cliff remained an avid attendee in court, hearing the BBC claiming they had simply been doing their job in covering the raid on his apartment and that their reporting had been 'accurate, in good faith, and a matter of legitimate public interest.'[533]

On Day 5 of the trial, BBC reporter Dan Johnson, under questioning, spoke of how he came to break the story and, by default, identify Cliff Richard. He explained how he had guessed the singer's name after a contact told him the police were looking at 'just one more major figure'. Johnson guessed this to be Cliff Richard, 'because of previous rumours I had heard about him. The contact confirmed I had guessed the right name.'[534] Johnson went on, 'The contact did not correct me,' he said. 'Because of the context of the other cases mentioned, and rumours I had heard about Sir Cliff's sexuality, I took from this the impression that it was an allegation of sexual abuse involving a boy and dating back some years. I also got the strong impression that the police were due to take further action.'[535]

Cross-examined by Justin Rushbrooke QC, Cliff's counsel, Johnson was asked, 'Do you accept your story has caused massive damage and distress to Sir Cliff?' To which Johnson replied, 'I accept that he has been upset and distressed about it,' before later adding: 'I accept the distress he feels, I don't accept it was caused by me uniquely. Obviously South Yorkshire Police were part of that and my colleagues at the BBC who were part of the story as well. I don't believe I was at fault, I just reported the facts of a story. I am sure the investigation would have been distressing.'[536]

Justin Rushbrooke QC later asked Dan Johnson if he was prepared to offer a personal apology in court to Cliff (who was present), but before he could answer Justice Mann intervened, saying the line of questioning was 'not helpful'.[537]

As questioning came towards a close, Dan Johnson was asked what thought he'd given to the privacy of Cliff Richard during the reporting. Johnson said his primary concern was around himself and his position when filming close to the singer's home, dismissing that he made any decisions about the helicopter being used and referring those decisions back to senior editorial staff in London. 'It wasn't for me to consider the bigger picture, the wider implications of what was being broadcast,' he said. 'It wasn't my responsibility and I hadn't seen everything that was being filmed. If you are talking about the general idea of having the helicopter there, then I thought that it was useful to tell people what was going on.'[538]

But by telling people what was going on and, more importantly, naming Cliff Richard, the BBC was throwing his name out into a pool from which wild – and baseless – accusations would emerge. 'I believe it was as a direct result of the publicity generated by the BBC that various people came out of the woodwork, and those allegations came to nothing eventually,' Gideon Benaim, one of the solicitors representing Cliff, told the court before later adding: 'The claimant has had an unblemished career over six decades and this was a massive issue. It was really critical and important to try and deal with these allegations and to prevent further damage as far as we could.[539]

The relationship between the BBC and South Yorkshire Police was a key pillar of the trial and, throughout, there was a theme that the BBC had colluded with SYP, even perhaps that the BBC, through Dan Johnson, had used strong-arm tactics to force a senior detective at SYP, Matt Fenwick (who, by now, had retired from the force), to provide information about the raid on the apartment in Berkshire and the identity of its owner.

Johnson denied this vehemently, stating any discussions with SYP '. . . wasn't a deal in a formal sense', while also denying any suggestions that he was 'strong-arming' the police and that his remark in an email he wrote that he had them 'over a barrel' was simply 'light-hearted'.[540]

Later in the trial, Gary Smith, who was UK News Editor for BBC News at the time, told Justice Mann that, had they not named Cliff Richard, the BBC may have faced criticism and been accused of not reporting a matter of high public interest with the high-profile figure involved, given the recent history of the Jimmy Savile allegations and knowledge within institutions that had not been made public. Smith went on to argue that the BBC had reported investigations into a number of high-profile figures including Rolf Harris, Max Clifford, Paul Gambaccini and Jimmy Tarbuck: none of them had attracted legal complaints related to a breach of privacy.

But, unlike Cliff Richard, none of them had had a helicopter hovering over their property with cameras zooming in to film officers going through personal items within. Why was Cliff so different? Why did the BBC deem it necessary to film the raid and identify him in such a sensational manner? While Gary Smith accepted the images filmed from the helicopter were an 'intrusion' into Cliff's privacy he added: 'There was a balance between the intrusion and the public interest. I'm saying there was a strong public interest in having pictures of what was happening inside the gated complex.'[541]

On the final day of the trial, David Crompton, who at the time of the raid was Chief Constable of South Yorkshire Police, gave damning evidence that was critical of the BBC and the way the raid was covered.

'I had thought that there may be some limited footage of my officers going into Sir Cliff Richard's property,' he said. 'What I saw was much more extensive and I thought it was intrusive.'[542] Later he commented on the nature of the relationship between SYP and the BBC after being told that Dan Johnson was aware of the investigation: 'I can remember very clearly thinking that there was a journalist who knew as much as I did about the allegations,' Crompton said. 'This information was deeply concerning to me, because I thought that a media report on a high-profile case, which was in its infancy, could fatally compromise SYP's ability to carry out a thorough investigation which, as I have said, was my priority. The thought of a journalist reporting on the investigation before SYP had been able to conduct the search was a particular concern.'[543]

Crompton believed that the story was 'bound to come out' and thought the BBC was likely to report it 'imminently', so providing the broadcaster with information about the search was a 'small concession' that he decided was necessary to 'protect the integrity' of the investigation. 'We were in a difficult position. I considered it to be of paramount importance that we were able to complete an unhindered and untainted investigation and one might say the relationship with the BBC became a shotgun wedding.'[544]

Of the coverage of the raid itself, which he watched on television while on holiday in Wales, Crompton said, 'I could never have imagined in my wildest dreams that the BBC would do what they did. I have never seen coverage like this ever in my police career,'[545] although, when it was put to him that SYP wanted publicity of its investigation into such a high-profile figure, Crompton replied, 'I fundamentally disagree.'[546]

At the close of Day 11, the case was adjourned to 8 May 2018, when closing legal submissions were made with Cliff's team seeking damages 'at the top end of the scale', while the BBC said its coverage of the story was in the public interest, its reporting fair and accurate and that they simply could not have sat on a story of this magnitude.[547]

There would now be a wait of a number of weeks while the judge considered the arguments set before him.

For Cliff it would be an anxious wait.

It would be a month or two before the judge delivered his verdict, and it would have killed me to have been sat twiddling my thumbs and stressing out as I waited. So, while he deliberated, I was hard at work in a studio in Miami.[548]

The recording sessions would be for a new album, one that Cliff hoped would reinvigorate his career in the wake of his trial. With songs such as 'Rise Up', 'Reborn' and 'Gonna Be Alright' amongst the tracks, it certainly looked to a brighter future.

But arriving back in the UK in July 2018, Cliff was unsure whether such an optimistic choice of songs was wise. Nobody but the judge knew which way the verdict would go, as reputations, future plans, the nature of journalism in the UK, and even judicial changes hung in the balance.

CHAPTER 29

On 18 July 2018, Cliff Richard was back in the High Court to hear the judgment being handed down in his legal action against the BBC. Dressed in a dark, sombre suit and spotted tie, he arrived in a grey people carrier and was greeted by cheers and shouts of good luck from a dozen fans and well-wishers outside the court when he emerged from the vehicle. Smiling his thanks to them and waving, he briskly entered the building where Gloria Hunniford and Paul Gambaccini were waiting for him to offer their support, as they had done throughout.

Sitting in the court, Cliff listened intently as Justice Mann delivered his lengthy verdict. It soon became evident that the judge was highly critical of the BBC. Amongst other aspects of their approach, Justice Mann was disparaging about the emphasis given by the BBC to the fact that Cliff was a public figure who had promoted his Christian beliefs in his writing and his public appearances, thus making him a legitimate target.

'Sir Cliff undoubtedly has those attributes,' commented Mann. 'However, on the facts of this case they do not detract from his reasonable expectations. A public figure is not, by virtue of that quality, necessarily deprived of his or her legitimate expectations of privacy.' Regarding the use of a helicopter during the filming of the raid, Justice Mann said, 'I consider that the filming into Sir Cliff's flat was an infringement of his English law privacy rights.'[549]

Of the argument put forward by the BBC that sexual abuse of children was and is a serious public concern, and abuse carried out by those in a public position and who had contact with children in that position was of a public concern at the time, Justice Mann stated, 'This is the only public interest defence put forward by the BBC in final submissions,' before adding, 'I think that they, or most of them [the minds of those at the BBC] were far more impressed by the size of the story and that they had the opportunity to scoop their rivals.'

As for the identification of Cliff by the BBC, Justice Mann commented, 'Knowing that Sir Cliff was under investigation might be of interest to the gossip mongers, but it does not contribute materially to the genuine public interest in the existence of police investigations in this area. It was known that investigations were made and prosecutions brought. I do not think that knowledge of the identity of the subject of the investigation was a material legitimate addition to the stock of public knowledge for these purposes.'[550]

With regards to Dan Johnson and information about the search, Justice Mann stated: 'The BBC's information trail started with the information provided by the confidential source, with its ultimate source in Operation Yewtree. From this Mr Johnson knew, or ought to have known, that the information was confidential and secretive. The BBC have accepted that, so far as SYP was concerned, the information about the investigation was information in respect of which Sir Cliff had a reasonable expectation of privacy, and the same applies as against the Metropolitan Police [Operation Yewtree]. It simply ought not to have been disclosed, as the provider of the information doubtless well knew.'

Later Justice Mann added: 'So far as the information about the search is concerned, Mr Johnson did not get that in a straightforward manner. He got it in the circumstances appearing above. No doubt when journalists get information, or get confirmation of information they believe they have, they will justifiably resort to subtle means from time to time, in the public interest of publishing justifiably publishable information. Mr Johnson might regard this sort of thing as "old-fashioned journalism", and in many circumstances there may ultimately be nothing too wrong about it when looked at in the round. However, in the present case Mr Johnson relied on a form of threat (not overtly made in a hostile manner but understood by SYP nonetheless) to get his information about the search and the confirmation he felt he needed. He knew the information was not volunteered by SYP, whether for its own purposes or otherwise. It matters not whether he was in a position, by himself, to carry out that threat. SYP thought it could be implemented.'[551]

Later, observing the singer's right of reply on the day of the raid, Justice Mann said, 'In my view it is also proper to give the subject [Cliff Richard] some sort of opportunity to challenge publication before it happens, whether by persuasion or injunction. The question arises as to whether the dealings between Miss Kitterick on the one hand and Sir Cliff's representatives on the other, prior to publication at 1 p.m., was in fact sufficient to give a fair opportunity for a statement or discussion before the broadcast or not. Bearing in mind the professed objectives of the right of reply opportunity, I do not think that it was.'[552]

Continuing his observations on Cliff's right of reply, Justice Mann offered, 'To that extent it can be said that the BBC did not quite comply with what it itself saw as the ethical requirements of its journalism at that stage. The real reason for that was, in my view, because it was giving a lot of weight, in its own deliberations, to preserving the exclusivity of its own scoop.'[553]

Referring to the actual news broadcasts themselves, Justice Mann suggested they were 'presented with a significant degree of breathless sensationalism' and that 'there was an attempt to lend drama to the broadcast by showing cars entering the property, and the helicopter shots added more, somewhat false, drama.'[653] Later, in a frank and forthright statement, Justice Mann said; 'In short, and insofar as it is relevant under this head, the BBC went in for an invasion of Sir Cliff's privacy rights in a big way.'[554] Given the litany of criticism aimed at the BBC in Justice Mann's verdict, it was little surprise that he found the BBC *had* infringed the singer's privacy: 'So far as the main claim in this case is concerned, I find that Sir Cliff had privacy rights in respect of the police investigation and that the BBC infringed those rights without a legal justification. It did so in a serious way and also in a somewhat sensationalist way. I have rejected the BBC's case that it was justified in reporting as it did under its rights to freedom of expression and freedom of the press. I did not find it necessary to rule on the claim under the Data Protection Act. Sir Cliff therefore wins on the privacy point and has established liability.'[555]

Justice Mann summarised, before going on to consider the level of damages.[556] These were likely to be substantial and Justice Mann wasted little time in describing how the allegations and broadcasting of the raid affected the singer: 'The impression he [Cliff Richard] had was that his life's work was being torn apart. The adverse publicity removed his status as a confident and respected artist and what he described as "a good ambassador for this country". He felt and still feels tainted. His health suffered, and he contracted shingles, which he put down to stress. Although there was no medical evidence as to that causation I accept that throughout the entire period he was the subject of severe stress, and that stress far exceeded the anxiety, and perhaps some levels of stress, that he would inevitably have been under from the investigation by itself had the news of it not been publicised.

'Although at the time of these events Sir Cliff was seventy-three, he was still working as an entertainer. However, as a result of these events that part of his life was, to an extent, put on hold, and his professional standing was diminished. Scurrilous material was published on the internet, which cannot have been pleasant. Sony, with whom he had intended to record an album in 2015, put the recording on hold. A planned release to coincide with his seventy-fifth birthday did not prove possible. An updated edition of his autobiography was shelved – a matter which arises under the special damages head, but I refer to it now to show the general effect on Sir Cliff's life.'[657]

He continued, 'Because of what he perceived as the stigma surrounding the revelations, Sir Cliff felt he could not or should not participate in other events, such as appearances at the London Palladium and at Canterbury Cathedral. Nor did he feel he could attend tennis tournaments (as a spectator), which he generally very much enjoyed. He claimed that retailers declined to stock one of his annual calendars because of the publicity (which, again, I refer to to show the general effect on his life, irrespective of any special damages claim that might arise out of it). Even after it was announced he would not be charged, a charity with which he had been concerned (Dreamflight) asked him not to appear at a 'waving off' of a flight of sick children because (he was told) his appearance might detract from a team of Paralympians who were doing the same thing. I accept all this evidence. It adds up to a life that was hugely affected for almost two years by loss of public status and reputation, embarrassment, stress, upset and hurt, with some consequential health effects.'[557]

It was a damning indictment of the manner in which the BBC reported the story and how they blatantly infringed the singer's privacy in the quest for a 'scoop' ahead of their rivals. The BBC were found liable and ordered to pay £210,000 in general damages, however the pay-out would likely be significantly higher once special damages were decided at a later hearing.

For Cliff, there was a feeling of relief rather than elation.

I didn't feel like standing up and punching the air. I just sat quietly, took a deep breath and absorbed his verdict.[558]

He emerged from the court to a rendition of 'Congratulations' from the gathering of his die-hard fans and was clearly too emotional to speak to the throng of reporters who had assembled wanting a quote, other than saying it was 'going to take a little while' and 'I hope you'll forgive me',[559] before he climbed into a taxi. He sped away, leaving his lawyer, Gideon Benaim, to speak on his behalf saying the impact on Cliff had been 'profound'.

'He [Cliff] never expected after sixty years in the public eye that his privacy and reputation would be tarnished in this way, and that he would need to fight such a battle,' Benaim said. 'Although he felt it necessary to pursue this case – and the sum awarded in damages is one of the highest ever in this area of law – Sir Cliff's motivation was not for personal gain, as he knew all along that he would be substantially out of pocket no matter what. His aim has been to try to right a wrong, and, to ensure as best he could, that no other innocent person would have to endure what he went through.'[560]

The ramifications of the singer winning the trial created, as expected, a shockwave through British media, who *en masse* questioned the impact Justice Mann's verdict might have on the future of journalism. First out of the blocks was the BBC, with Director of News, Fran Unsworth, offering a statement.

We are sorry for the distress that Sir Cliff has been through. We understand the very serious impact that this has had on him. We have thought long and hard about how we covered this story. On reflection there are things we would have done differently; however, the judge has ruled that the very naming of Sir Cliff was unlawful. So even had the BBC not used helicopter shots or ran the story with less prominence, the judge would still have found that the story was unlawful; despite ruling that what we broadcast about the search was accurate. This judgement creates new case law and represents a dramatic shift against press freedom and the long-standing ability of journalists to report on police investigations, which in some cases has led to further complainants coming forward. This impacts not just the BBC, but every media organisation. This isn't just about reporting on individuals. It means police investigations, and searches of people's homes, could go unreported and unscrutinised. It will make it harder to scrutinise the conduct of the police and we fear it will undermine the wider principle of the public's right to know. It will put decision-making in the hands of the police. We don't believe this is compatible with liberty and press freedoms; something that has been at the heart of this country for generations. For all of these reasons, there is a significant principle at stake. That is why the BBC is looking at an appeal.[561]

Unsworth was quickly joined by other notable media figures, all pouring scorn on the verdict's implied threat to British journalism. Tim Shipman, the *Sunday Times* political editor, called the ruling 'an atrocity for a free media', adding it would 'dramatically restrict the freedom to report,'[562] while Ian Murray, the Executive Director of the Society of Editors, said, 'The ruling to make it unlawful that anyone under investigation can be named is a major step and one that has worrying consequences for press freedom and the public's right to know.'[563]

Commenting on the verdict, the *Sun* said: 'The privacy ruling in Sir Cliff Richard's favour is profoundly dangerous and a devastating affront to press freedom. Effectively handing all suspects a new right to anonymity until charged is also far too fundamental a change to be made by one judge at the stroke of a pen. Not only must the BBC appeal and win, the Government must legislate so police can name suspects once arrested, with the press able to report it.'[564]

Of course, for anonymity of those accused to become law it would need to be passed by Parliament, but it's questionable whether Government had a desire for such a move.

'Concerning anonymity,' says John Harding, a leading solicitor in the field of serious assault allegations, particularly offences of a sexual nature, 'any change in the law would require Parliament to accept that sexual allegations are more damaging to an individual than offences of murder or theft. Parliament has shown no appetite in the past to recognise such and it shows no appetite to amend the law in the future. Nonetheless, such allegations *can* be more damaging. The simple allegation carries a stigma like no other offence. If the Government itself has recognised this by granting complainants in such cases anonymity, why not extend it to defendants?'[565]

On the very day Justice Mann gave his verdict, Anna Soubry, then a Conservative MP, took an opportunity in Prime Minister's Questions to call for Theresa May, then Prime Minister, to introduce such a law to stop police suspects being named by the media until they are charged. Soubry, a barrister herself, suggested it could be called 'Cliff's Law', asking Theresa May, 'Would the Prime Minister look again now at changing the law so that a suspect is not named by the media, except in exceptional cases, until such time as they're charged?'

Soubry had history with attempting to introduce such a law. In 2010 she had tabled the Anonymity (Arrested Persons) Private Members' Bill to the House of Commons seeking to introduce legislation dealing with the naming of a person arrested until he/she is charged or a Crown Court judge deems it's in the public's interest to name him/her. The bill never got beyond its second reading.

Soubry didn't have much luck in 2018 either, with Prime Minster Theresa May saying in response to her call for 'Cliff's Law': 'This is a difficult issue, it does have to be dealt with sensitively. There may well be cases where actually the publication of a name enables other victims to come forward and therefore to strengthen the case against an individual.'[566]

Cliff surfaced later that night to give an interview to ITV

News. During it he commented on the furore surrounding the implied threat to freedom of speech resulting from his victory.

I just hope the press don't think the freedom of speech is in danger here. It's not. It's their abuse of it that's in danger. That's what I'll always fight. The worst thing [the BBC] *did, the most disastrous thing they did, which has now been ruled by the judge, the most unlawful thing they did was to name me before I was charged.*[567]

He also commented on how his life had been shattered by the accusations, the BBC infringement of privacy and the subsequent trial, which gave him sleepless nights and resulted in bouts of ill-health.

I'm sure I'll recover. There are aspects in my life I recognise now for instance. In Wimbledon there is a tunnel between Centre Court and Court One. I used to use it regularly to go and see the matches I was interested in on Court One and it went right past the ball boys' dressing room. I won't go there now. I won't go anywhere near children. Why? I've spent my whole life hugging people's grandchildren. But because of this thing now . . . There's aspects of my life now even when I'm having photographs taken, I try not to make contact.[568]

Cliff's victory in court was, however, tinged with sadness. During the lengthy judicial process, he had lost people close to him. His sister Donella had died in 2016 and, the year before, his veteran tour manager David Bryce had passed away. Also in 2015, tragically young, his niece Linzi had lost her fight against cancer at the age of just thirty-five. All of them died while Cliff's name was being dragged through the dirt. And then, of course, there was Cilla Black, perhaps Cliff's closest showbiz friend, who had died following a fall in Malaga in 2015. Cliff wished Cilla, like all the others, had been alive to see him cleared.

It would have been fantastic to share it with her. We'd have had to have cracked open a bottle, no doubt about it. She would have come in with her heels on; with Cilla there was always high heels. She was fantastic. So full of life. Cilla would have been great to share this with because she was very much on my side.[569]

In time, the BBC would appeal against the verdict, which meant the lurid accusations would be dragged up once more, Cliff's name smeared across the newspapers in connection with them again – even though he had been cleared – and the anxiety and stress returning to the singer as he awaited the result and all its ramifications.

But that would be in the future. Now, in the summer of 2018 with the trial over, Cliff vindicated and damages settled, the singer wanted to put the entire episode behind him, move on and resurrect his career, which had been in limbo since the allegations first surfaced in 2014.

However, that would be easier said than done.

I have got past it, but I don't think I will ever get over it. Not fully. It did too much damage and it left too much of a stain on my life. It's certainly not the kind of thing you can ever just forget.[570]

CHAPTER 30

If you can't forget, is it ever possible to move on?

The previous four years had been intensely traumatic for Cliff; from the moment he watched the raid on his apartment via a TV screen in Portugal to finding out the allegations he was facing. Then there was the media scrutiny, the salacious headlines, the internet gossip, the conspiracy theories. All the while Cliff's accusers hid behind anonymity while his name was bandied across the world. His career came to a standstill, opportunities were lost, not to mention the millions of pounds he spent fighting his corner. He became ill, suffered intolerable stress and feared he would forever be tainted by the abuse allegations.

Of course, some would point to the fact that Cliff, in the circumstances, was fortunate: he had considerable wealth to draw on to fund his legal battle and he had a close group of friends offering their support, people such as Gloria Hunniford, Paul Gambaccini and John McElynn.

And his name was cleared.

Eventually.

But mud sticks and he feared his legacy might be forever tainted. The music industry is littered with those whose misdemeanours are more readily remembered than their music. Jerry Lee Lewis might have given us 'Great Balls of Fire', but his marriage to his thirteen-year-old cousin continues to haunt his legacy. Michael Jackson might once have been the King of Pop, but now his name is forever linked to allegations of sexual abuse against young boys. R Kelly is known more for doing time for sexual abuse than any of his hits and PJ Proby is probably best-known for his trousers ripping on stage in a provocative dance rather than any of his hits in the sixties.

Was this a fate awaiting Cliff? Would the allegations of sex abuse – even when proved without foundation – be his abiding legacy despite him selling over 250 million records, having numerous Number 1s and charting in eight continuous decades? Would his charitable work, his knighthood, and decades of being a respected family entertainer count for nothing?

A study by the University of Oxford Centre for Criminology opens with a quote saying: 'Accusations of serious criminality, especially alleged wrongdoing, are often their own convictions in the high court of public opinion, because the stigma is so severe, and because definitively proving innocence in a disputed sex case is often impossible.'[571]

Such accusations can have catastrophic results on the alleged perpetrator, damaging their career, their personal life, their relationships and their health, leaving their lives in tatters. And regardless of any reputational suffering, the psychological scars of those wrongly accused can last indefinitely. A 2020 study found 60 per cent of those wrongly accused had an increase in paranoia and anxiety; self-stigma became an issue as did mental health, with depression, panic attacks and even suicidal thoughts present. Over 50 per cent exhibited signs of PTSD and when looking at relationships with others, 87 per cent reported becoming socially withdrawn and isolated, often due to a sense of alienation, or deliberate withdrawal due to fear of being burdensome to others.[572]

Two years after the raid on his Berkshire apartment, Cliff described suffering similar symptoms.

> *The fact of the raid; the false insinuation that I was guilty, knowing that I was innocent; and, of course, the worldwide press coverage that followed the BBC's decision to cover the raid, caused me a long period of distress, humiliation, anxiety and illness. As you would expect, I had trouble carrying on with life as normal.*[573]

And what of the accusers of these false crimes, those who hide behind anonymity for the rest of their lives while their victims – for that is what they are – are left to pick up the pieces? Often, the accusers have a history of criminality themselves, are experienced in lying to authorities or have made fraudulent claims. They are often mentally unwell and their accusation or accusations are usually a way to cover up other behaviour often to pursue emotional gains.

Then, of course, there's calculated deception, where accusers knowingly bring false charges purely out of self-interest such as financial gain, career advancement, legal victory or simply wishing to see someone else fall. Narcissists and sociopaths are more inclined towards manipulation and these personality types lack moral hesitation around weaponising lies against their targets. By willingly trading another person's wellbeing for their own profit, these accusers demonstrate the darkest motivations.

And it's all so easy.

Matthew Scott is a criminal law barrister with forty years' experience. In his blog he illustrates this perfectly in connection to a chance encounter with Cliff Richard in the 1970s: 'I was 15 when I met Cliff Richard. I was a pupil at a boys only boarding school. Every Sunday – this was back in the 1970s – we all had to attend a religious service. Mostly these took place in the school's wonderful chapel but every so often speakers were invited to give a religious talk in a more secular setting. One of these was Cliff Richard. He was a star, albeit no longer a very trendy one, and there was great excitement as the day of his visit approached. Not only would the great man sing, play his guitar and entertain us in his characteristic happy-clappy-Jesus-loves-you sort of way, he would also answer questions, so it was said, "about anything you like." Of course, nobody would have dared ask him about his sexuality. You didn't ask visiting speakers about such things and – even though we were all, of course, pretty obsessed by sex in general – I don't remember any particular interest being expressed in Cliff's sex life. Instead, encouraged by the promise of a no holds-barred debate, I went to the meeting, shyly prepared to bowl him a deistic doosra. "Why does a perfectly good God allow famines?" or some such enigma. Sadly, I never got the chance to cross-examine the great man, or even to try out my question. Cliff set himself up on stage and displayed no apparent desire to hob-nob with any of the hundreds of starstruck adolescent boys. Indeed, as far as I could see he tried to insulate himself from any direct contact with us at all. Instead of engaging directly with the seething mass of teenagers gathered in the hall, all questions were "moderated" through a trusted side-kick who announced that the only questions allowed would be those posed to Cliff by *him*, on our behalf. So it was all a bit of a disappointment. Cliff strummed his guitar, thumped his tambourine and crooned out a few gospel numbers while running through an obviously rehearsed catechism routine with his assistant. Even though we'd not had to shell out our pocket money to listen to him, I think most of us came away feeling slightly short-changed. There were no conversions, healings or speakings in tongues, and at least one member of the audience left the hall very slightly disillusioned about the Christianity that Cliff clearly believed in so strongly. The best that can be said is that he made absolutely no attempt to molest me, or indeed anybody else. I daresay that rather dreary Sunday morning session made considerably less of an impact on Cliff than it did on me. In fact, it wouldn't surprise me if he'd entirely forgotten coming to the school.'

Later in the blog, Scott describes how, if he had been so minded, that event could have been exploited decades later in the era of bandwagoning: 'If I had a pressing need for money I would have a motive, and if I was of a dishonest disposition my meeting with Cliff in the 1970s could now provide me with an opportunity. I would feel emboldened by the announcement that another man has apparently made a sexual complaint against him.' He continues: 'I now have the perfect opportunity to present myself as a victim and solve some financial problems. I could go to the police alleging that after his dreary talk Cliff indecently assaulted me. I can surmise that there is at least one other complaint from a teenage boy – because the police or the BBC or both have already publicised the fact. I can dredge up all sorts of details from the depths of my memory – or imagination – that might give it the ring of truth. It would be a lie, but who would know? If Cliff has forgotten that he ever came to my school (which is perfectly possible), so much the better.

His denial might be uncovered, he would be seen as a liar and I would be vindicated. What is more, save in the unlikely event that a prosecution was brought against me, I could not be publicly named, whatever the result of any trial.[574]

No one can possibly defend sexual abuse, but the manner in which people can be accused of historic sexual offences, sometimes without any supporting evidence at all, must be questioned. Firstly, that allegation is magnified by their name being released as a result of the 'shaking the tree' approach adopted by the police. Then add in the current climate of the time, in Cliff Richard's case the post-Jimmy Savile era. Throw into the mix the almost inevitable inability of those accused of historic sex abuse to prove their alibi (who can recall what they were doing on a specific date a month ago, let alone three decades ago?) and a single uncorroborated allegation can become increasingly persuasive in the court of public opinion.

This was one of the reasons Cliff threw his efforts into a campaign to give sexual offence suspects full anonymity until charged. The campaign was spearheaded by Falsely Accused Individuals for Reform (FAIR) and was an initiative led by Daniel Janner QC, whose late father, Lord Janner, was the subject of twenty-two sexual offence charges, but who was deemed unfit to stand trial. It later emerged that one of those accusing Lord Janner was Carl Beech, the serial fantasist known as 'Nick', who had accused Leon Brittan, Lord Bramall and Sir Edward Heath falsely and was now serving an eighteen-year prison sentence for perverting the course of justice.

'Beech maintained in this trial that my late father raped him in the Carlton Club,' said Daniel Janner. 'The jury would have nothing of it. It is impossible to get over the hurt which such ghastly alleged acts of violence have on a law-abiding family like mine. They are corrosive. They lie on the internet with ignorant people saying that there is no smoke without fire. We loved our late father. He died an innocent man. He was a force for good and justice.'[575]

FAIR's aim was to gather 100,000 signatures in order to force Parliament to consider debating the topic of anonymity for those accused of sex abuse crimes until charged. 'It's about the rebalancing of the criminal justice system and in particular preventing the unique stain of sexual allegations sticking with people who turn out to be innocent,' commented Janner. 'It is stopping prominent people being, in Sir Cliff's words, "live bait" served up for false accusers who then come forward asking for compensation. This will not prevent genuine claimants coming forward after a person is charged.'[576]

Of his part in the launch, Cliff said:

I will be helping to launch this Parliament petition on 1 July to ensure that no one is ever again treated as appallingly as I was when my name was wrongfully exposed in the media. There must be anonymity before charge in sexual allegations unless there are exceptional circumstances. That is why FAIR's campaign is right and why I am supporting it. It should be a criminal offence to name a suspect before charge.[577]

As well as Cliff, the campaign also had the support of Paul Gambaccini and Harvey Proctor, but they were faced with criticism from the charity Rape Crisis England & Wales, whose spokesperson, Katie Russell, stated: 'Giving these suspects exceptional treatment compared to those suspected of similarly serious and stigmatising crimes would inevitably reinforce the public misconception – which is unsupported by evidence but

THE LIFE AND TRIALS OF CLIFF RICHARD

nonetheless widely held – that those suspected of sexual offences are more likely to have been falsely accused than those suspected of other types of crime. There are no grounds for changing the law specifically in relation to those suspected of sexual violence and abuse crimes.'[578]

More criticism came from Harriet Wistrich, director of the Centre for Women's Justice. She commented: 'There are believed to be a significant number of men who target vulnerable women deliberately, often by using drink or drugs and other means to ensure they are incapacitated. These sorts of cases are notoriously difficult to charge and preventing the naming of suspects will be of great assistance to such serial offenders.'[579]

Rachel Krys, of the End Violence Against Women Coalition, said: 'Very few rapes tend to result in convictions, there is a real risk this would make it worse. This would have a chilling effect on victims' ability to seek justice.'[580]

As it happened, the campaign only gathered 27,000 signatures. Part of this was put down to having to abandon the petition when the 2019 General Election was called,[581] but the campaign was perhaps not helped by Cliff's comments during an appearance on ITV's *Loose Women* the previous year, when he said:

> *Some people have spent two years in prison and been innocent. It's the danger if we don't change the law, it's going to keep happening to innocent people. When I was in the court with the BBC, I saw a quote that I loved, a Judge Blackstone from way back, said: 'I would rather ten guilty people escape than one innocent person suffer.'*[582]

While Cliff's anonymity campaign stalled – for now – there was one victory that he could at last claim, as the final chapter in his ongoing battle with the BBC closed.

In July 2018, following Cliff winning the High Court Judgement against the BBC infringing his privacy, and being awarded £210,000 in the process, the broadcaster sought leave to appeal the verdict arguing the ruling could put press freedom at stake. However, Justice Mann refused the BBC's attempt to mount an appeal, saying it did not have a real prospect of success and added that there was no other compelling reason why Court of Appeal judges should consider the case.[583]

It also emerged that, during the hearing, the corporation had agreed to pay £850,000 towards Cliff's legal fees.[584] By September 2018, the figure that the BBC had to pay towards the singer's legal costs had risen to £2 million, although Cliff suggested he was still 'substantially out of pocket'.[585]

Following legal advice, the BBC decided it did not have a realistic chance of overturning the judgement and that any appeal 'would inevitably mean an expensive legal *cul de sac* and one that would simply prolong Sir Cliff's distress'.[586] Finally, after four years, it was finished.

What the BBC did was an abuse. They took it upon themselves to be the judge, jury and executioner. If heads roll then maybe it's because it's deserved. The BBC knew the police were not going to name me. It seemed to me there was a great deal of arrogance there in that they took no notice of the police, they obviously didn't read again the Leveson report.[587]

As far as Cliff was concerned, it really was time to move on.

CHAPTER 31

Career-wise, Cliff had effectively been in limbo since the allegations first came to light in August 2014. There had been a few concerts here and there, while his album *Just... Fabulous Rock 'n' Roll*, which he had somehow summoned the strength to record in the early days of the scandal, had been released to limited fanfare in 2016 and was followed up a year later with a compilation album, *Stronger Thru The Years*, which sold only 60,000 copies.

But there'd been no album of new original music since 2004 and, with the court case over and 2018 being the sixtieth anniversary of the release of 'Move It', Cliff was determined to do something special.

A UK tour had been planned for later in the year to celebrate the anniversary, but it was the news of an album of brand new songs that really generated excitement for his fans. The album had been recorded immediately following the trial and during the period Justice Mann was considering his verdict, a period of uncertainty for Cliff as he waited for the result. Nevertheless, he had flown to Miami to record twelve brand new tracks, even roping in old friend Olivia Newton-John to perform a duet with him. The album stayed under wraps until the trial was done and dusted and it was finally released in November 2018.

It's going to be called Rise Up!, *which for me feels the right title to have, because after the bad period of two years in my life where I couldn't sleep and think about anything, it seems to me that I've managed to rise up, so I feel it's a good title for the album and the songs are good as well. I'm so thrilled with it. I'm hoping that it will be a revival for me, not only for me personally as a person, but maybe as someone who could be recognised by some of these younger people to be a valuable artist. I'm not messing around with it, it's for real and you should really close your eyes when you listen to new records 'cause you don't need to know how old I am. And I'm not going to tell you.*[588]

The UK music scene had shifted immeasurably since Cliff had last released any original material in 2004. Now the charts were dominated by artists such as Drake, Cardi B, Calvin Harris and Ariana Grande. Cliff had scored ten Number 1 singles before any of these had even been born. Songs and albums were written by committee now rather than individuals and, consequently, a level of uniqueness had disappeared from the mainstream music scene. Successful songwriting teams hopped from artist to artist offering their services, but simply came up with soundalikes based on what had worked before.

It was a far cry from the early days of rock 'n' roll when Cliff burst onto the scene with his distinct style, albeit copied from Elvis. Whether Cliff's new album could be a platform for his 'revival' remained to be seen. Perhaps disappointingly, he too had succumbed to the quest for a hit by employing teams of songwriters, particularly Scandinavian writers-for-hire such as Sigurd Rosnes and Martin Sjolie, who had written for Sigrid and Cher amongst others, and Carl Falk, who had composed songs for One Direction and Demi Lovato.

Perhaps this accounts for Alexis Petridis saying in his review of the album, 'The light entertainer's first album of new material for fourteen years is a bet-hedging hotch-potch of styles and ideas.' 'Listening to the album there is no individuality, no identity, no real theme to the record. It is safe in its searching for a hit, and a veil of desperation with wanting to be liked by his current fans, while seemingly trying to coax a younger audience, hangs like a shadow over the album.' [589]

One almost wishes that Cliff had gone leftfield in his 'comeback', perhaps in the way Rick Rubin stripped down Johnny Cash for his *American Recordings* or how Martyn Ware and Glen Gregory of Heaven 17 took Tina Turner from Vegas showgirl to synthpop seductress on 'Let's Stay Together', paving the way for her *Private Dancer* album and her stratospheric comeback. Similarly, Tom Jones was reintroduced to new audiences when he teamed up with Art Of Noise to record a version of Prince's 'Kiss' – and he's never looked back since.

For whatever reason, Cliff couldn't reinvent himself or didn't want to reinvent himself. As a result, rather than being thrust back into the limelight, he blended into the background, reverting to a light entertainer, a crooner, a safe interpreter of other people's songs written for the masses but appealing only to the faithful. One of the only songs on the album not to be written by a team of Scandinavian guns-for-hire was the title track and lead single, 'Rise Up', which was composed by

Terry Britten and Graham Lyle, both well-known to Cliff as Britten had been Cliff's guitarist for many years and had co-written 'Devil Woman' while Lyle had composed 'What's Love Got to Do With It', the worldwide hit for Tina Turner. Alex Petridis referred to the song 'Rise Up' as being one of the 'good things' on the album, but upon its release as a single it spent just one week in the singles chart at Number 30 before disappearing (although it did spend one week at the top of the vinyl-only singles chart).

This was despite getting rare airplay on BBC Radio 2, where it was premiered on Ken Bruce's show. The album fared little better, spending a debut week at Number 4 before sliding down to Number 97 after nine weeks. It wasn't really the 'revival' Cliff had hoped for.

And neither was there any evidence of the new album influencing younger artists or them recognising him as 'a valuable artist' as Cliff himself had hoped. In fact, the sole celebrant of Cliff in the music world continued to be Morrissey. In a later interview with *Medium*, Morrissey was asked about his own difficulties with the mainstream press and whether there was an artist he felt a kinship with. 'Cliff Richard,' he answered immediately. 'Mostly because I understand the terror he endured at the hands of the press who had him executed pre-trial. But also, he had something like sixty hits over five decades yet no radio station would play his music which struck me as unjustifiable because radio is a public service. Five years ago I wrote a song called "Knockabout World" with Cliff Richard in mind. Under such terrible circumstances I think he's done incredibly well.'

So, it seemed, despite his hoped-for career revival with *Rise Up*, Cliff remained on the periphery, his relevance in the world of modern popular music perhaps more questionable than ever.

Not that his diehard fans seemed to care. They packed out the venues in late 2018 as Cliff hit the road on his *60th Anniversary Tour*, with an additional 100,000 fans watching the performance from Manchester's Bridgewater Hall in cinemas worldwide as it was livestreamed.

The set list saw him draw not only on his classic hits and tracks from his *Rise Up* album, but also some of the rock 'n' roll standards that inspired him, songs such as 'Peggy Sue', 'Heartbreak Hotel' and 'Wake Up Little Susie'. While any reference to the BBC was met with resounding boos from the audience, reviews for the concerts were reasonably well received. The *Nottingham Post* wrote, 'With a voice that has defied the test of time, he put it to good effect unloading endless payloads of pop perkiness,'[590] while writing in The *Telegraph*, Neil McCormick said, 'Sir Cliff's comeback seems assured. He sang pop classics from every decade of his astonishing career, and his voice was as smooth, rounded and pristine as ever.'[591] Dave Simpson wrote in the *Guardian*, under a headline proclaiming, 'From ghastly to sublime in determined return', that 'The chronological, two-hour performance traces a mercurial if at times bonkers trajectory from "Move It's "British Elvis" to later horrors such as "The Millennium Prayer", which turns the venue into something akin to a religious rally.'[592]

From the UK the tour moved to Denmark for three concerts before returning to England for a special one-off concert for BBC Radio 2's *In Concert* series in November. However, the stress and the strain of the year, the trial and the appeal, not to mention the recent run of shows, where Cliff gave his all, as ever, had taken its toll on the 78-year-old singer. It was discovered he had developed laryngitis, which forced him to withdraw from the show.

It was a rare moment of ill-health for Cliff who had kept

himself fit and in good shape throughout his career. He plays tennis two or three times a week, visits the gym regularly, controls his diet, and he rarely touched alcohol until he purchased his vineyard. Even so, he won't drink to excess, limiting himself to two glasses if, and when, he does drink. It is a regime that made him appear ageless, allowed him to keep his 30-inch waistline throughout his career and earned him the nickname 'The Peter Pan of Pop'.

> *It's hard work staying in shape. But you have to work at everything if you want to stay fit.*[593]

The singer admits to colouring his hair with a light brown tint to stop any signs of greying and to taking nine tablets and capsules a day to keep him healthy.

> *I think maybe one of them is keeping me alive, but I don't know which one it is. So, I'll keep taking them all.*[594]

And his complexion is kept youthful thanks to tips picked up when appearing on television.

> *The make-up girls on* Top of the Pops *used to recommend things to me and I'd go and buy a gallon of the stuff. I knew they knew what was good for the skin.*[595]

But ageing catches up with us all, and even the Peter Pan of Pop can't hold back the ravages of time.

> *It is a stressful thing now. I know I cannot possibly be the Peter Pan of Pop because I don't look eighteen anymore. I can try to*

look good, but I can't compete with Brad Pitt. He is young and great-looking. All I can do is make the best of what I've got. People say the press is obsessed with the way I look, but not as obsessed as I am. But I do believe people who age well think and act young. I still feel eighteen inside.[596]

In 2020 he celebrated his eightieth birthday. The year should have been dominated by his '*Great 80 Tour*', which would take in ten locations across the UK and culminate in two nights at the Royal Albert Hall, with the final performance there on the eve of his actual birthday. But, with the world under the shadow of Covid, plans had to be scrapped. An announcement on his official website said: 'I'm dismayed to announce the postponement of my 2020 shows – we'll have to hold on to the thought that we can party together in 2021 for an even bigger and better 80th birthday celebration! I cannot wait to see all my fans! Stay safe!'

With Covid ravaging the globe and with Cliff having lost a number of those nearest and dearest to him in the previous few years, it would only be natural if Cliff occasionally dwelt on his own mortality. But death couldn't be further from his mind.

If you can prolong your life and hold off death for a while, why not? It is what I try to do. I would like to play tennis for my 100th birthday and I will.[597]

However, having watched his mother die of dementia, Cliff knew all too well the devastating effects the disease had on the individual's standard of living and he revealed openly that he'd had discussions with other close family members about the possibility of euthanasia if he was struck down with dementia. In an interview he stated that he had made a death pact with one of his sisters, a surprising admission given his faith and the church's stance of being against assisted suicide.

> *I said, look if this happens to me, I'll do the same for you if you'll do it for me, don't let it go on too long. And just make sure I'm looked after, because I don't want to be a burden on anybody else.*[598]

For the time being, Cliff was in good health and any dramatic headlines about death pacts were just that, newspaper headlines.

He spent lockdown at his home in Barbados, but kept busy by putting the finishing touches to his autobiography, performing a 'lockdown set' for the Royal Albert Hall Home season to raise money for the venue which, like so many others, was shut during the crisis, and recording tracks via Zoom for a new album.

Titled *Music... The Air That I Breathe*, it featured five previously recorded duets with artists Bonnie Tyler, Albert Hammond, Sheila Walsh, the Bellamy Brothers and the Piano Guys that had not been released on an album before, five newly recorded covers, and two brand new songs, 'Falling For You', co-written by Chris Eaton who had previously composed 'Saviour's Day' , and 'PS Please', which featured Mark Knopfler on guitar.

> *I'm so thrilled with it because it's a very diverse album. I just hope, even if you're not a Cliff Richard fan listening, you might find something on here that you like because they're all quite different.*[599]

The album was released on 30 October 2020, and entered the album charts at Number 3, his highest charting album in ten years.

It was his 46th Top 10 album, which bettered Elvis in the UK, and by breaking into the Top 5 it meant that Cliff became the first artist ever – and very probably the last – to score a Top 5 album in eight consecutive decades. It was a phenomenal achievement that began on 25 April 1959, when the album *Cliff* entered the Top 5 behind the original soundtracks to *South Pacific, Gigi, My Fair Lady* and Elvis Presley's LP *Elvis Presley Rock 'n' Roll.*

When I was told that I had had a top five album in eight consecutive decades, in fact my feet have not touched the ground since, because you can't plan that.[600]

It wasn't until a year later that Cliff could finally embark on his *The Great 80 Tour* following its Covid cancellation. It would prove to be an emotional journey; many of those involved had been due to take part the previous year and had seen their lives and livelihoods decimated by the pandemic. Fans, too, were eager to experience the communion-like atmosphere of a live concert after having been in lockdown for so long and seen their day-to-day activities curtailed or stopped altogether. Now, over thirteen dates across England and Scotland fans, technicians and performers could come together to belatedly celebrate Cliff's eightieth birthday.

The tour kicked off in Sheffield where adoring fans, some wearing Cliff T-shirts while others wore Cliff facemasks, watched a singer obviously thrilled to be back on stage as he bounded through an effortless two-hour set. By the time the tour had reached the Royal Albert Hall – practically Cliff's second home – it had become a well-oiled machine.

'There aren't many sights more utterly delightful in modern entertainment than seeing Britain's oldest pop star lead 5,000 fans of a similar vintage in a spirited singalong of "Young ones, darling we're the young ones",' wrote Neil McCormick in his *Daily Telegrap*h review. 'Sir Cliff still has all the moves: the twirls, shoulder shifts, finger points, leg shakes, hip swivels, bum wiggles and the truly terrible amateur dramatics in which he enacts disappointment at being unable to deliver a letter during "Carrie", indicates the relative sizes of speakers in "Wired for Sound" and does the evil eyes in "Devil Woman". It might be corny, but it is exactly what the audience came to see.[601]

Despite giving the concert four stars out of five, McCormick did note one concession to age in the performance. 'Let's just say the quality and sound of the lead vocals fluctuated suspiciously throughout, with certain songs evidently relying on pre-recorded parts. For me, it's a pity Richard feels the need to rely on such showbiz trickery, because it is clear that his voice is still pliant and tuneful.'[602]

Nevertheless, McCormick reported a joyous event, and it was similar throughout the tour, and he concluded by writing: 'As he launched into a flashy version of "We Don't Talk Anymore", his aged fans rose to their feet in approval, and a section of the crowd rushed to the front of the stage. Well, I say rushed. Not everyone in the venue was quite as sprightly as the star. But when their old idol sang, time melted away. That is the magic of music.'[603]

The concerts were a runaway success for Cliff and it wasn't just the tour that ensured Cliff ended 2021 on a high note. Since his first calendar was released in 1979, his enthusiastic fanbase had flocked to buy them with over 1.5m being sold. Now it emerged that his calendar for 2022, which included the 81-year-old posing shirtless for August in only swimming trunks, had beaten everyone from Elvis Presley to Kylie Minogue to Harry Styles to the top spot.

Cliff was showing no signs of slowing down and, it seemed, the chance of him retiring wasn't even under consideration.

I don't know if I ever want to retire. I don't mind stopping. Stopping would mean that I could absolutely change my mind any time I wanted to, or phone my office and say, 'Can you get us a couple of nights at the Royal Albert Hall?' So, retiring is not in my vocabulary, but stopping is good for me – I can work whenever I want to, if I want to.[604]

There appeared little chance of him stopping in 2022 with his own calendar bulging with projects. A Christmas album was planned, which would be recorded in April; Cliff was to be part of Queen Elizabeth II's Jubilee pageant later in the year, where he would ride an open-topped double-decker bus through London's streets as an icon of his era, the 1950s; and BBC2 had granted him his own Christmas TV show, an hour-long special imaginatively titled *Cliff at Christmas*.

He had also agreed to take part in a major documentary for Channel 4, called *The Accused: National Treasures On Trial*. In this film, Cliff would appear alongside Paul Gambaccini and Neil Fox as they reflected on their ordeals in being falsely accused of historic sex crimes and publicly hung out to dry by the police and the press, which resulted in their lives and reputations being upended.

It had been eight years since the allegations against Cliff had emerged, six years since he was cleared, and four years since he had been victorious over the BBC in his privacy trial. Whatever he said, whatever he did, it seemed Cliff couldn't totally move on despite his best intentions. Always, the shadow of the allegations would lurk in the background; despite all he could say, despite the ruling of the courts, there would be those who said 'no smoke without fire'.

By appearing in *The Accused: National Treasures On Trial*, Cliff was perhaps continuing to fan the flames, but he knew the allegations were absurd and untrue. British justice had proved it so. Those who didn't believe it would never be converted, their prejudice against him ingrained. What he could achieve by appearing in such a documentary was to highlight the question of anonymity until charged for those accused.

In 2022, alongside Gambaccini and Daniel Janner QC, Cliff renewed his attempts to get MPs to grant anonymity for sexual offence suspects before they are charged. They had tried in 2019 to get the topic debated in Parliament but failed. This time they managed to get the Anonymity of Suspects Bill debated in October 2022, following an impassioned plea by Cliff to MPs and peers. His case was championed by Sir Christopher Chope MP, who had attended the meeting at which the singer spoke and was 'impressed by what was said at that gathering because, essentially, it is a campaign by people who have been falsely accused and whose lives have been completely wrecked as a consequence.'[605]

During the debate, Sir Christopher read what Cliff had said to the meeting in June:

I am pleased to support the new pressure group Falsely Accused Individuals for Reform . . . Being falsely accused myself and having that exposed in the media was the worst thing that has happened to me in my entire life. Even though untrue, the stigma is almost impossible to eradicate. Hence the importance of FAIR's campaign to change the law to provide for anonymity before charge in sexual allegations and hence my continued work with FAIR in the future. Had this proposed change in the law been enacted when the police decided to raid my apartment following the allegations of a fantasist, the BBC would not have been able to film this event, name me, (even though the South Yorkshire Police had decided not to) and so plunge my life and those close to me into fear and misery.[606]

Sponsoring the Bill, Sir Christopher went on: 'It took a long time for Sir Cliff to be able to clear his name and I think it's clear even now he still bears the scars of that ordeal, which should never have happened. This Bill is designed to prevent other people similarly being afflicted because somebody makes an accusation anonymously, sometimes the police then act upon it and then they tip off the media or brief the media or social media as to what has happened, thereby destroying the principles – which I think should be there – which are that people are innocent until proved guilty, and that they should be able to enjoy anonymity until such time as they might be charged with an offence."[607]

Sadly, the Bill ran out of time for consideration in the chamber and the debate was adjourned, meaning it failed to progress and is unlikely to be considered in its current form.

Despite Cliff's best intentions the fight, for the time being, was over.

CHAPTER 32

The singer, meanwhile, had another battle on his hands in 2022, and this time with a rather unexpected opponent.

Rapper, singer and songwriter Stormzy had had a meteoric rise to fame in 2014 as an independent artist before signing to Warner and then being poached by Universal Records in 2020 for £10 million at a time when everything he touched seemed to turn to gold. But after winning a MOBO for Best Grime Act, his first album for Universal saw him drop his trademark hard rapping style and switch to a gospel sound for a collection of Christian-influenced songs. 'People are now calling him the Cliff Richard of hip-hop,' a source told the *Daily Mail*.[608]

Stormzy was set to release his new album, *This Is What I Mean*, on 25 November 2022, the same day that Cliff was launching his new record, *Christmas With Cliff*. With such a title, it was blatantly obvious that Cliff was after the coveted Christmas Number 1 album.

The singer's first wholly Christmas album since 2003, *Christmas With Cliff* contained thirteen new recordings of Christmas music such as 'It's the Most Wonderful Time of the Year', 'Joy to the World' and 'Rockin' Around the Christmas Tree'. It also contained three brand new songs, one of which was 'Six Days After Christmas (Happy New Year)', co-written with AJ Brown by his familiar collaborator Chris Eaton.

> *The record company requested a Christmas album and I thought, well, I haven't done one for years. I didn't realise it was nearly twenty years ago. They then sent me about 100 titles or more. I didn't realise there were that many Christmas songs that have been released over the years. So I picked nine, and then I found three new ones. They were very happy to add the new ones. That's where the single comes from. It's just an exciting time.*[609]

Now in the twilight of his career, to many people Cliff had become synonymous with Christmas. Every festive playlist would likely contain 'Mistletoe and Wine' or 'Saviour's Day' and shops would pump these songs through their speakers to provide a festive backdrop to eager spenders in the run-up to Christmas. But for Cliff, he laughs at the notion of being known as the 'King of Christmas'.

> *Everybody thinks I own Christmas. I don't! I've had four number ones, which doesn't mean you own anything. I consider myself fortunate.*[610]

Stormzy had, himself, launched attempts in the past decade to have a Christmas Number 1, particularly with singles. In 2015, in the face of stiff competition from *X Factor* winner Louisa Johnson's cover of Bob Dylan's 'Forever Young', Stormzy had campaigned to get his grime single 'Shut Up' to the top of the charts at Christmas. 'Grime music has been having an amazing couple of years,' Stormzy told *Fader* magazine. 'But this would be one of those things – like, "Oh, you don't respect grime? But we got a Christmas number one." How can you not respect a genre that has a Christmas number one?'[611]

In the end Stormzy lost out to Lewisham & Greenwich NHS Choir's mash-up of 'Bridge Over Troubled Water' and 'Fix You'. Four years later, Stormzy's 'Own It' was pipped to the Christmas Number 1 by LadBaby's 'I Love Sausage Rolls' while, the same year, the rapper's album *Heavy Is the Head* had to settle for Number 2 in the Christmas album charts being beaten to the top spot by veteran crooner Rod Stewart's *You're In My Heart*.

Perhaps 2022 would be his year. The scene was set for a Christmas showdown between Cliff and Stormzy.

It was the season of Mistletoe and Grime.

I don't know Stormzy. I'm going up against the most popular artist today, and I'm still able to compete. I'm really happy about it. I should say 'may the best man win', but I won't in case he does.[612]

Christmas With Cliff was an instant success, going straight into the album charts at Number 2, his highest ever chart position since 1993 when *The Album* hit the top spot and only the second time one of his non-compilation studio albums had reached Number 2 since 1961's *21 Today*. It was an impressive debut for the album. The only problem was that Stormzy had pipped Cliff by just 600 chart units to go straight into the charts at Number 1.

'Everyone loves a tight number one race, and this week's battle between Sir Cliff Richard and Stormzy has been an absolute classic, pitching two of our musical icons head-to-head,' said Martin Talbot, Chief Executive of the Official Charts Company. 'We at Official Charts are of course delighted to congratulate Stormzy on his big win, but it is also only right to doff our chart cap to Sir Cliff too. It takes two to make a classic chart race and that has certainly been the case this week. Great work, both!'[613]

Stormzy's album quickly dropped out of the Top 10, but *Christmas With Cliff* continued to hover around the top of the charts giving him hope of the coveted Christmas top spot. But despite a late surge that pushed his album back up to Number 2 in the Christmas week, Cliff was ultimately beaten to Number 1 by Taylor Swift's *Midnights*.

However, it's interesting to note that Cliff's late surge back up the charts was boosted by nearly 16,000 physical sales in the week running up to Christmas, the only act in the entire charts to break the 10,000 physical sales barrier (Taylor Swift sold 9,216 physical copies of her album). It points, perhaps, to the demographic of Cliff's fanbase; the older generation still wedded to CDs rather than streaming technology and, as such, an audience delighted to receive a physical copy of Cliff's album as a last-minute Christmas present.

The disappointment of not reaching Number 1 with his album was nothing compared to Cliff's sadness later in the month at hearing the news of the death of Bill Latham at the age of eighty-four. Latham was an integral figure in Cliff's life, essentially as his right-hand man from 1978 when he left Tearfund to become part of the singer's management team until 2010.

Dear all, yet another loss. This time, someone I feel as though I've known forever has left this life and moved on to a better

one. Many, if not all of you, will know of whom I write . . . Bill
Latham. He is the one who led me on to that spiritual pathway
that changed my life fully and completely. He showed me how
important it was to be charitable and also be brave enough to
speak openly of my faith. Bill was one of those people who you
could reliably lean on and I did, many times.[614]

Cliff had first met Latham in the sixties and, of course, their friendship became the topic of much tabloid fare when Latham moved in with the singer giving rise to unfounded stories of a relationship, stories Cliff repeatedly denied and which were somewhat quashed when Latham moved out to live with his wife; the singer giving them a house as a wedding present.[615]

Latham was one of the core group of friends around Cliff who kept him grounded, thereby avoiding the fate of superstars like Elvis. 'Cliff has always had good advice down the line, and good people around him,' commented DJ Mike Read. 'Elvis was surrounded by people who wouldn't say boo to him. They were all on the gravy train, all yes men. But Cliff has always been surrounded by friends who have a sense of reason, a sense of wellbeing.'[616]

Bill Latham was one of those, as was Cilla Black, as was his sister Donna. So was Olivia Newton-John. Now they had all passed away.

Olivia Newton-John, whom Cliff had been so close to and to whom there were rumours of romance, posthumously appeared on Cliff's most recent album, 2023's *Cliff with Strings – My Kinda Life*. Spanning his entire career, the album saw orchestral reworkings of some of his classic hits such as 'Living Doll', 'Summer Holiday' and 'We Don't Talk Anymore', alongside

Cliff's versions of 'Everything I Do (I Do It For You)', 'Peace In Our Time', and 'Suddenly' from the film *Xanadu*, using vocals he had recorded with Olivia Newton-John in 2015.

> *After sixty-five years in the business, it is really an emotional journey to listen back to some of my original vocals and hear just how young I was, and how my style changed over the years. These tracks mean a lot to me and they are so refreshed with the orchestral arrangements. The most emotional track on the album for me is 'Suddenly' with my dear friend Olivia Newton-John. We recorded this version together live for my 75th birthday in 2015 and it always strikes me how well our voices sounded together, and the crystal gentility that Olivia always managed to exude. I'm glad I was able to highlight this great performance again.*[617]

To support the album, which entered the charts at Number 5 before disappearing from view, a short tour was announced. Titled *The Blue Sapphire Tour*, it was an eight-date tour with six of the concerts at London's Eventim Hammersmith Apollo. It was becoming increasingly noticeable that Cliff's live dates were getting fewer and farther in-between.

He hadn't undertaken a really extensive tour since 2013 and his foreign shows had all but stopped. Time was catching up with him, but it should be remembered he was approaching his eighty-third birthday. Despite his age, reviews for *The Blue Sapphire Tour* were positive.

'With no big screens to show close ups of wrinkles, the ageless octogenarian looked and sounded unchanged from his prime, albeit it's a prime that lasted longer than most pop stars entire careers,'[618] wrote Neil McCormick in the *Daily Telegraph*, while Fergal Kinney in *The Quietus* commented: 'Dressed in a dark glitter shirt tucked into leather-effect trousers and glitter trainers, Richard moves with an energy that lays waste to his eighty-three years.'[619]

Like Paul McCartney, Mick Jagger, Keith Richards, Neil Young, Roger Daltrey and Bob Dylan and all the other septuagenarians and octogenarians continuing to tour and performing the songs they wrote during their youth, Cliff can't retire. 'These artists *live* to perform,' says Ray Waddell, who has covered the concert business for over thirty years. 'You can sell, or download, millions of records, but that's no substitute for 20,000 people loving every move you make. Very few people get to experience anything that powerful.'[620]

The shows may be fewer and shorter, but there's no way Cliff's going to stop performing. Like the others, it's in his blood, it's what he lives for. As an artist, there's no real innovation in what Cliff does, it's the same as its always been. He's been singing the same songs the same way for over sixty years, but he's been doing it with consummate professionalism and that's all his fans want. It's become nostalgia, not art. Was it ever art?

The fans don't seem to care. Sharon Matthews and her mum, Jean Firth, have been following Cliff up and down the country for forty years and, between them, have seen him in concert one thousand times.[621] But that's nothing compared to Colette Williams and her mother Ray, who have seen him in concert ten thousand times between them over fifty years.[622] Diehard fans such as these are why he continues to sell out venues in the UK year after year. They'll follow him as long as possible and, with a future tour of the UK, Australia and New Zealand announced, it seems Cliff will continue to go on as long as his voice, his body and his mind will let him.

I love the impact you have on fans who have supported you throughout the years. The feeling of love you get when you get on stage literally hits you. I'd like to take my friends on stage, so they can feel it too. It's so physical.[623]

But as Peter Pan himself acknowledged: 'Time is chasing after all of us.'

EPILOGUE

*People will forget what you said, people will forget what you
did, but people will never forget how you made them feel.*
MAYA ANGELOU

It is now over sixty years since Cliff Richard burst onto the music
scene. In doing so he opened the doors for all that followed. As
John Lennon said: 'Before Cliff Richard and "Move It", there was
nothing worth listening to in England.'[624]

With the release of that song, Cliff became Britain's rock 'n'
roll pioneer and a career was born which, at the time of writing,
had seen him record fourteen Number 1 singles and seven
Number 1 albums. Sixty-eight of his singles have reached the Top
10 and, combined, his albums and singles have spent over forty
years on the charts. He's the only singer to have five Number 1
singles in the UK in five consecutive decades and he became the
first act to reach Number 1 twice with two versions of the same
song, 'Living Doll'. He's sold 21 million singles in the UK alone,
just behind Elvis and the Beatles and an estimated 250 million
albums worldwide. These figures alone are staggering enough, but
he's also hosted TV specials, appeared in movies and musicals,

raised huge sums for charity, received an OBE and a Knighthood and been part of the fabric of British culture for eight decades.

Yet . . . Despite a career and life in the limelight, Cliff Richard remains an enigma to all and, to many, something of a figure of fun. Being an enigma is something he relishes, as he revealed back in 2008. But a figure of fun – pop's punchline – less so.

In the fifties, when he burst onto the scene as Britain's first rock 'n' roll star, there appeared nobody more threatening with his rebellious image borrowed from his American idols. But in the decades since, Cliff has morphed into many versions – some cool, many less so – in his constant quest for success and, perhaps, relevance as the music world shifted about him.

By the mid-sixties, Cliff's first golden age had faded as the acts that followed in the wake of his pioneering rock 'n' roll hit adapted and innovated the genre, quickly overhauling him both commercially and artistically. John Lennon, who had been fulsome in his praise of 'Move It', by 1963 was finding Cliff cringeworthy: 'We've always hated him, he was everything we hated in pop.'[625]

In fact, it could be suggested that 1963 was the beginning of Cliff's demise as a serious pop act. Yes, he had other hits in the sixties, but as the Beatles and the Rolling Stones, amongst others, started to dominate the music scene, Cliff began to drift away, reinventing himself subtly by moving into movies and pantomime alongside his singing career.

In doing so he assumed the mantle of a family entertainer rather than rock 'n' roll rebel. His open proclamation of faith and his seemingly sexless sex-life in the swinging sixties only cemented his image as a clean-cut showman, directly opposite to the unruly rockers getting stoned, throwing TVs out of hotel rooms and taking full advantage of their groupies. Remember, Cliff was still in his mid-twenties at this point, and while the Beatles had released

Sgt Pepper and the Beach Boys their *Pet Sounds*, both embracing innovation in pushing technological and creative boundaries, Cliff was about to represent the UK in the Eurovision Song Contest with the upbeat yet lyrically naive 'Congratulations'.

By now, his credibility was definitely gone.

He had also, of course, discovered Christianity during this decade and announced it to the world. A pop star with faith? Certainly, the idea of a rock 'n' roller talking about his religious beliefs didn't fit the image and added more fuel to the fire for those who were beginning to ridicule the singer. The seventies saw Cliff find a new soft-rock groove as a balladeer and host of TV specials. Rock 'n' roll was in his distant past as he became firmly established as a middle-of-the-road entertainer.

'The fear of Cliff is the fear of showbiz,' says Tom Ewing of pop blog *Freaky Trigger*. 'It's the lurking fate that all British entertainers want to avoid, but usually don't. Cliff was happy to be swallowed up by showbiz. He's the only person I can think of who would have done exactly the same thing if there had been no Beatles.'[626]

His forays into synthpop in the eighties, complete with roller-skating videos and lurid costumes, took themselves too seriously. He couldn't compete with the Human League, Soft Cell or Heaven 17, and their darker underbelly rooted in real life. Cliff's synthpop was light, forgettable, the sound you hear faintly in lifts and shopping malls, while the others made music that was seedy, sinister and equally at home in sordid sex clubs as it was in the corners of underground discos.

By the nineties Cliff was firmly on the outside, desperately relying on Christmas hits to sustain a chart presence, and as the millennium came and went, his career since then has been sustained by a loyal and die-hard fanbase making sure his shows sell-out, his calendars fly off the shelves, and his CDs tickle the Top 10 album charts.

Naturally, his treatment at the hands of South Yorkshire Police and the BBC gained him – on the most part – the nation's sympathy, but even an injustice on this scale couldn't forever rid Cliff of the jibes constantly being aimed at him.

Maybe it's because he lacks the artistic gravitas he seems to want so badly. In interviews he does appear to take himself and his career seriously, and why shouldn't he given all he's achieved (which is unlikely ever to be rivalled). But there is a touch of over-sensitivity in criticism or sneery condescension of him, his music or his career.

It's not helped, of course, by some of the comments he has made in interviews about wine or Jesus or Tony Blair, or how rock 'n' roll he is, or by criticising radio stations for not playing his records. More recent comments – which may be down to age – about singing without 'artificial insemination', or opting not to have his photo taken with Elvis because his hero had put on 'a lot of weight', have shown him to be out of touch maybe, arrogant perhaps, or simply old. It's hard to make a serious judgement of someone when they spoil the moment with such regularity.

Why does he keep going?

Probably because, despite everything, he still feels he's got something to prove. His career has been his life, he has sacrificed so much for it, yet he finds his music not being played on the radio and reviews are often barbed. His audience is dwindling with age, with few signs of regeneration from newer fans. Young artists don't seem to want to admit being influenced by him and there appears to be no sign of a Rick Rubin-type figure riding over the hills to revitalise his career with a fresh, innovative sound.

And perhaps that's the crux of the problem. Cliff is Cliff, always has been, singing the same songs to the same fans the same way. There's been no attempt to innovate or to push boundaries, and such reluctance means a new audience will not find him. Johnny Cash and Neil Diamond were thrown lifelines by Rick Rubin and their careers soared later in their careers. There's no sign of Cliff following their path.

And unlike Cash and Diamond, and other veterans such as Paul McCartney, Paul Simon, the Rolling Stones, Neil Young, even to a lesser extent Rod Stewart, Cliff isn't a songwriter. He's a singer, an interpreter of other people's songs. Yes, he's written a few, but there's no 'Yesterday', no 'Jumpin' Jack Flash', no 'The Sound of Silence', no 'Maggie May'. Therefore, no real artistic legacy to leave behind.

He's a crooner, albeit a good one, but when a singer dies their voice dies with them and what records of Cliff's will hold up in ten, twenty, thirty years' time? While 'Mistletoe and Wine' and 'Saviour's Day' will undoubtedly still crop up on Christmas compilations, it's probably only 'Move It' that will be remembered. And so it should, because it's a fantastic record and a trailblazing one at that. And without it we may not have had the Beatles or the Stones and everything and everyone who has come since.

It's shameful that Cliff's later years have been dominated by false sex abuse allegations, disgraceful that he should have been hauled through the justice system such as it is. Even now, we understand, Cliff has not been formally told which of the allegations laid against him were sent to the CPS. As he has said himself, he's tainted by it forever and maybe his legacy will be tainted by it also.

He doesn't deserve that. For all the jibes, for all the ridicule, for all the condescension, Cliff Richard is a national treasure. What he has achieved in his career will almost certainly never be equalled and for that alone he should be celebrated.

But there is more to Cliff: despite his insistence he enjoys being an enigma, we know he's devoted to his sisters and his close friends, we know he donates large amounts of his income to charity, we know he respects his fans, we know he's the consummate professional on stage and in the recording studio and we know that he's devoted to his faith. There's no reason to ridicule anyone for any of that, especially someone who's given so much enjoyment to so many people throughout his lifetime.

Maybe the only real loser in Cliff's life is Cliff himself in respect of family and relationships. He has said on numerous occasions he has enough nephews and nieces to make up for never having a family and he's stated that he feels he would have been a good father, but it wasn't to be.

He sacrificed it all for his career; sacrificed love, sex, a family. Maybe it's because he's asexual. His fleeting heterosexual relationships are in the distant past and, surely, if he was homosexual somebody, somewhere would have spilled the beans. As we have seen, Vicki Wickham observed that his friendship with John McElynn appears, to anyone looking on, as being a gay couple, comfortable in their relationship, but also that there seemed nothing sexual about it.

Cliff has said he simply craves company and friendship.

Perhaps that's all he wants in a life where career comes first.

I know that I looked quite cool when I started out, and that helped, but since then I've been seen as cool at some times, then very uncool at others. And, when it comes down to it, I don't think it really means anything. What is cool? I think the only true measure of coolness is success. So, I haven't done too badly.[627]

ACKNOWLEDGEMENTS

We wish to thank everyone who has been involved or who has contributed to the creation of this book. With Cliff having a career spanning nine decades of popular culture it is impossible to thank individually all the authors, biographers, journalists and commentators from which we have drawn inspiration but we acknowledge our debt to them. Special thanks must also go to Morrissey, Tris Penna and the entire team at Bonnier, especially Ciara Lloyd, who has provided so much enthusiasm, encouragement and support for this publication.

Matt & Mark

SOURCE NOTES

Prologue

1   Christopher Hitchens, *Hitch-22: A Memoir*, Atlantic Books, 2010.

2   Darren Shan, *Sons of Destiny*, HarperCollins, 2009.

Chapter 1

3   Interview with Cliff Richard, *Northern Life*, 23 March 2021 .

4   Ibid.

5   Cliff Richard, *The Dreamer: An Autobiography*, Penguin RandomHouse, 2020.

6   Cliff Richard, *Which One's Cliff?*, Hodder & Stoughton, 1977.

7   *Daily Mail*, 1 November 2011.

Chapter 2

8   Cliff Richard, *The Dreamer: An Autobiography*.

9   Steve Turner, *Cliff Richard: The Bachelor Boy*, Carlton Books, 2008.

10   *Desert Island Discs*, BBC Radio 4, 20 December 2020.

11   Interview with Cliff Richard, *Northern Life*, 23 March 2021.

12   Steve Turner, *Cliff Richard: The Bachelor Boy*, Carlton Books, 2008.

13   Ibid.

14   Cliff Richard, *The Dreamer: An Autobiography*.

15   Ibid.

16   Billy Bragg, *Roots, Radicals & Rockers: How Skiffle Changed The World*, Faber & Faber, 2018'

17   Russ Hamilton was one of the first pop singer-songwriters to come out of Liverpool and had had huge success in the UK and the USA charts in 1957 with 'We Will Make Love' and 'Rainbow'.

18   Richard, *The Dreamer*.

19   Turner, *The Bachelor Boy*.

20   Richard, *The Dreamer*.

21   Turner, *The Bachelor Boy*.

22   'Abbey Road: When UK Rock & Roll Was Born', 24 July 2021, abbeyroad.com.

23   *Melody Maker*, 14 June 1958.

24   'Classic Tracks: Move It', Richard Buskin, *Sound On Sound* magazine, November 2003.

25   *Sold On Song*, Patrick Humphries, BBC Radio 2.

26   Interview with Jack Good, *Sounds Of The 60s*, BBC Radio 2, 5 July 2014.

27   'His Violent Hip Swinging Was Revolting', John Pidgeon, *Guardian*, 26 September 2008.

28   *Sold On Song*, Patrick Humphries, BBC Radio 2.

Chapter 3

29   'Preacher & The Pop Star', Gordon Malnick, *Irish Independent*, 15 August 2014.

30   'Cliff Richard, Billy Graham & a Rally for the Faithful', Rebecca Camber, *Daily Mail*, 14 August 2014.

31   Ibid.

32   Ibid.

33   'Cilla Black Defends Cliff Richard', Ella Alexander, *Independent*, 20 August 2014.

34   *Studio 10*, Network 10, 27 March 2015.

35   'Sir Cliff Richard Tells Police He Was Never Alone With Boys', Stephen Wright & Sophie Jane Evans, *Daily Mail*, 7 November 2015.

36   *Studio 10*, Network 10, 27 March 2015.

Chapter 4

37   'Meeting Cliff Changed My Life', Simon Evans, *Choice* magazine.

38   Richard, *The Dreamer*.

39   Turner, *The Bachelor Boy*.

40   Ibid.

41   Ibid.

42   Cliff Richard, *It's Great To be Young*, Consul/World Distributors, 1961.

43   Cliff Richard, *Which One's Cliff?*, Hodder & Stoughton, 1977.

44   Turner, *The Bachelor Boy*.

45   Richard, *The Dreamer*.

46   Ibid.

47   Ibid.

48   Cliff Richard, *My Life, My Way: The Autobiography*, Headline Review, 2008.

49   'Cliff Richard Stole My Wife', Jenny Johnston, *Daily Mail*, 13 December 2008.

50   'Sir Cliff Is Accused of Ignoring Dying Plight of Jet', Ben Todd & Peter Robertson, *Daily Mail*, 21 March 2011.

51   'I Want to Know If I Am the Secret Love Child of Cliff Richard', Lianne Kolorin, *Daily Express*, 9 December 2013.

Chapter 5

52   'How Cliff Richard Wrote Dear John Letter to Dump Melbourne Dancer in the 60s', Paul Harris, *Daily Mail*, 9 April 2010.

53   Ibid.

54   'Sir Cliff Richard Picked Music Over Love', BBC News, 10 April .

55   Richard, *The Dreamer*.

56   'Music Matters', Pete Chambers, *Coventry Observer*, 16 October 2020.

57   Now called Urban Saints, Crusaders was a Christian youth organisation formed in 1906 that aimed to help young people follow and become like Jesus and be agents of change and transformation in their world.

58   Cliff Richard, *Which One's Cliff?*.

59   Turner, *The Bachelor Boy*.

60   *The Real Cliff Richard*, Channel 4, 2003.

61   *Sir Cliff Richard – 60 Years in Public and Private*, ITV, 2018.

62   Richard, *Which One's Cliff?*.

63   Ibid.

64   Richard, *The Dreamer*.

65   'The Pop Star & Preacher Who've Been Friends For 48 Years', *Daily Mail*, 16 August 2014.

Chapter 6

66   Bruce Welch, *Rock & Roll: I Gave You The Best Years of My Life: A Life in The Shadows*, Penguin, 1990.

67   Chris Culverson, *Me & My Shadows* website.

68   Richard, *The Dreamer*.

69   'Homes Around the World But Never a Lasting Love To Share Them With', Alison Boshoff, *Daily Mail*, 14 August 2014.

70   Richard, *The Dreamer*.

71   Ibid.

72   Turner, *The Bachelor Boy*.

73   'He Changed My Life Fully & Completely', Emma Powell & Richard Eden, *Daily Mail*, 30 December 2022.

74   Katelyn Beaty, *Celebrities For Jesus: How Personas, Platforms & Profits Are Hurting The Church*, Brazos Press, 2022.

75   *Gaga: Five Foot Two*, directed by Chris Moukarbel, Netflix, 2017.

76   'Why More And More Pop Stars Refuse to go on Tour', Carlos Megía, *El Pais*, 7 June, 2023.

77   'The Big Pop Stars Are All Lonely', Nick McGrath, *Guardian*, 18 April 2015.

78 Turner, *The Bachelor Boy*.

79 In 1970 Cliff did release an album of gospel and Christian songs titled *About That Man*. It failed to chart.

80 Richard, *The Dreamer*.

81 Turner, *The Bachelor Boy*.

82 Ibid.

83 Richard, *The Dreamer*.

84 Ibid.

85 Turner, *The Bachelor Boy*.

86 Interview with Cliff Richard, *Record Collector*, 27 November 2018.

87 Richard, *The Dreamer*.

88 Interview with Tris Penna, 22 January 2025.

89 Interview with Cliff Richard, *Record Collector*, 27 November 2018.

90 Turner, *The Bachelor Boy*.

91 "How We Made New Rose" by Dave Simpson (*Guardian*, 19 March, 2018)

92 "Far From Fun" by Dale Maplethorpe (*Far Out Magazine*, 2 September 2024)

93 Ibid.

94 How We Made New Rose', Dave Simpson, *Guardian*, 19 March, 2018.

95 Richard, *The Dreamer*.

96 Turner, *The Bachelor Boy*.

97 Richard, *The Dreamer*.

Chapter 7

98 'Public Support Operation Yewtree', *Rochdale Online*, 3 March, 2014.

99 'DJ Neil Fox Cleared of Sex Assaults', BBC News, 14 December 2015

100 'Jim Davidson Feared Operation Yewtree Would End His Career', Katherine Heslop, *Daily Mirror*, 12 February 2023.

101 'Jimmy Tarbuck Breaks Down in First TV Interview Since Historic Sex Abuse Claims Were Dropped', Jennifer Ruby, *Evening Standard*, 21 September, 2015.

102 'Freddie Starr Will Not Be Prosecuted Over Sex Offence Allegations Says CPS', Josh Halliday, *Guardian*, 6 May, 2014.

103 'Jimmy Savile: How the Police Investigation Grew', Vikram Dodd, *Guardian*, 28 October 2012.

104 'We Got Things Wrong Admits Savile Police Chief to NSPCC', *Halifax Courier*, 12 November 2015.

105 Because the allegation was a single incident within a particular police area it was proposed to hand the investigation over to South Yorkshire Police, in whose area the incident allegedly took place.

106 Witness statement of David Crompton, 30 November, 2017.

Chapter 8

107 'Labour Call for Orgreave Enquiry', BBC.co.uk, 22 October 2012.

108 Ibid.

109 Ibid.

110 'Ex-South Yorkshire Police Chief: "I Was Stabbed In The Back"', David Rhodes, BBC News, 20 June, 2017.

111 Approved Judgement, Case HC-2016-002849, 18 July 2018.

112 'Cliff Richard Leak Denied by Police, Vikram Dodd, *Guardian,* 15 August 2014.

113 'Independent Review Commissioned by the Police & Crime Commissioner for South Yorkshire Police Into the Disclosure of Information to the BBC', Andy Trotter, 29 September, 2014.

114 In Justice Mann's findings he concludes: 'There are some grounds for finding that it is likely that his informant was a police officer or involved in a police force (probably the Metropolitan Police).' Approved Judgement, Case HC-2016-002849, 18 July 2018.

115 'Police Probe Claims They Were the Source of Leak of Sir Cliff Richard Investigation', Tom Pettifor, *Daily Mirror,* 1 March, 2017.

116 Letter from David Crompton to Chair of the Committee, 22 August 2014.

117 Witness statement of David Crompton, 30 November 2017.

118 Dates vary for this initial phone call: while Andy Trotter's commissioned report states it is 14 July, Justice Mann's observations suggest it is on or around 9 July. Given the further information and dates in Justice Mann's report, it is likely 9 July is the correct date.

119 'I Acted Fairly, says BBC Reporter', BBC News, 18 April 2018.

120 Approved Judgement, 18 July 2018.

121 Letter from Carrie Goodwin to Chair of the Committee, 17 September 2014.

122 Ibid.

123 Approved Judgement, 18 July 2018.

124 Ibid.

125 Witness statement of David Crompton, 30 November 2017.

126 Ibid.

127 Ibid.

128 Approved Judgement, 18 July 2018.

129 Ibid.

130 Ibid.

131 Ibid.

132 In Justice Mann's report it states that Sir Cliff's property was in Surrey, which is incorrect. It appears that the address South Yorkshire Police had presumed was Sir Cliff's at this stage of the investigation was wrong.

133 Ibid.

134 Approved Judgement, 18 July 2018.

135 Ibid.

136 Ibid.

Chapter 9

137 'Gary Smith Appointed Head of News and Current Affairs', bbc.co.uk, 26 October 2015.

138 Approved Judgement,18 July 2018.

139 'BBC Editor Defends Report', BBC News, 23 April 2018.

140 'BBC Editor Joked About Cliff Richard Playing 'Jailhouse Rock'', Jim Waterson, *Guardian*, 20 April 2018.

141 Approved Judgement, 18 July 2018.

142 Ibid.

143 'BBC Reporter Was Toast of the Newsroom', Joseph Curtis, *Daily Mail*, 19 April 2018.

144 Approved Judgement, 18 July 2018.

145 Witness statement of David Crompton, 30 November 2017.

146 Approved Judgement, 18 July 2018.

147 Ibid.

148 Richard, *The Dreamer*.

149 The BBC also sent a reporting team to Sir Cliff's property in Barbados, a six-bedroom villa on the ultra-exclusive Sugar Hills Tennis Resort.

150 Witness statement of Lesley Card, 30 November 2017.

151 Approved Judgement, 18 July 2018.

152 Witness statement of Lesley Card, 30 November 2017.

153 Approved Judgement, 18 July 2018.

154 Ibid.

155 Ibid.

156 Ibid.

157 Ibid.

158 'Court Papers Reveal How Police Tipped Off BBC Reporter', Rebecca Camber, *Daily Mail*, 26 October 2016.

Chapter 10

159 'The Producers', Chas de Whalley, *International Musician & Recording World*, December 1986.

160 Interview with Scott Gorham, nuclearblastrecords.com, 8 September 2019.

161 'Living In Harmony', originally recorded by Olivia Newton-John, 'Hey Mr Dream Maker' and 'Green Light'.

162 Turner, *The Bachelor Boy*.

163 Richard, *The Dreamer*.

164 Turner, *The Bachelor Boy*.

165 Interview with Cliff Richard, *Record Collector*, 27 November 2018.

166 Interview with Cliff Richard, *Solid Gold Sunday*, KISS FM, 23 August 2015.

167 *Breakfast With Frost*, BBC TV, 28 April 2002.

168 Turner, *The Bachelor Boy*.

Chapter 11

169 'Cliff Richard Pays Tribute to the Friend and Former Manager He Lived With for 30 Years', Emma Powell, *Daily Mail*, 30 December 2022.

170 'Is Cliff Richard In Crisis?', Alison Boshoff, *Daily Mail*, 10 July, 2010.

171 Ibid.

172 Richard, *The Dreamer*.

173 'The Way the Police Have Treated Cliff Richard is Completely Unacceptable', Geoffrey Robertson QC, *Independent*, 20 August 2014.

174 'Cliff Richard Case Redraws the Boundaries of Media Law', Jim Waterson, *Guardian*, 18 July 2018.

Chapter 12

175 Witness statement of David Crompton, 30 November 2017.

176 Spears500.com

177 'Operating From the Top of the PR Tree', *Independent*, 5 February 2007.

178 Ibid.

179 Ibid.

180 Approved Judgement, 18 July 2018.

181 Ibid.

182 Ibid.

183 Ibid.

184 Ibid.

185 Witness Statement of Lesley Card, 30 November 2017.

186 Approved Judgement, 18 July 2018.

187 Ibid.

188 Ibid.

189 Ibid.

190 Ibid.

191 Ibid.

192 Ibid.

193 Ibid.

194 'Cliff Richard Case Redraws Boundaries of Media Law', Jim Waterson, *Guardian*, 18 July 2018.

195 Ibid.

196 Approved Judgement, 18 July 2018.

197 Ibid

198 Ibid.

199 Ibid.

200 Ibid.

201 Ibid.

202 Ibid.

203 Ibid.

204 Closing Skeleton Argument of the First Defendant, Claim No: HC-2016-002849.

205 Case Report: Day 5, Sir Cliff Richard v BBC, inform.org, 19 April 2018.

206 Approved Judgement, 18 July 2018.

207 Ibid.

208 Ibid.

Chapter 13

209 Approved Judgement, 18 July 2018.

210 'Cliff Richard Felt Violated By BBC', BBC News, 17 April 2018.

211 'Sir Cliff Richard Insists: I Am Not A Paedophile', Martin Evans, *Daily Telegraph*, 14 August 2014.

212 Case Report: Day 5, Sir Cliff Richard v BBC, inform.org, 19 April 2018.

213 Richard, *The Dreamer.*

214 *Desert Island Discs*, 20 December 2020.

215 Richard, *The Dreamer.*

216 'Edwardian House at the Heart of a Long Simmering Sex Scandal', Tom Watson, *Observer*, 5 July 2014.

217 'Witnesses Allege Senior Tories Involved in Sex Abuse Scandal', *Socialist Worker*, 31 December 2012.

218 Richard, *The Dreamer.*

219 'Social Worker Who Accused Leon Brittan And Other VIPs As Being Members of an Alleged Paedophile Ring Was Convicted of Fraud in 2011', Sam Tonkin, *Daily Mail*, 27 September 2015.

220 Independent Inquiry Into Child Sexual Abuse, 2022.

221 Approved Judgement, 18 July 2018.

222 Ibid.

223 Ibid.

224 Witness statement of David Crompton, 30 November 2017.

225 *Desert Island Discs*, 20 December, 2020.

226 Richard, *The Dreamer.*

227 Ibid.

228 Ibid.

Chapter 14

229 'Cliff Richard: *Daily Telegraph's* Sensationalist Headline is a Nasty Spin, Roy Greenslade, *Guardian*, 15 August 2014.

230 *Desert Island Discs*, 20 December 2020.

231 Cliff Richard interview, *Jonathan Ross Show*, ITV, 16 November 2018.

232 *Desert Island Discs*, 20 December 2020.

233 Cliff Richard interview, *Piers Morgan's Life Stories*, ITV, 25 October 2020.

234 Approved Judgement, 18 July 2018.

235 David Gray & Peter Watt, 'Giving Victims A Voice', Joint MPS & NSPCC Report, January 2013.

236 'Newsnight's McAlpine Scandal', Roy Greenslade, *Guardian*, 19 February 2014.

237 'BBC Reaches Settlement With Lord McAlpine', BBC News, 15 November 2012.

238 'Newsnight Consigned Me to Lowest Circle of Hell', Josh Halliday, *Guardian*, 15 November 2012.

239 'The Moral Panic That Ruined Lives', Luke Gittos, Spiked.com, 14 August 2018.

240 Approved Judgement, 18 July 2018.

241 Sir Bernard Hogan-Howe was then the Metropolitan Police Commissioner. Later, Paul Gambaccini, referring to his arrest and the false allegations of sexual abuse aimed at him, described Hogan-Howe as 'the villain of my life': 'Paul Gambaccini Threatens Legal Action Against "Vile" Met Police', *Guardian*, 20 October 2016.

242 Approved Judgement, 18 July 2018.

243 'South Yorkshire Police Complain to the BBC, *Guardian*, 17 August 2014.

244 Approved Judgement, 18 July 2018.

245 In his witness statement Johnson said he made these remarks in jest. In his observations Justice Mann suggested, 'I think it unlikely that there was any such jest. It would be a very odd remark to make in jest.' Approved Judgement, 18 July 2018.

246 'Cliff Richard: The Moral Annihilation of a Celebrity, Frank Furedi, Spiked, 18 August 2014

247 'Cliff Richard Leak Denied By Police', Vikram Dodd, *Guardian*, 15 August 2014.

248 Closing Skeleton Argument of the First Defendant, Claim No: HC-2016-002849.

Chapter 15

249 'Why Live Aid Was the Greatest Show of All', Mark Beaumont, *Independent*, 11 July 2020.

250 'Live Aid Memories', *Independent*, 13 July 2010.

251 'What Is Sir Clifford Richard Doing With This Lot', William Shaw, *Smash Hits*, 12–25 March 1986.

252 'Single of the Week', jonkutner.com, 6 October 2024.

253 William Shaw, *Smash Hits*, 12–25 March 1986.

254 Turner, *The Bachelor Boy*.

255 Richard, *The Dreamer*.

256 *Philadelphia Enquirer*, 10 May 1986.

257 *Ottawa Citizen*, 23 January 1987.

258 Turner, *The Bachelor Boy*.

259 Ibid.

260 Richard, *The Dreamer*.

261 Interview with Cliff Richard, Gary James, Classicbands.com.

262 Interview with Tris Penna, 24 January 2025.

263 'I Wrote That', Jim Ottewill, *M Magazine*, 2 December 2024.

264 Ibid.

265 'Mistletoe and Wine's Political Beginnings', John McKie, BBC News, 14 December 2013.

266 Jim Ottewill, *M Magazine*, 2 December 2024.

267 *Desert Island Discs*, 20 December 2020.

268 John McKie, BBC News, 14 December 2013.

269 Ibid.

270 'How Much Do Popstars Earn From Their Christmas Songs Every Year', Joe Sommerlad, *Independent*, 27 December 2022.

271 John McKie, BBC News, 14 December 2013.

272 *Record Mirror*, 19 August 1989.

273 *Music Week*, 19 August 1989.

274 'Old Music: Van Morrison & Cliff Richard – Whenever God Shines His Light', Greg Freeman, *Guardian*, 21 September 2012.

275 Interview with Van Morrison, *Record Collector*, Issue 481, 11 June 2018.

276 This was a re-recording of Band Aid's 1985 charity single 'Do They Know It's Christmas' put together by Stock, Aitken and Waterman and featuring artists such as Kylie Minogue, Lisa Stansfield, Jason Donovan, Matt Goss and Cliff Richard. Like its predecessor it reached Number 1.

277 Written by Julie Gold, it was recorded by Nanci Griffith in 1987 and became a minor hit in Ireland. Bette Midler recorded it in 1990 and it became a Top 3 hit in the USA. Cliff released a live version in October 1990, which peaked at Number 11 in the UK charts.

278 Turner, *The Bachelor Boy*.

279 It was actually the fourth time Cliff had spent Christmas at the top of the charts. As well as 'Mistletoe and Wine' and 'Saviour's Day', he was part of Band Aid II's 'Do They Know It's Christmas?' in 1989 and in 1960 he topped the charts at Christmas with The Shadows and their song 'I Love You'.

280 'If It's Christmas It Can Only Be Sir Cliff Of Richard', Nick Harper, *Guardian*, 19 December 2003.

281 Album Review by Alan Jones, *Music Week*, 24 April 1993.

Chapter 16

282 Richard, *The Dreamer*.

283 Turner, *The Bachelor Boy*.

284 '4 Out of 5 Musicals Failed Their Investors', Gregory Bresiger, *New York Post*, 25 January 2015.

285 'Inside Cliff a Violent Baddie Is Lurking', Hunter Davies, *Independent*, 4 April 1994.

286 Ibid.

287 'Cliff's Oxygen of Bad Publicity', David Lister, *Independent*, 13 April 1997.

288 Ibid.

289 'Over the Top With Cliff', David Lister, *Independent*, 16 October 1996.

290 Turner, *The Bachelor Boy*.

291 Interview with Cliff Richard, *TFI Friday*, Channel 4, 2 October 1998.

292 Richard, *The Dreamer*.

293 'Cliff's Contract Goes Pop As His Latest Album Flops', *Sunday Mirror*, 28 February 1999.

294 'Sir Cliff Foils Radio Ban', BBC News, 11 October 1998.

295 'Field of Dreams', Tony Cummings, *Cross Rhythms* magazine, 1 February 2001.

296 'Last Laugh For Cliff', Helen Carter, *Guardian*, 29 November 1999.

297 'Michael Brand's Cliff Campaign Vile', BBC News, 10 December 1999.

298 Ibid.

299 Tony Cummings, *Cross Rhythms* magazine, 1 February 2001.

300 'Michael Brand's Cliff Campaign Vile', BBC News, 10 December 1999.

Chapter 17

301 'I Lay On The Floor Crying, I Thought I Was Going To Die', David Wigg, *Daily Mail*, 20 June 2016.

302 'Cliff Richard Pulls Out Of Charity Event In Wake Of Sex Abuse Allegation', Gerard Couzens & John Twomey, *Daily Express*, 19 August 2014.

303 Gloria Hunniford Interviews Cliff Richard, *Lorraine*, ITV, 24 June 2016.

304 'The Police Tip-Off & Cliff Richard', Dominic Crossley, *Legal Week*, 15 August 2014.

305 *Lorraine*, ITV, 24 June 2016.

306 'More People Contact Police After Sir Cliff Richard's Home Searched', Gordon Rayner, *Daily Telegraph*, 15 August 2014.

307 Ibid.

308 'Cliff Richard: The Moral Annihilation of a Celebrity, Frank Furedi, *Spiked*, 18 August 2014.

309 Ibid.

310 'Treated Like A Guilty Man', David Wigg, *Daily Mail*, 21 June 2016.

311 Ibid.

312 Ibid.

313 'Cliff Richard Interviewed By Police Over Sex Crime Allegation', *Guardian*, 23 August 2014.

314 Ibid.

Chapter 18

315 Richard, *The Dreamer*.

316 'Cliff Richard Cancels His Performance at Cathedral Charity Concert', Martin Williams, *Guardian*, 19 August 2014.

317 'Sir Cliff Richard Recalls How He Feared Heart Attack After Sex Assault Claims', Flora Thompson, *Evening Standard*, 8 June 2022.

318 Richard, *The Dreamer*.

319 'Cliff Richard "Poured My Heart Out To God" After Allegations', Susan Gately, catholicireland.net, 12 August 2018.

320 Richard, *The Dreamer*.

321 'Vatican: Same-sex Couples Ruling Is Not Endorsement of Homosexuality', Angela Giuffrida, *Guardian*, 4 January 2024.

322 'Pope Francis Says Homosexuality Is a Sin But Not a Crime', Nicole Winfield, Associated Press, 25 January 2023.

323 'Cliff: Church Must Accept Gays Exist', *Irish Examiner*, 18 December 2005.

324 'Sir Cliff Speaks Frankly About His "Companion The Ex-Priest"', Chris Green, *Independent*, 6 September 2008.

325 Richard, *My Life, My Way*.

326 'Cliff Richard: My Sexuality Is Private And I'll Take It To The Grave', Nick Duffy, *Pink News*, 2 February 2024.

327 'I Love Olivia Says Cliff', Lydia Slate, *New Idea* magazine, 20 January 1996.

328 Turner, *The Bachelor Boy*.

329 Ibid.

330 Ibid.

331 'Cliff Richard & Sue Barker's Relationship Explored', Shivon Watson, *Daily Star*, 14 October 2022.

332 'Sue Barker Shares "Frustrating" Reason She Wishes She'd "Never Gone Near" Ex Cliff Richard in the 1980s', Jacob Stolworthy, *Independent*, 7 September 2022.

333 Ibid.

334 Turner, *The Bachelor Boy*.

335 Ibid.

336 Ibid.

337 'Mum And Pine Trees Keep Cliff Richard Young', Sandra Jobson, *Sydney Morning Herald*, 2 January 1982.

338 Interview with Bryan Chambers, March 2025.

339 'Sir Cliff Richard Puts The Record Straight On God, Infidelity, And Those Gay Rumours', *Evening Standard*, 12 April 2012.

Chapter 19

340 'They Think I'm Going to Die on Stage', Lieven Mathys, usabyrv.wordpress.com, 11 December 2013.

341 Interview With Cliff Richard, *Lorraine*, ITV, 11 November 2016.

342 'Cliff Richard On Elvis Presley: He Sounded Like He Had Secrets You Needed To Learn', *Guardian*, 30 October 2023.

343 *Lorraine*, ITV, 11 November 2016.

344 Letter from David Crompton to Keith Vaz MP, 10 February 2015.

345 Ibid.

346 Richard, *The Dreamer*.

347 'Cliff Richard's Lawyers Hit Out At MPs For Publishing Sex Abuse Claims Letter Causing Star "Further Damaging Coverage"', Khaleda Rahman *Daily Mail*, 27 February 2015.

348 Ibid.

349 Ibid.

350 'Cliff Richard Investigation 'Increased Significantly And Involves More Than One Allegation' Says Police Chief", Kashmira Gander, Independent, 25 February 2015.

351 'I'm Addicted to Being an MP: The Surprise Return of Keith Vaz', Abigail Buchanan, *Daily Telegraph*, 1 July 2024.

Chapter 20

352 'What's Sadder Than an Ageing Rocker', Nigel Jones, *Spectator*, 4 November 2024.

353 Richard, *The Dreamer*.

354 'Sir Cliff Still a Bachelor Boy', BBC News, 23 February 2000.

355 Ibid.

356 Turner, *The Bachelor Boy*.

357 'Success Story: Cliff Richard', Kay Goddard, *Daily Mail*, 13 December 2008.

358 Ibid.

359 Cliff Richard interview, *Woman's Hour*, BBC Radio 4, 6 December 2001.

360 Turner, *The Bachelor Boy*.

361 *Desert Island Discs*, 20 December 2020.

362 Richard, *My Life, My Way*.

363 'Ex-priest at Cliff's Side As He Fights Sex Claims', Alison Boshoff, *Daily Mail*, 16 August 2014.

364 'Sir Cliff to Sell Up and Leave Britain', Angella Johnson & Sharon Churcher, *Mail On Sunday*, 9 April 2006.

365 Ibid.

366 'Ex-priest at Cliff's Side', Alison Boshoff, *Daily Mail*, 16 August 2014.

367 'Sir Cliff To Sell Up', Angella Johnson & Sharon Churcher, *Mail On Sunday*, 9 April 2006.

368 Ibid.

369 Ibid.

370 'My Close Friendship With the Former Priest Who Shares My Life', *Evening Standard*, 12 April 2012.

371 Ibid.

372 'If I Was Gay Would It Make Any Difference?', Tom Payne, *Independent*, 20 April 2014.

373 Interview with Cliff Richard, Sky News, 12 September 2008.

374 *When Piers Met Sir Cliff*, ITV1, 26 September 2009.

375 'Cliff Richard: The Problem With Bachelorhood', Nicola Harley, Gulf News, 15 September 2018.

376 Michael Bywater 'Lost Worlds: What Have We Lost And Where Did It Go?' Granta Books, 2005

377 Interview with Vicki Wickham, January 2025.

Chapter 21

378 *Still Cliff*, ITV, 6 December 2003.

379 'Me and My Wine: Cliff Richard', *Guardian*, 13 October 2002.

380 'Christmas Number One Tops Cliff's List For Santa', *Irish Examiner*, 1 October 2003.

381 'Decca Signs Up Cliff Richard', (*Irish Examiner*, 6 September 2004.

382 'Cliff Richard Took Swipe At 'Arch Rivals' Beatles For "Being Step Behind Bee Gees"', Josh Saunders, *Daily Express*, 10 February 2021.

383 'Cliff Richard: *Somethin' Is Goin' On* Review', Dave Simpson, *Guardian*, 22 October 2004.

384 'Cliff Richard Blames Radio Ban For Ending His Recording Career', Xan Brooks, *Guardian*, 21 September 2005.

385 'Blackburn Victory Over Cliff Ban', BBC News, 24 June 2004.

386 'My Campaign For Cliff', Tim Dowling, *Guardian*, 21 September 2005.

387 'Blackburn Victory Over Cliff Ban', BBC News, 24 June 2004.

388 'Classic U-Turn On Cliff Richard Ban', Claire Couzens, *Guardian*, 24 June 2004.

389 'Not So Golden Oldies', *The Economist*, 6 January 2005.

390 'Sir Cliff Backs Royalty Campaign', BBC News, 18 April 2006.

391 'Sir Cliff Cost Us Copyright Battle', Andrew Orlowski, Theregister.com, 25 January 2007.

392 'Blair Sings Along to Cliff's Summer Holiday', Robert Winnett, *The Times*, 30 July 2006.

393 'PM Makes Secret Donation After 26-Night Stay at Sir Cliff's', Andy McSmith, *Independent*, 17 November 2005.

394 'Holidaying Blair in Conflict of Interest Over Copyright Law', James Chapman, *Daily Mail*, 30 July 2006.

395 'Revealed: Why Sir Cliff Gave Blair a Summer Holiday', Mark Brown *Guardian*, 24 August 2006.

396 'MPs Come to the Defence of Cliff Richard's Copyright', Paul MacInnes, *Guardian*, 16 May 2007.

397 'Musicians Celebrate Victory', Patrick Foster, *The Times*, 13 February 2009.

398 Richard, *The Dreamer*.

Chapter 22

399 'Will Cliff Make No. 1 For a Sixth Decade in a Row?', Stephanie Condron, *Daily Telegraph*, 19 December 2006.

400 Ibid.

401 'Why Cliff Hangs On', Daniel Bardsley, *Gulf News*, 28 January 2007.

402 'Cliff Fans Control Album Cost', BBC News, 30 October 2007.

403 Richard, *My Life, My Way*.

404 'Sir Cliff Richard's Mother Dies After Long Battle With Alzheimer's', *Daily Mail*, 18 October 2007.

405 'Sir Cliff Defiant At 50 Not Out', Kevin Young, BBC News, 10 September 2008.

406 Cliff Richard Interview, *The Final Reunion* DVD, 2009.

407 'Out Of The Shadows: Jet Harris Isn't Invited as Cliff Richard and the Boys Reunite For Tour', Simon Cable, *Daily Mail*, 6 December 2008.

408 'Shadows Guitarist Jet Harris Left Out of Comeback Gig', Duncan Eaton, *Southern Daily Echo*, 14 December 2008.

409 Interview with Hank Marvin, GMTV, 18 September 2009

410 Interview with Cliff Richard, Officialcharts.com, 16 November 2011.

411 *Soulicious* album review, *Record Collector*, Issue 394, 28 September 2011.

412 'Cliff Richard Review: The O2 London', Michael Hann, *Guardian*, 27 October 2011.

413 'Sir Cliff Honoured to Support Morrissey', BBC News, 13 February 2014.

414 'Morrissey Q&A', M. Tye Comer, *Billboard*, 27 February 2014.

415 'Sir Cliff Richard to Stage Free Solo Show in New York', BBC News, 17 June 2014.

416 'Cliff Richard at the Gramercy Theatre Reviewed', Iman Lababedi, Rocknyc.com, 22 June 2014.

Chapter 23

417 Richard, *The Dreamer*.

418 'Cliff Richard Is Praying For His Accusers of Historic Sex Offences, Says Broadcaster Paul Gambaccini', Corline Frost, *Huffington Post*, 15 September 2015

419 'The Met Behaved Like the Mob', Stephen Wright, *Daily Mail*, 30 October 2020.

420 Aleksander Solzhenitsyn, *The Gulag Archipelago*, Harvill Press, 2003.

421 Paul Gambaccini , *Love, Paul Gambaccini: My Year Under the Yewtree*, Biteback Publishing, 2015.

422 Ibid.

423 'Historic Sex Investigations Are Based on "Rumour and Accusation" Rather Than Evidence', Martin Evans, *Daily Telegraph*, 15 September 2015.

424 'Sex Allegations Cost Me £200,000 – But I Won't Sue the Police', Angela Wintle, *Daily Telegraph*, 15 November 2015.

425 'Paul Gambaccini and the Lessons of Pre-Charge Bail', Kate Goold, www.bindmans.com, 17 September 2015.

426 Ibid.

427 'Paul Gambaccini Says Lord Hogan-Howe Should Be Imprisoned For "Destroying His Life"', Sophie Barnes, *Daily Telegraph*, 23 December 2018.

428 'Cliff Richard, Killarney INEC Review', Ed Power, *Daily Telegraph*, 27 September 2015.

429 Richard, *The Dreamer*.

430 Ed Power, *Daily Telegraph*, 27 September 2015.

Chapter 24

431 'Cliff Richard Abuse Probe Cops "Ready to Hand Evidence File to Prosecutors"', Simon Wright, *Daily Mirror*, 3 October 2015.

432 'Treated Like a Guilty Man', David Wigg, *Daily Mail*, 21 June 2016.

433 Ibid.

434 'Fresh Agony For Sir Cliff', Rebecca Camber, *Daily Mail*, 1 September 2016.

435 Ibid.

436 'I Lay On The Floor Crying, I Thought I Was Going To Die', David Wigg, *Daily Mail*, 21 June 2016.

437 Ibid.

438 Richard, *The Dreamer*.

439 'I Lay On The Floor Crying', David Wigg, *Daily Mail*, 20 June 2016.

440 Gloria Hunniford, *My Life*, John Blake Publishing, 2017.

441 'How Cliff Was Smeared By a Serial Rapist, a Blackmailer and Even a "Dodgy Minister"', Richard Pendlebury & Stephen Wright, *Scottish Daily Mail*, 25 June 2016.

442 'Hung Out Like Bait', Mike Sullivan, *Sun*, 17 June 2016.

443 Richard, *The Dreamer*.

444 'Sir Cliff's Accuser Was Arrested on Suspicion of Blackmail', Aaron James, *Premier Christian News*, 20 June 2016.

445 'Serial Rapist Made Sex Abuse Claim Against Sir Cliff Richard', *Star*, 17 June 2016.

446 'Sir Cliff Richard's Child Sex Accuser "Is One of Britain's Worst Serial Rapists"', Keiligh Baker, *Daily Mail*, 17 June 2016.

447 'How Cliff Was Smeared By A Serial Rapist', Richard Pendlebury & Stephen Wright, *Scottish Daily Mail*, 25 June 2016.

448 'Sir Cliff Richard's Child Sex Accuser', Keiligh Baker, *Daily Mail*, 17 June 2016'

449 'How a Self-Promoting TV Detective Obsessed With Celebrity Sex Abusers Helped Ruin the Lives of Sir Cliff and a String of Other Famous Faces . . . Who All Turned Out to Be Totally Innocent', David Rose & Rosie Waterhouse, *Mail on Sunday*, 23 November 2018.

450 Ibid.

451 Ibid.

452 'Sir Cliff Put Through Hell By Police', Richard Madeley & Judi Finnegan, *Daily Express*, 13 February 2016.

453 'Cliff To Sue BBC For Using Film of Him With Savile', Arthur Martin, *New Zealand Herald*, 5 March 2016.

454 Ibid.

455 'Cliff Richard Child Abuse Accuser Claims Cops Haven't Spoken to Him in Three Months', Nick Dorman, *Daily Mirror*, 1 May 2016.

456 Ibid.

457 Ibid.

458 'Sir Cliff Put Through Hell By Police', Richard Madeley & Judi Finnegan, *Daily Express*, 13 February 2016

459 'Cliff Richard: Crown Prosecution Service Receives "Full File" of Evidence in Child Sex Abuse Investigation', Tom Morgan, *Daily Telegraph*, 10 May 2016.

460 'Police Hand Cliff Richard Sexual Abuse Claims to Prosecutors, Sources Claim', Jamie Grierson, *Guardian*, 10 May 2016.

Chapter 25

461 'BBC Stars Reveal What They'd Heard About Jimmy Savile', Jon Dean, *Daily Mirror*, 25 February 2016.

462 'Jimmy Savile Police "Reluctant to Investigate Because of Celebrity Status"', Josh Halliday & Haroon Siddique, *Guardian*, 12 March 2013.

463 'Giving Victims a Voice', David Gray & Peter Watt, MPS & NSPCC Report, January 2013.

464 'Ten Years on From Operation Yewtree and the Accused Still Bear the Scars', Jasper Rees, *Daily Telegraph*, 24 August 2022.

465 'Yewtree No Witch-hunt', *Belfast Telegraph*, 13 August 2013.

466 'Ten Years On From Operation Yewtree', Jasper Rees, *Daily Telegraph*, 24 August 2022.

467 'Tom Watson Must Quit', Martin Robinson & Joel Adams, *Daily Mail*, 23 July 2019.

468 'Carl Beech: Liar, Fraudster and Paedophile', BBC News, 26 July 2019.

469 'Carl Beech Made Up Paedophile Ring Claims, Jury Finds', Simon Murphy, *Guardian*, 22 July 2019.

470 'How Tom Watson's Championing of "Nick" Sparked a Major Inquiry Into a Paedophile Ring That Didn't Exist', Robert Mendick & Martin Evans, *Daily Telegraph*, 23 July 2019.

471 Vikram Dodd, *Guardian*, 22 July 2019.

472 'How Carl Beech's Web Of Lies About VIP Sex Abuse Convinced MPs, Police and Investigators He Was the Real Deal', Martin Evans, *Daily Telegraph*, 22 July 2019.

473 Ibid.

474 'Operation Midland: How the Met Lost Its Way', Rajeev Syan & Sandra Laville, *Guardian*, 21 March 2016.

475 'Revealed: How Carl Beech the Accuser Became the Abused', Simon Murphy, *Guardian*, 22 July 2019.

476 'How Carl Beech's Web of Lies About VIP Sex Abuse Convinced MPs, Police And Investigators He Was the Real Deal', Martin Evans, *Daily Telegraph*, 22 July 2019.

477 'Carl Beech: "VIP Abuse" Accuser Jailed For 18 Years', BBC News, 26 July 2019.

478 'Sir Edward Heath: The Filipino Brother Keeper Who Sparked Child Sex Abuse Inquiry', Martin Evans, *Daily Telegraph*, 4 August 2015.

479 'Devil Worship, Murder and a Thirst For Blood: The 35 "Fantasy" Allegations Dismissed By the 1.5m Ted Heath Probe', Martin Robinson & Rebecca Camber, *Daily Mail*, 7 October 2017.

480 'The Allegations Of Child Sex Abuse Against Sir Edward Heath Are driven By Hysteria', Charles Moore, Daily Telegraph, 14 August 2015

481 'The Paedophile Panic Has More Than a Hint of Homophobia to It', Brendan O'Neill, *Spectator*, 1 September 2015.

482 'Cyril Smith, The Serial Paedophile to Whom the Establishment Turned a Blind Eye', Martin Evans, *Daily Telegraph*, 18 February 2020.

483 'Social Media Gossip Fuels Bigotry As UK Investigates Sex Abuse', Catherine Mayer, *Time*, 16 August 2014.

484 'Cliff Richard Case: Police Assisted BBC "Too Much"', BBC News, 26 April 2018.

Chapter 26

485 'MPs Criticise DPP Alison Saunders Over Collapse lOf Rape Trials', Owen Bowcott, *Guardian*, 20 July 2018.

486 'Our Police Have Been Brainwashed ByAlison Saunders' View Of Rap', Allison Pearson, *Daily Telegraph*, 6 February 2018.

487 'Young Lives Were Ruined and Justice Was Betrayed – Alison Saunders Was a Zealot, But We Finally Beat Her', Allison Pearson, *Daily Telegraph*, 3 April 2018.

488 'Alison Saunders: When Law Becomes a Crusade', Luke Gittos, *Spiked!*, 4 April 2018.

489 'CPS Must Explain Why Savile Probe Was Dropped', *Independent*, 25 October 2012.

490 'Sir Cliff Richard Speaks Out After Prosecutors Drop Child Sex Abuse Case', Martin Bentham, *Evening Standard*, 16 June 2016.

491 'Sir Cliff: I Wept After Being Cleared of Sex Abuse Allegations', Jane Matthews, *Daily Telegraph*, 5 November 2016.

492 'Gloria Hunniford Shares Her Relief As Close Friend Sir Cliff Richard Is Cleared of Historic Sexual Abuse Allegations', Natalie Corner, *Daily Mirror*, 16 June 2016.

493 'BBC Statement Regarding Sir Cliff Richard', BBC, 21 June 2016.

494 'BBC's Hollow Apology to Cliff', Sam Greenhill, *Daily Mail*, 21 June 2016.

495 'I Lay On The Floor Crying', David Wigg, *Daily Mail*, 20 June 2016.

496 'Sir Cliff Richard Cleared of Historic Sex Assault Claims After Prosecutors Drop Case', Martin Evans, *Daily Telegraph*, 16 June 2016.

497 Ibid.

498 Ibid.

499 'Was There Any Way Not to Traduce Cliff Richard?', Matthew Parris, *Spectator*, 25 June 2016'

500 'Sir Cliff Richard's Last Goodbye to Dying Sister Donna As He's Left "Utterly Devastated" By Sibling's Death', Halina Watts, *Daily Mirror,* 9 August 2016.

501 'Sir Cliff Richard Tells Fans He Is "Back To My Best" After Sister Dies In "Absolutely Depressing" Year For Singer', *Daily Telegraph*, 24 August 2016.

502 'Second Person Challenges CPS Decision Not to Charge Sir Cliff Richard', *Guardian*, 9 September 2016.

503 'Decision To Drop Cliff Richard Case Upheld By CPS', BBC News, 27 September 2016.

504 Ibid.

505 'Rock On! Cliff Richard to Release Classic Rock 'n' Roll Covers Album', Rebecca Hawkes, *Daily Telegraph*, 29 September 2016.

506 Cliff Richard Interview, Celebrity Radio, 30 November 2016.

Chapter 27

507 'Cliff Richard Stands Out At Wimbledon As He Flashes Huge Smile After Confirming He's Suing BBC and Police', Rebecca Pocklington & Ben Russell, *Daily Mirror*, 10 July 2016.

508 'When Cliff Was Controversial', *Record Collector*, 18 August 2008.

509 'BBC's Fury At £900k Pre-Action Legal Costs of Sir Cliff Richard', John Hyde, *Law Society Gazette*, 4 May 2017.

510 'Sir Cliff Richard's £3.5m Luxury Mansion That Singer Put On the Market After Cops "defiled" It Has Sold', Mark Hodge, *Sun,* 23 June 2016.

511 'Cliff Richard Buys £800k New York Pad With Best Pal As He Quits UK Over Sex Slurs', Christopher Bucktin, *Daily Mirror*, 25 May 2019.

512 'Sir Cliff Richard Quits Britain For "Anonymity" In New York After Baseless Sex Abuse Slurs', Hannah Hope, *Sun*, 24 May 2019.

513 'Sir Cliff Richard Settles Row With South Yorkshire Police Over Raid On His Home', *Daily Telegraph*, 26 May 2017.

514 Approved Judgement, 18 July 2018.

515 Richard, *The Dreamer*.

516 'Sir Cliff Richard Settles Row With South Yorkshire Police', *Daily Telegraph*, 26 May 2017.

Chapter 28

517 'Sir Cliff Richard To "Sue BBC For Up To £1.5m"' As Damning Texts Between Cops And BBC Over Raid On His Home Are Revealed', Tom Wells, *Sun*, 25 October 2016.

518 '"Sue Those Bastards": Angry Rod Stewart Backs Pal Cliff Richard Over Child Abuse Smears Legal Fight', Halina Watts, *Daily Record,* 16 October 2016.

519 'I Lay On The Floor Crying,', David Wigg, *Daily Mail*, 21 June 2016.

520 'Singer Makes Prayer Sign Ahead of BBC High Court Trial', Minnie Wright, *Daily Express*, 12 April 2018.

521 'Cliff Richard v BBC Privacy Trial, Day 1, Opening Submissions', inform.org, 13 April 2018.

522 Richard, *The Dreamer*.

523 'Sir Cliff Richard Breaks Down In Tears As he Gives Evidence During BBC Trial', Sky News, 14 April 2018.

524 'Cliff Richard: BBC Raid Report "Shocking And Upsetting"', BBC News, 13 April 2018.

525 'Cliff Richard v BBC Privacy Trial, Day 1, Sir Cliff's Evidence', inform.org, 13 April 2018.

526 Ibid.

527 'BBC Raid Report "Shocking And Upsetting"', BBC News, 13 April 2018.

528 Richard, *The Dreamer*.

529 'Why Cliff Richard's Case Against the BBC Should Worry Us All', Roy Greenslade, *Guardian*, 17 April 2018.

530 Ibid.

531 'Sir Cliff Richard's Case Against the BBC Could Have a Great Impact on Future Privacy Law', Tracey Singlehurst-Ward, hughjames.com, 12 April 2018.

532 'Cliff Richard Is Right to Seek Anonymity For Those Accused of Sex Crimes', Simon Jenkins, *Guardian*, 1 July 2019.

533 Richard, *The Dreamer*.

534 'Cliff Richard v BBC: Day 5, Sir Cliff Faced "Crisis Situation", Reporter "Guessed the Singer's Name"', inform.org, 19 April 2018.

535 Ibid.

536 Ibid.

537 Ibid.

538 Ibid.

539 Ibid.

540 'Cliff Richard v BBC: Day 6, Reporter Denies Forcing Detectives' Hand', inform.org, 20 April 2018.

541 'Cliff Richard v BBC: Day 8, Editor: BBC Could Have Faced Criticism For Not Reporting Investigation', inform.org, 24 April 2018.

542 'Cliff Richard v BBC: Day 11, 'Footage Of Raid Was Intrusive Says Ex-police Chief', inform.org, 27 April 2018.

543 Ibid.

544 Ibid.

545 Ibid.

546 Ibid.

547 'Sir Cliff Awaits Judgement On Legal Battle With BBC', Lucy Cotter & Amy Hitchcock, Sky News, 9 May 2018.

548 Richard, *The Dreamer*.

Chapter 29

549 Approved Judgement, 18 July 2018.

550 Ibid.

551 Ibid.

552 Ibid.

553 Ibid.

554 Ibid.

555 'Sir Cliff Richard Privacy Ruling: Giving Suspects Anonymity Could Stop Other "Victims" Coming Forward Says Theresa May', Hayley Dixon & Danny Boyle, *Daily Telegraph*, 18 July 2018.

556 Approved Judgement, 18 July 2018.

557 Ibid.

558 Richard, *The Dreamer*.

559 'Cliff Richard BBC Case: Singer Awarded £210,000 After Successfully Suing BBC For Invasion Of Privacy', Tristan Kirk, *Evening Standard*, 18 July 2018'

560 'Sir Cliff Richard: Reaction to High Court Ruling', BBC News, 18 July 2018.

561 'Sir Cliff Richard Privacy Ruling', Hayley Dixon & Danny Boyle, *Daily Telegraph*, 18 July 2018.

562 'Reaction To High Court Ruling', BBC News, 18 July 2018.

563 Ibid.

564 'Free Speech Falls Off Cliff', Tom Wells & Mike Sullivan, *Sun*, 18 July 2018.

565 'Guilty Until Proven Innocent: Life After a False Rape Allegation', Jonathan Wells, *Daily Telegraph*, 28 October 2015.

566 Hayley Dixon & Danny Boyle, *Daily Telegraph*, 18 July 2018)

567 'Media Experts Alarmed at Consequences of Cliff Richard Ruling', Jim Waterson, *Guardian*, 18 July 2018.

568 Hayley Dixon & Danny Boyle, *Daily Telegraph*, 18 July 2018.

569 'Sir Cliff Richard Sex Abuse Allegations Made Him Confused And "Crazy"', David Wigg, *Daily Mail*, 22 June 2016.

570 Richard, *The Dreamer*.

Chapter 30

571 'The Impact of Being Wrongly Accused of Abuse In Occupations of Trust: Victims' Voices, Carolyn Hoyle, Naomi-Ellen Speechley & Ros Burnett, University of Oxford Centre For Criminology.

572 'Psychological Impact of Being Wrongfully Accused of Criminal Offences: A Systematic Literature Review', Samantha K Brooks & Neil Greenberg, *Medicine, Science & The Law*, Vol. 61 (1), 2021.

573 'Cliff Richard Says He Is "Forever Tainted" By Abuse Allegations', *Guardian*, 17 October 2016.

574 'Sir Cliff Richard and Historic Sex Cases: Is Our Justice System Fair To Old Men?', Matthew Scott, barristerblogger.com 3 September 2014

575 'Met Police "Fanned the Flames" of Carl Beech's False Allegations of Westminster Paedophile Ring', Tony Diver, Jamie Johnson, Hayley Dixon, *Daily Telegraph*, 29 July 2019.

576 'Sir Cliff Richard Urges MPs to Give Suspects Accused of Sexual Offences Anonymity – But Critics Say 'Chilling' Move Could Allow Rapists to Go Free', Rebecca Camber, *Daily Mail*, 10 May 2019.

577 Ibid.

578 'Rape Crisis Responds to Sir Cliff Campaign For Anonymity In Law For Sexual Offence Suspects', TRC Sexual Abuse & Rape Support Greater Manchester, 5 July 2019'

579 Rebecca Camber, *Daily Mail*, 10 May 2019.

580 Ibid.

581 'Sir Cliff Richard and Paul Gambaccini Revive Campaign For Anonymity For Suspects', FloraThompson, *Evening Standard*, 8 June 2022.

582 'Outrage As Sir Cliff Richard Claims He'd Rather See 10 Criminals Go Free Than One Innocent Person Suffer', Patrick Grafton-Green, *Evening Standard*, 28 November 2018.

583 'BBC Is Refused Leave to Appeal Against Cliff Richard Privacy Ruling', *Guardian*, 26 July 2018.

584 'Sir Cliff Richard: BBC Agrees To Pay £850,000 Towards Legal Costs', BBC News, 26 July 2018.

585 'Sir Cliff Richard: BBC Pays £2m in Final Settlement After Privacy Case', BBC News, 4 September 2019.

586 'BBC Will Not Appeal Against Cliff Richard Privacy Victory', Jim Waterson, *Guardian*, 15 August 2018.

587 'BBC Licence Fee Payers Foot £2million Legal Bill After Sir Cliff Richard Payout From Privacy Battle With Broadcaster More Than Doubles', Ross Ibbetson, *Daily Mail*, 4 September 2019.

Chapter 31

588 Interview with Cliff Richard by Paul Gambaccini, abbeyroad.com, 30 August 2018.

589 'Cliff Richard: *Rise Up* Review – Don't Call It a Comeback', Ale Petridis, *Guardian*, 22 November 2018.

590 'Sir Cliff Richard at Nottingham's Royal Concert Hall', Kevin Cooper, *Nottingham Post*, 10 October 2018.

591 'Cliff Richard: Royal Albert Hall Review', Neil McCormick, *Daily Telegraph* 15 October 2018

592 'Cliff Richard Review: From Ghastly To Sublime In Determined Return', Dave Simpson, *The Guardian* 5 October 2018

593 'A New UK Tour, a New Album, But Maybe the Last of His Hit Calendars', David Wigg, *Daily Mail*, 26 April 2013.

594 Ibid.

595 Ibid.

596 Ibid.

597 'How I Stayed Healthy Over 50 Years of Showbiz', Kay Goddard, *Daily Mail*, 13 December 2008.

598 'I Have a Death Pact With My Sister: Sir Cliff Richard Reveals They Have Agreed Suicide If They Get Dementia Like Their Mother', Ben Todd, *Daily Mail*, 17 October 2011.

599 Interview with Cliff Richard, cliffrichardradio.com, 30 October 2020.

600 'Cliff Richard & Stormzy Compete For No. 1 In UK Albums Chart', Nadia Khomami, *Guardian*, 22 November 2022.

601 '"Darling, We're the Young Ones": Sir Cliff Richard Proves He's Still Got the Moves', Neil McCormick, *Daily Telegraph*, 24 October 2021.

602 Ibid.

603 Ibid.

604 'Cliff Richard Shares His Secrets to Staying Young As He Appears at Wimbledon', Zara Woodcock, *Daily Mirror*, 30 June 2022.

605 Anonymity of Suspects Bill Debate, *Hansard*, Vol. 721, 28 October 2022)

606 Ibid.

607 'Avoid Sir Cliff Richard Ordeal Repeat By Granting Anonymity For Suspects, MP Says', Kit Sandeman, *Yorkshire Post*, 28 October 2022.

Chapter 32

608 'Did Stormzy Get Too Big For His Boots?', Alana Khosla, *Daily Mail*, 22 March 2025.

609 Interview With Cliff Richard (*Good Morning Britain*, ITV, 2 December 2022)

610 'Sir Cliff Richard Thinks of Christmas Every Day', uk.news.yahoo.com, 27 December 2024.

611 'Stormzy On His Bid For Number 1', Aimee Cliff, *Fader*, 14 December 2015.

612 'I Don't Know Stormzy', Rebecca Davison, *Daily Mail*, 29 November 2022.

613 'Stormzy Beats Cliff Richard to Top Spot With Third Number One Album', Ellie Iorizzo, *Evening Standard*, 2 December 2022.

614 'He Changed My Life Fully and Completely', Emma Powell, *Daily Mail*, 30 December 2022.

615 Ibid.

616 'Cliff Richard Mourns Live In Friend Who helped Him Escape Elvis's Terrible Fate', Stefan Kyriazis, *Daily Express*, 31 December 2022.

617 'Sir Cliff Richard Announces New Album Featuring "Very Emotional" Olivia Newton-John Duet', George Simpson, *Daily Express*, 29 August 2023.

618 'Cliff Richard, Hammersmith Apollo, Review: Ageless Rock and Roll Idol Is Unchanged From His Prime', Neil McCormick, *Daily Telegraph*, 6 November 2023.

619 'Middle England Gospel: Cliff Richard at the Hammersmith Apollo', Fergal Kinney, *The Quietus*, 13 November 2023.

620 'The Road Will Kill You: Why Older Musicians Are Cancelling Tours', Jum Farber, *Guardian*, 2 March 2020.

621 'Cliff Richard Superfans Finally Get to Meet Their Idol', BBC News, 13 October 2011.

622 'We're the Cliffettes', Sadie Nicholas, *Daily Express*, 17 June 2019.

623 'Cliff Richard, 83, Hints at When He Would Consider Quitting in Five-Word Update', Matt Jackson, *Daily Express*, 3 July 2024.

624 'John Lennon Gave Damning Opinion Over Cliff Richard's Music', Callum Crumlish, *Daily Express*, 1 August 2022.

625 'Cliff Richard At Hammersmith Apollo', Fergal Kinney, *The Quietus*, 13 November 2023.

626 'Cliff Richard – Why We've Got Him All Wrong', Bob Stanley, *Guardian*, 17 September 2009.

627 Richard, *The Dreamer*.